PRODUCTIVE WORK – IN INDUSTRY AND SCHOOLS

Becoming Persons Again

Arthur G. Wirth

Foreword by

Irving Bluestone, Vice President (retired)
United Auto Workers Union
and

Arthur Brown, President
The John Dewey Society for the
Study of Education and Culture

UNIVERSITY
PRESS OF
AMERICA

LANHAM • NEW YORK • LONDON

Co-published by arrangement with
the John Dewey Society

To

Dave, Hal, John

and

'the fat lady'

The great task of our time is to become
persons again.   -Martin Buber

ACKNOWLEDGMENTS

I am keenly aware of the many persons who made indispensable contributions to the work. To mention a few does not mean that I am unaware of the others to whom I am indebted.

The research upon which the study is based was made possible by research fellowships from the John Dewey Foundation. Jo Ann Boydston, Director of The Center For Dewey Studies, Southern Illinois University (Carbondale) not only administered the fellowships, but acted as a friend and adviser. I am grateful for the intellectual interchange of colleagues who challenged my thinking and reacted critically to my writing: William Connor, Raymond Callahan, Louis Smith, Gary Natriello, Robert Boguslaw, Martin Levit, Michael Katz, Arthur Brown, Hal Zimmerman, and William Caspary. Barry Anderson knew how to lighten my teaching at important stages. I am particularly grateful to Marilyn Cohn, Ordia Harrison and Rita Roth who let me learn from their important research studies and permitted me to make generous use of their writings.

Key persons who freely gave of their time and insights to help me see the significance of pioneering new work projects were: Jon Frode Blichfeldt and Max Elden, of Work Research Institutes in Norway; Richard Ramsay of the Project Staff of the Work Improvement Program in Bolivar, Tennessee; and David J. Doherty, my guide to auto industry projects in Flint and Detroit. Mike Cooley, on a memorable morning in London, England, recreated for me the struggle of union leaders in Lucas Aerospace Industries, who have raised a new order of questions about corporate life - questions about the rights of workers to engage in socially useful work.

Becky Torstrick sustained me by her unflagging faith in the significance of the work, and by her consummate skill in guiding the manuscript to completion. Fred Zweig helped me understand the underlying grounding of our personal dignity and power upon which we can build new institutions.

My wife, Marian, freely provided the patience and the caring which made it all possible. She believes that I can learn to write a clean sentence.

I wish to acknowledge permission from the following publishers to quote from copyright materials cited in the text:
Addison-Wesley Publishing Company
AMACOM
The Continuum Publishing Company
Macmillan Publishing Company
Pergamon Press
South End Press
Tavistock Publishers Ltd.
University of California Press.
William Morrow and Company

Chapter IV is based on research for my previous study, <u>Education In the Technological Society</u>. (Washington, D.C.: University Press of America, Inc., 1980).

Chapter V appeared earlier in <u>Economic and Industrial Democracy</u> (Volume 2, no. 2, May 1981) as "Exploring Linkages Between Dewey's Educational Philosophy and Industrial Organization."

TABLE OF CONTENTS

The John Dewey Society is pleased to endorse
this book by Arthur Wirth. It reflects Dewey's deep
concern about the relationship between education and
culture.

Arthur Brown, President
The John Dewey Society

In addressing one of our society's long-standing
dilemmas, Arthur Wirth has demonstrated that harmonizing essential democratic values and the demand for
productive efficiency is not a utopian vision. It has
been achieved in work places in many different parts
of the world. But Wirth does more than just point to
cases. He elaborates also on the practical and
philosophical justifications for work place democracy
and on its implication for education. In this regard,
he has made a major contribution to our understanding
of the relationship between school and society.

Although our professional backgrounds are different -- industry and education -- each of us, in
arguing for the sorts of reforms Wirth writes about,
has had to contend with the view that democracy in the
work place is ineffective and inefficient. This view
is based on what we regard to be unsupported and
unsupportable presuppositions about human nature, the
basic differences between persons, and the essential
character of complex human organizations. These
presuppositions include the ideas that (1) only a
relatively few are capable of making judicious management decisions; (2) workers/faculty will not exert the
effort necessary for the process of managing; (3)
workers/faculty are driven by self-interest and have
little or no concern for the larger good; (4) productivity depends on a division of labor which in turn
rationalizes an authoritarian system and a hierarchical organizational structure.

To the contrary, ample empirical evidence is
available to support what each of us has personally
found to be the case: When workers/faculty are given
the opportunity to deliberate on important institutional matters, when they are sufficiently informed,
when they are convinced that the conclusions they draw
will be taken seriously, and when they can voice their
views without fear -- in a word when they are full
participants in the decision-making process -- they
will devote an extraordinary amount of time to the
task and come up with fair and responsible proposals.

Without doubt Platonic theories about basic human
differences and Hobbesian ideas about human nature,
together with mechanistic and positivistic philosophies, have over the years profoundly affected our
world views. But one must wonder why, in an age of
science, knowledge about the relative inefficiency of
the hierarchical structure of social institutionas is
not more widely acted upon. No doubt, fear is a

factor, particularly on the part of persons in positions of authority who feel threatened with a loss of status and power. But even those in subordinate positions are often fearful, at least skeptical, about their own ability and the ability of their peers to exercise the kinds of intelligence required for participation in the managerial process. Among other inhibiting factors are institutional inertia, cultural habits, legal questions, and a natural reluctance to depart from traditional and orthodox modes of production.

Nonetheless, whether business institutions, at least, should organize in accordance with the scientific management model or in accordance with the participatory model may not be an option for much longer. The evidence is clear that participatory principles, properly implemented, result in enhanced efficiency, hence increased profit. And as international and intranational economic competition becomes more intense, it is compelling that we utilize fully the intellectual capacities and creative energies of employees at all levels in business organizations -- in effect make every employee a manager. There will be, of course, resistance by those who are fearful, skeptical, or self-serving, but in a relatively free economy such resistance must inevitably wither away.

A somewhat different situation exists in educational institutions. The purpose of educational institutions is far more complex and the "bottom line" far less clear than is the case with business institutions. The directive power of profit does not apply. The overriding objective of many administrators in education is persuading governing boards and the public at large that they are doing a good job. Hence, they see public relations as the key to their success, and, therefore, the participatory nature of the decision-making process is of little, if any, concern to them.

And so, beset as they are these days by budget cuts and public clamor for efficiency, educational institutions are moving away from traditional collegial relationships and toward a hardening of the lines of authority between administration and faculty. Presidents and deans often feel that they alone can and must make the "tough" decisions, and they are turning for advice not so much to faculty, but to money managers, credit counters, and public relations experts. Faculty members are being asked to tend to their academic knitting whilst those hired to do the job manage. As a result, morale among faculty has

xii

fallen precipitously; many feel depreciated and out of control -- an irony not only in light of the history of academia but also in light of the fact that the principles of participation grew in large part out of studies done in the university.

Much the same situation exists in the public schools. Research shows that of all the sources of frustration felt by teachers -- and there are many -- those they regard to be the most stressful are (1) the limited opportunity to participate in making school decisions and (2) poor teacher/administrator relationships. Compounding the problem are new demands for proof of efficiency in the form of scores on uniform assessment tests which have been imposed on teachers as a result of legislative pressure. The results are predictable. Scores are rising because teachers, reluctantly, are teaching for the test and, unfortunately, undermining genuine education in the process. And it is genuine education, not bits and pieces of information, which the democratized work place, let alone the larger society, requires.

It seems odd to say this, but we can only hope that the enlightenment which is beginning to dawn on the business world will have its effect on the educational world. Surely any major contradictions between the purpose and organizational style of business and educational institutions must, in the long run, be mediated. How much damage will have been done in the meantime to the institutions and to the process of education, as well as to society, is a serious question.

Our discussion thus far has focused on technical efficiency, what Professor Wirth calls "vulgar efficiency." It is, of course, a matter of great importance. But an even more significant issue is the interrelationship between the values of society and the values which inhere in its institutions. No society, especially a democratic society, can long endure disjunctions and discontinuities in the values of its major institutions without suffering serious consequences. Conversely, if a society is to strengthen its primary values, it must actively encourage the institutions which comprise it -- family, business, school -- to operate in a manner consistent with those values. For institutions, as Wirth rightly observes, are learning communities. In the process of living and working in them, we acquire certain values and understandings, certain dispositions and attitudes. If it is democracy we prize, we must recognize that it is not just a political system which grants us the franchise and certain civil rights. It is also an ethical system, a way of relating to one another, a way of solving problems together informed by a sense of fraternity and a respect for persons. When that spirit permeates our social institutions, the cause of democracy will have indeed been served.

Irving Bluestone

Arthur Brown

Wayne State University
May, 1983

CHAPTER ONE

INTRODUCTION

I began this study when I was repelled by what
I saw happening to teachers and students in the mid-
1970's. I saw demoralization and alienation resulting
from efforts to define education as a cost/benefit
production function in order "to improve efficiency."
Schools were being brought under the grip of the
values and techniques of technocratic ideology that
were prevalent in industry. On the encouraging side I
found, as a response to economic crisis, the emergence
of significant instances of democratic redesign of
work. If technocratic values from industry can exert
powerful influences on schools, countermovements
toward industrial democracy might support different
ideas about learning and school life.

As an educator, I decided I needed to learn
more about the leaders in industry who, in searching
for answers to their own productivity problems, were
rejecting the narrow "scientific efficiency" model
embraced so avidly by educational policy makers. The
investigation led me to explore parallel tensions in
both education and industry, between two major value
orientations in American life: values of technocratic
efficiency and values of the democratic tradition. At
issue is what we choose to become as a people, as we
prepare to enter the twenty-first century.

In industry, challenges to the main-line scientific efficiency model were coming from a cluster of
developments associated with a loosely defined phenomenon of industrial democracy. Since this concept is
central to the themes of the book, it is important to
deal with definitional problems in some detail before
we begin. One will look in vain for precise, univer-
sally agreed on definitions of terms like industrial
democracy, work-place democracy, socio-technical work
theory, and quality of work life. While these terms
have been associated with the restoration of democratic values at work, their mere usage does not guarantee such an end. Like other terms that become popular
in American life, they can quickly degenerate into
empty, deceptive slogans - in this case clichés for
maintaining manipulative practices to support the
status quo. I shall try briefly to clarify my own
conceptions, but a more adequate explication will
depend on the unfolding of the narrative which
follows.

We might note, to begin with, the wide range of

1

usage of industrial democracy terminology. Industrial democracy is a heavily overworked term in the litera- ture of social scientists and political activists. As Joep F. Bolveg pointed out in Job Design and Industri- al Democracy, the term has been used in recent years in connection with autonomous work groups in Norway; the model of workers' self-management in Yugoslovia; co-determination in Germany; the general tradition of trade union collective bargaining in the U.S.A.; and factory occupation by protesting workers at the Lip company in France.[1] These are very different, but there is a common value perspective underlying all of them: the assumption that peoples' interests are not adequately represented in the decision-making pro- cesses of organizations; and an aspiration by persons at work to increase their influence over decisions which are of concern to them.

In the usage just referred to, one may note that industrial democracy may be related to fundamen- tal challenges to capitalist ownership. The Webbs in Industrial Democracy (1902), for example, pointed to a society in which industry would be run by workers under a charter negotiated with government to protect community interests. Anarchists like Kropotkin and Bakunin argued that workers' seizure of power at the local level was necessary, both to improve work conditions, and to act as protection against coercive state power. The young Marx deplored the alienated condition of workers and saw the transfer of power away from capitalists as the only solution. Nine- teenth century syndicalists aimed at industrial democracy and the abolition of the state; but, instead of peaceful change through collective bargaining, advocated a general strike and public agitation, by which trade unions would achieve control over the economy. More recently, European New Left Maoists or anarchists have re-embraced many of these ideas.

In this study, industrial democracy is primar- ily used in the much narrower sense of work-place democracy. This is so because I am interested in examining realistic prospects for institutional change in the United States. American unions, in general, have chosen to follow Samuel Gompers' tradition of working within a system of private ownership. Since that is the reality from which moves toward further democratization may emerge, I describe what in fact is developing and attempt to identify the growing points which could lead to further extensions of democratic principles and practice.

Reference to American unions provides a key

2

point for distinguishing legitimate from bogus aspects
of "industrial democracy." Unions have found that
various unilateral developments like job enrichment,
"human relations", and quality circles may be ploys to
by-pass or subvert worker organizations. A central
issue, therefore, is to determine whether "industrial
democracy" practices are aimed at undermining or
protecting a strong, active role for democratic
unions. I accept as legitimate only those approaches
which provide adequate union safeguards.

More specifically, I concentrate on versions
like those which grew out of pioneering efforts by
Einar Thorsrud and his colleagues in the Norwegian
Industrial Democracy Projects (1960-70's), and Quality
of Work Life, ideas developed collaboratively by
Michael Maccoby and Irving Bluestone (Vice President
of the United Auto Workers Union) in the United
States.*

Thorsrud's version of industrial democracy
concentrated on winning more dignity and participation
for people at work. It avoided ideological positions
on the ultimate form of society or on issues between
capitalist or socialist economic systems. It operated
within a general Social Democratic reform orientation
and tended to reflect the pragmatism characteristic of
the dominant outlook of U.S. unions. In practice,
Thorsrud's orientation assumed that solutions
regarding increased worker participation can be sought
within a mixed but basically privately owned economy.
It assumed further that widespread worker involvement
in the values and practice of work place democracy was
an important ground work for exploring broader social
extensions of the idea. Unless capitalism enters a
stage of break-down, the push is to seek a more
humane, democratically oriented private enterprise
system.

Socio-technical work design was the functional
tool designed to implement the goals. Socio-technical
theory, pioneered thirty years ago at the Tavistock
Institute of Human Relations in England and in Norwegian Industrial Democracy Projects, provided the
conceptual frame for challenging dominant "Taylorist"
scientific management, and for analyzing work in ways
to combine broader worker participation with technical
design to support it.

---

*Joep F. Bolveg in Job Design and Industrial Democracy
(p. 123) points out that there is great similarity
between American "Quality of Work Life" efforts and
Norwegian work design theory and practice.

The democratic thrust of this version of socio-technical theory distinguishes it from a variety of forms of "job enrichment and human relations" schemes that were emerging at the same time. These typically are unilateral changes prescribed by management to increase productivity. Norwegian type socio-technical theory, on the other hand, assumes that the goal of democratization will be filled only if four principles are met: (1) The workers and their representatives must influence decisions during the planning and change process; (2) the changes must lead to increased worker autonomy; (3) the workers must share in economic benefits; and (4) the workers must be able to withdraw if they no longer evaluate the changes positively.[2]

Furthermore, the assumption is that traditional collective bargaining will be retained to protect worker interests. Direct worker participation in decisions at the work site is seen as an extension of democratic unionism. While American union leaders are split in their attitudes toward "quality of work life", the U.A.W. Vice-President Irving Bluestone articulates the case for it. "While the worker's rate of pay may predominate his relationship to his job, he can be responsive to the opportunity for playing an innovative, creative, and imaginative role in the production process."[3]

I describe at some length, features of the theory and practice of this version of industrial democracy, to which important American industries are turning in their moment of crisis. My hunch, as an educator, is that significant shifts in the master economic institution will have effects for teachers and schools. The philosophy of industrial democracy of the Thorsrud democratic socio-technical type, is rooted in value orientations with implications for concepts of society and education that deserve serious thought. The industrial democracy prototype departs in significant respects from current technocratic efficiency emphases.

All of this involves political questions regarding the actual and desired state of a democratic society. If work and education are inextricably connected, the issue of "What kind of political economy?" becomes a critical question. I want to say a few words about the political orientation I work from.

As stated in the text, I operate from the value preference articulated by Kalman H. Silvert in The Reason for Democracy: a democratic political economy

4

must see the person-in-society as both end and means, "combining his reason and his actions in empowered participation." From that perspective I see the two dominant world political economies: Marxist-Leninist state socialism and multi-national corporate capitalism, as fundamentally flawed. In differing ways, the power-elites which govern them are beyond responsible control, and their destructive effects on nature and human beings make them untenable as systems for entering the twenty-first century.

I am persuaded by the argument of Leszek Kolakowski in Main Currents of Marxism, that the ideals of Marxist humanism are betrayed by Marxist-Leninist doctrine, which centers truth and authority in the monolithic power of the Communist Party. The seeds of Marxist-Leninist authoritarianism may be embedded in Marx's own work.

Where capitalism is concerned, apart from its recent shaky performance in keeping people at work, and its failure to reduce shocking economic inequities, there is the danger identified by Admiral Rickover in his retirement address (January 28, 1982): "Through their control of vast resources ... large corporations have become, in effect, another branch of government ... without the checks and balances inherent in our democratic system."[4] This has corrosive effects on our efforts to maintain democratic political life under late-industrial conditions at home. It has led us to be passive observers as multi-national corporations subvert democratic processes in countries beyond our borders.

There are, moreover, basic flaws in the economic determinism doctrines of both corporate capitalism and Marxist-Leninist communism. The underlying "greedy little pig ethic" of classical laissez-faire theory is too destructive for handling the complexities of our overcrowded, interdependent planetary home. It fails to honor sufficiently what is most distinctive about humans and the major source of our strength - our capacity, as Ernest Becker put it, to act as homo poeta - as meaning makers, creative problem solvers, capable of making conscious plans to replace destructive policies with life-nurturing ones.

Marxist-Leninist economic determinism, on the other hand, assumes that capitalism is vulnerable to its own inner contradictions. But, since the wielders of power will not relinquish their privileges peacefully, people must turn to the dictatorship of a vanguard party. Twentieth century experience provides little hope that democratic ends will derive from

5

dictatorial means placed beyond the people's reach.

Both determinisms reject the democratic Enlightenment faith that the core value is to respect the dignity of persons and their capacity for being on-going learners; that the capacity for free examination of ideas and critical, collaborative participation provides the best means for confronting the challenges of change unleashed by science and technology. Control needs have led to fear of participative involvement which is open-ended and unpredictable.

As the rate of ecological decay and human alienation increases, there is growing disillusionment with both multi-national corporate capitalism and classical socialist state ownership. My own position is that we need to explore pluralist third ways which support the values of democratic humanism: individuality and community. Those are the values intrinsic to many aspects of industrial democracy; they are values intrinsic to humane education. The turn to democratic participation opens an opportunity to find out if it is possible to "go through" private corporate institutions, to transform them so that they will be more conserving of nature, more responsive to public interest, and more sustaining of the creative energies of the work force. Related possibilities include the expansion of producer cooperatives as workers take over ownership of failing companies. As John Dewey saw the issue, the question is whether needed economic and social changes can be created that will also preserve and develop the democratic ideals of the earlier liberalism: intellectual and moral freedom, freedom of inquiry and expression, freedom of association in work, recreation and religion; or whether social controls are to be instituted by coercive state prescription in ways to threaten those values.[5]

Work place democracy, of course, is not enough. It will gain credibility as a reform movement only if it becomes, as some of the Norwegians argue, one of the "leading edges" for raising questions about "the quality of life" beyond the work place. This inevitably will involve controversial political questions about the location and allocation of power and resources. I turn to some of those possibilities in the final chapter.

Where education is concerned, the argument is that concepts of learning and schooling will be significantly affected by the outcome of the tension between technocratic efficiency and democratic renewal. In Chapters IV and V, I describe how that issue was present at the opening of the twentieth century in contentions between educational social- efficiency theorists, and John Dewey as articulator of the "progressive" tradition. In Chapters VI, VII, and VIII, I describe the contemporary revival of that debate. I recount efforts in the 60's and 70's to define education as a cost/benefit production function; and I describe critiques and alternatives which reflect the values of a democratic social philosophy.

Finally, I explore how tensions between technocratic efficiency and industrial democracy orientations in the work world reveal options we confront in both education and the larger society as we close out the century.

I write then of the possibility of a resurgence of a neglected part of American experience - the democratic ideal: having respect for the dignity of persons, having confidence that people of diverse abilities and roles can communicate to create answers to problems of living. In the midst of our economic crisis, significant leaders are sensing that renewal of our strength depends on revitalizing that ideal.

In all candor, recent history suggests that the odds are against our taking the opportunity seriously. We seem to prefer to follow other banners: to design institutions to control people for narrow pursuit of profit; to create schooling for limited skill mastery; to fixate on material accumulation in ways which divert us from contact with ourselves and from creative solutions to the injustice and ugliness that remain within the society; to pursue chauvinistic policies overseas which ally us with brutal militarists because they protect U.S. corporate interests.

There is no guarantee that we shall reinvigorate the democratic ideal which once captured the imagination of the world's people. There is a hunger, however, for guiding visions which will bring meaning to the lives of contemporary men and women. The democratic ideal still remains part of a living American heritage. I write to point to evidence of green shoot renewals which, if nurtured, might act as a force to free untapped hopes and energies of our people in work and in education. There is the far-fetched possibility that we would choose to transform a post-industrial America into a high democratic society.

NOTES

1.   Joep F. Bolweg, <u>Job Design and Industrial Democracy</u>. (Leiden: Martinus Nijhoff Social Sciences Division, 1976), p. 87.

2.   Ibid., p. 100.

3.   Ibid., p. 116.

4.   Admiral Hyman Rickover, Testimony before Joint Economic Committee of U.S. Senate, January 28, 1982. (See <u>New York Times</u>, January 29, 1982, p. A-17.)

5.   John Dewey, <u>Intelligence in the Modern World</u>.   ed., Joseph Ratner (New York: Modern Library, 1939), p. 425.

CHAPTER II

INDUSTRY AND EDUCATION IN
AMERICA - INTEGRAL VS. VULGAR EFFICIENCY

Living on the threshold of a new age, we
squabble among ourselves to acquire or retain
the privileges of bygone times, we contemplate
changing almost anything on this earth but
ourselves.... A new single insight must dawn on
people: you do not solve world problems by
applying technological fixes within the framework of narrowly self-centered values. Coping
with mankind's current predicament calls for
inner changes... for mobilizing new values and
new aspirations, backed by new levels of
personal commitment and political will.[1]
Ervin Laszlo, United Nations Institute for
Training and Research.

This book is written from the conviction that
the remaining years of this century face us with challenges which concern survival and well-being on the
planet. We are at the beginning of a momentous
transition from a petroleum to a multi-energy based
society. Historically, every such major energy
transition, e.g., the shift from wind and water power
to coal, and then from coal to petroleum has affected
the whole quality of human experience. We may envisage the energy crisis as the forerunner of a number
of shortages and failures in technological systems
that will force far-reaching changes in the way we may
manage our societies and conduct our lives.

Changes of this magnitude cannot be managed by
technique alone; at bottom we are required to change
the fundamental ways we relate to nature and to each
other. One urgent need is for simultaneous redesign
of two critical institutions - work and education, in
ways congruent with the values of a less destructive,
more sustainable society. Work is critical because it
involves the ways we relate to the world to produce
survival materials, and education is a major means to
effect changes in attitudes and values. The changes
must occur concurrently because values taught by
educators are vitiated if practices in work contradict
them.

The substantive changes required will include:
(1) shifts from dominance-exploitation relations
toward nature to synergistic-symbiotic relations. We
have to learn to see ourselves as living systems

9

within other systems. The health of one depends on the health of others. (2) shifts in ways we relate to our "boundless resource" - the most highly educated human work force in history.

Our task is to ask how we can use this resource to create "good work." E. F. Schumacher reminded us that "good work" embraces both a conserving attitude toward what happens to people at work as well as to material produced. The function of "good work" is to give a person a chance to "utilize and develop his faculties; to enable him to overcome his ego-centeredness by joining with others in a common task; and to bring forth the goods and services of a becoming existence," i.e., goods and services that meet the criteria of "permanence, health and beauty."[2]

In contrast, we are aware that Western societies in both work and schools are marked by parallel symptoms of malaise: waste and low-quality work, absenteeism, apathy or hostility, and alcohol or drug abuse. There is widespread concern about the decline of productivity and the quality of life in both industry and schools. I agree with Ervin Laszlo, of the United Nations Institute for Training and Research, that a major source of our distress lies in an insistence on clinging to a "modernist" technocratic efficiency tradition in both economic and school life which embraces the "technological fix" error - the error which assumes that problems of all systems - natural, mechanical or human can be solved by technical solutions designed by outside experts. In the words of Ervin Laszlo, "modernism" brought us enormous material progress, and has become a threat to life and well being. Its technique is embedded in a set of beliefs:[3]

> --that in this world it is each man for himself, with the strongest and the most resourceful earning rightful privileges.

> --that nature is nothing but a collection of objects to be exploited for endless material growth.

> --that science discovers "facts" and that they alone are what count: values are merely subjective.

> --that true efficiency is maximum quantitative productivity for each machine, each enterprise, and each human being.

--that we can know all we need to know about people by applying a systems-efficiency, "cost-benefit" model to evaluate their performances and behaviors.

--that our responsibilities end with assuring our own welfare and that of our country - and that we should let the next generation fend for itself as we have had to.

--that human happiness consists of having the most sumptuous, powerful products and that the signs of progress are bigger, more mechanized cities, farms, industries and institutions.

The spirit of "technocratic modernism" has dominated our twentieth century efforts in industry and education.

In industry, the dominant mode of production emerged as "scientific management" or "Taylorism," named after Frederick W. Taylor, author of the enormously influential The Principles of Scientific Management (New York, 1911). It was Taylor, the industrial engineer, who became a crusader for the idea that human efficiency at work could be increased enormously by substituting scientific analysis by management for traditional worker skills and rule of thumb procedures. He was an imaginative engineer who, as Raymond Callahan pointed out, "in his work with metals exhibited the creative imagination, the persistence, and the singleness of purpose of a scientist."[4] But it was his style of redefining the nature of work for people which made him famous.

His keen eye spotted glaring weaknesses in the early modes of factory production. He attributed low efficiency to poor concepts of management and tendencies toward "soldiering" by the workers. The details of Taylor's philosophy and methods are available elsewhere and are not necessary for our purposes. But since they had long-standing influence that continues to this day and illustrate a concept of efficiency which will come under criticism in this book, we summarize briefly main features of the rationale.

Taylor began by finding the flaw in the best management practice of his day which he called the initiative and incentive system. Under this system workers were given freedom and encouragement to produce more by various incentive systems. For Taylor, the basic difficulty was that workingmen, through lack of education or mental ability, were incapable of understanding the scientific basis

11

underlying the job. The remedy was for management to step in and assume duties consistent with the principles of scientific management. The new role for management was an active role of analyzing, planning, and controlling the whole work process in detail.

Taylor demonstrated job analysis by conducting time and motion studies with a stop watch to identify all of the specific moves and procedures in a unit of work. After identifying time saving changes, he tested them out with a first class worker. When a job analysis was identified which produced better results, he standardized the steps. Each worker received an instruction card which described in detail "not only what was to be done but how it is to be done and the exact time allowed for doing it." Once the time and motion prescriptions had been objectively and scientifically determined, it was the task of management to set definite tasks for each day and to create detailed supervisory procedures to assure compliance and control. The ideal of work design was to plan the job flow so that the work of each person would be "confined to the performance of a single leading function."[5]

Taylor firmly believed that there was "one best way of doing a job and this method could be determined only through the scientific study of that job by experts with proper implements..." He saw his theory as providing an "almost equal division of the work and the responsibility between the management and the workmen." For Taylor this meant that "one type of man is needed to plan ahead and an entirely different type to execute the work." Managers were to analyze, plan and control. The worker's "equal division" was to do what he was told by management. A mechanic working under Taylor reported that Mr. Taylor told him he was "not supposed to think; there are other people paid for thinking around here."[6]

The statement is a classical example of the mind set and structural conditions which Harry Braverman described as "leading to the degradation of work", i.e., where thinking, conceptualizing, intellectualizing about the work process was made a prerogative of management, while people at work were limited to the execution of prescribed, limited tasks under the scrutiny and control of supervision.[7]

From the beginning there were people like Samuel Gompers who found Taylor's ideas humanly demeaning. But Taylor was concerned that there was a "bottom line" dimension to his work that, in the crunch, would bring all parties to accept it. The

size of the productive pie would increase under his
system, as would the slice received by each member of
labor and management. John Kennedy later restated the
point in saying that all boats would rise with a
rising tide. It followed that all rational participants would be content and grateful for the results.

When the Taylorist rationale produced marvels
of quantitative production, its advocates assumed it
had a magic potency for other institutions. The
public schools, as Raymond Callahan points out in
Education and the Cult of Efficiency, were pulled
under its influence early in the century. More
recently, as clamors about school inadequacies mount-
ed, educators again were pushed to seek solutions
through its application. C.A. Bowers has pointed out
that in the schools, technocratic efficiency ideology
increasingly asserts itself in the form of "teacher
accountability and competency-based instruction."[8] It
sees itself as concerned with the neutral goal of
improving learning efficiency, defined as increased
measurable output. It tends to assume that only
observable behavior is real, that anything real must
be measurable, that learning consists of mastery of
discrete components, and that the good person is
operationally defined by scoring well on expert-
designed tests. It is the competititve achievement
model designed to help winners get ahead vocationally
and to reinforce the attitude that in this world it is
each person for her/himself.

There is, however, an irony involved, for as
schools have turned toward refined versions of Taylorist efficiency, that model was being declared dysfunctional by a number of thoughtful leaders in industry.
Educators ought to be alert to this development, for
their experience with "Taylorism" in education has
taught them that schools are affected by values of the
work world.

My own interests in looking at education/work
relations grew out of observations of some consequences of the accountability development in schools
in the mid-seventies. Where "accountability" reduced
teaching to the idea that "only test scores count,"
committed creative teachers were demoralized or
leaving, while many of the rest were cheating. (A
model of which children did not need yet another
example.)

As a parent I had developed confidence that the
best bet for getting our own children "hooked on
learning" was when they could work with committed
teachers, whose creative energies were engaged - who

demonstrated by the way they lived in the schools that they themselves were enthusiastic learners - people working from what the Greeks called their <u>entheos</u> - the personal God within which was the source of <u>enthusiasmos</u> or enthusiasm.[9]

If the new reductionist emphasis - "teaching is 'teaching for tests'" did damage to that, and in addition taught kids that adults will cheat when fearful, then I assumed that something crazy and crazy-making was going on.

At the same time I was reading accounts about the decline of productivity and morale in American industry - a decline at the very center of that rational efficiency model.

A set of questions began to form in my mind. Might "scientific management," being applied so forcefully in both industry and education, itself be a cause of lowered quality of work? If we think of schools as work places for children and teachers, what makes them "good work" places from the scientific management perspective? What makes them "good work" places from the E.F. Schumacher perspective with which we began the chapter? If there was a flaw in the scientific management rationale which had crazy-making effects for schools, was anyone in industry questioning its effects? Were alternative theories for securing good work in industry being seriously tried anywhere? If so, could these theories have relevance for how to get good work in schools?

A bit of searching led me to Paul Dickson's <u>The Future of the Work Place</u> (1975) which described serious doubts among a few leaders in industry about the dominant model. I soon discovered that a lusty challenger to "scientific management" was emerging: socio-technical theory for work redesign, associated with ideas of industrial democracy. At that time pioneering was limited to Scandinavia, and a few industries here and there in a number of countries. But there was also an international network of supportive theory and research emerging from such sources as The Work Research Institutes in Norway, the Tavistock Institute in England and from the writings of persons like Einar Thorsrud and P. G. Herbst in Norway, Pehr Gyllenhammar (President of Volvo in Sweden), Fred Emery in Australia, and Eric Trist, Michael Maccoby and Louis Davis in the United States. By 1980, when survival was threatened by Japanese competition, corporations in major American industries, like steel and automaking, were turning seriously in this direction - with General Motors taking the lead.

14

General Motors, for example, used to boast that
the production line had been designed so that every
task could be taught in fifteen minutes or less;
efficiency could be guaranteed by designing work tasks
so that any idiot could do them. If morale and
workmanship were poor, the answer was to step up
supervision and control. But in 1980, on our campus,
Dr. William Duffy, Director of Research in Work
Innovation at General Motors, said G.M. was now
convinced that a model based on "increased control by
supervisors, of a reluctant work force which produces
shabby products, is not viable for survival." General
Motors, with a commitment of 45 billion dollars for
plant redesign by 1985, is moving strongly in the
direction of the socio-technical model. In looking at
education/work relations, I shall argue that understanding the philosophy and values of socio-technical
theory is important for leaders of both institutions.
For the moment, it is sufficient to say that the main
criticism of traditional scientific management by the
socio-technical theorists, is that it is guilty of the
"technological fix" error, i.e, the assumption that
all problems will yield to technical-type solutions.
But the reality of human work is "socio" as well as
"technical," and "socio" refers to the inner, purpo-
sive, intentional, evaluative, idea-generating,
communicative-collaborative aspects of human beings.
The mainline efficiency model is out of touch with
these distinctive, human dimensions of reality. It
fails because it fails to engage the personal enthusiasms and commitment of whole human beings, and their
capacities for the learning required to meet the
challenge of turbulent change. Traditional job
design, which relies on task fragmentation and detailed supervisory control, is breaking down. To treat a
socio-technical system as nothing but a technical
system is to be out of touch with reality, i.e., to be
crazy - which leads to trouble. A clue to the common
source of trouble in industries and schools may be
found in the Old Norwegian root word of crazy: krasa,
which means crushed or fragmented - to atomize a whole
which belongs together.
We can expect the tension between the contend-
ing concepts of work to be sharp and abrasive because
it is related to a basic value split in American
culture.
Daniel Bell in "Schools in American Society"
perceives the split as follows:
There is a widening tension between an economic, technical order oriented to functional

15

rationality and efficiency, organized on the simple principle of economizing - of least costs and optimization of production and profits; and counter trends concerned with reaches for "wholeness of persons" and "self-realization." (Bell sees hedonism in the latter, while I see it as related to the democratic ethos with its insistence on persons being treated as ends rather than as means only.)

Bell points out that the structural principle of utilitarian efficiency is bureaucratization. "You divide people into roles, you segment them, you specialize them. People then become subordinated within the structure so as to facilitate the greater output of goods and greater efficiency in the use of resources."[10]

We now witness, simultaneously, powerful efforts to make bureaucratic efficiency the dominant fact in all phases of our lives, and a growing resistance to it.

At a more philosophical level, Karl Popper uses a potent metaphor to identify the underlying issue. He says that there are three ways of conceptualizing human reality: as a clock, as a cloud, and as a system of plastic control.

What we need for understanding rational human behavior is something intermediate between perfect determinism - something intermediate between perfect clouds and perfect clocks.... What we want is to understand how such non-physical things as purposes, deliberations, plans, decisions, intentions and values, can play a part in bringing about changes in the physical world.[11]

The solution is the idea of "plastic or flexible" control which is the idea of combining freedom and control in contrast to cast-iron control.

At this point it may appear that the enemy is being defined as "efficiency." Yet efficiency can hardly be described as unqualified evil. One dictionary definition of efficient is simply "having and using requisite knowledge, skill and industry." But efficiency in cultural practice is not a single thing.

I think it is useful to follow Denis Goulet in his analysis of "the two edged sword" of technological efficiency which enables us to make a distinction between "vulgar efficiency" and "integral efficiency."[12] In his analysis of Western technology, Goulet says it must be seen as both a bearer and a

16

destroyer of human values; and as bringing both
freedom from traditional restraints and new determinisms. One of the values central to Western type
technology is a particular conception of efficiency:
a viewpoint drawn from a productivity perspective of
industry in which productivity is measured as a
proportion of input to output. This represents an
engineer's way of defining efficiency within closed
circuit mechanical systems. It fits with another
dictionary definition of efficiency as "the ratio of
the work done by a machine, engine etc. to the energy
supplied to it." Within this framework, assessors of
efficiency compare measures of input and output.
Decisions necessarily must be made as to what to
include or exclude from comparisons. Certain elements
are treated as "externalities" to the efficiency
calculus. These are items not included as relevant to
the system. Others which are included in the calculations, are labeled as "internalities." Thus safety
belts were not included as "internalities" in auto
design for many years; or factory managers, until
recently, did not include anti-pollution devices among
cost/benefit calculations; pollution was treated as a
mere "externality." As Goulet observes:

> The exclusion of this and similar values is
> easy to explain: Given the socio-economic
> system within which Western technology ma-
> tured, the production of goods by firms was
> treated in accord with a profit-maximizing
> calculus. Quite logically, therefore, impor-
> tant social values were systematically exclud-
> ed. Behind this form of reasoning lies a
> mechanistic engineering mentality. [13]

This limited way of perceiving efficiency, and
associated concepts of rationality and problem-
solving, comes out of a peculiar Western tradition of
science and economic life that has not been shared by
most other human cultures. We are so used to it,
however, that it has a "taken for granted" quality
that puts it beyond question.

To help us see that other conceptions of efficiency are possible, Goulet decribes the idea about
"efficient work" of two Bedouin tribes in the Sahara.
For them it was a way to work which permitted them to
recite Koranic prayers seven times daily and to reduce
physical energy during Ramadan fasting periods. And
the "efficient" path to take their flocks to pasture
was not the shortest route but one which permitted
them to practice Koranic hospitality toward the poor
along the way. [14]

The engineering mentality could not but label these distractions as "externalities." On the other hand a non-Western perspective enabled these tribes to "internalize" religious and ethical values in their assessment of "efficiency."

The example may be overly dramatic but it illustrates Goulet's point that we are beginning to be aware that the technological tradition of the West, which limits definitions of efficiency to what can be accommodated by the "closed systems" mental set of the engineering tradition, is not our only option. There is, in fact, a growing sense that it is dangerous to our well-being. Conceptually it may be clear that the time for change has arrived. We need to recognize also that the difficulty of implementation is enormous.

> Huge vested interests, not the least of which is the intellectual security produced by two centuries of thinking in familiar patterns, stand in the way. Most moderns simply do not know how to be efficient without destroying the environment, alienating workers or reinforcing technological determinism. Out of habit they judge the efficiency of machines and processes by systematically excluding important social values. The balance is difficult to redress because a host of problems press for solution on the old terms. That is why efficiency needs to be redefined via political consultations which bear directly on value priorities and the allocation of social costs. It is no longer correct to label some procedure efficient if it exacts intolerable social costs, proves grossly wasteful of resources, or imposes its mechanistic rhythms on its operator. [15]

We may, I believe, appropriately label these destructive tendencies of the limited engineering mentality as "vulgar efficiency."

The urgent need now, says Goulet, is to create "new modes of operating efficiently, simultaneously solving problems in the conventional style and optimizing social values hitherto externalized but now needing to be internalized."[16] It may be necessary, for example, for purposes of quantitative-material growth to include competition and accountability. One may recall how even in a Marxist society like China, there is "socialist emulation," with public posting of records of production performances by outstanding work brigades. Kindly social intentions cannot take the place of getting good work accomplished efficiently. But Goulet adds, "managers and designers of technology will need to explore ways of becoming integrally efficient, that is, of producing efficiently while optimizing social and human values. This they must do with as much passion, singlemindedness, and practical sense as they now devote to making profits or creating new products." [17]

Thus we may see that for our time a basic issue has become not efficiency vs. inefficiency but "vulgar" - limited engineering-type efficiency vs. "integral efficiency."

Much of what follows in this book revolves around the argument that constructive action for human welfare, and perhaps survival, depends on creating policies which establish tensional balances between freedom and control. The evidence is mounting that important sectors of the work world, populated now with a more highly educated, less acquiescent work force, are malfunctioning because of a fixation on efforts to attain efficiency by the "control model of a perfect clock." In education also, the "clock control" model has become a dominating paradigm. Educators have followed the tendency to confront trouble by stepping up controls, so that we spend tens of millions of dollars on school guards - armed and unarmed. But controls, without commitment of students and teachers, do not produce impressive results. American educational history would lead us to expect that eventually calls for alternatives to the futility of "clock control"/"vulgar efficiency" in schools will be made. The cultural tension between bureaucratic rationality and "wholeness of persons" is as deeply embedded in education as it is in any other institution. The controversy between the educational tradition of a positivist science of education and democratic progressivism or "humanistic education" has raged throughout the century, and runs parallel to the contentions between Taylorist efficiency and industrial democracy in economic life. In Chapter IV we shall examine one of the struggles, as the century opened, to bring schools under the discipline of scientific management. The specific issue centered on the question of the nature and role of vocationalism in the schools, and involved exchanges between John Dewey and progressive era democrats, versus social efficiency philosophers championing an efficient training model of schooling. In brief, vocationalists wanted public schools to reflect the values, attitudes and techniques of scientific management and the engineering mentality of corporate capitalism. Dewey championed a counter version of science as "freed intelligence," an exemplar of the moral values of social democracy which could transform both schooling and industry.

My argument is that the tension between the values of technological efficiency and democratic-humanist values have been in contention in American life thoughout the twentieth century. We confronted these issues as the century opened and we will be confronting them as the century comes to a close.

I entertain the belief that the dominant scientific management model is, or will be, brought under challenge again. In industry, an emerging challenger is democratic socio-technical theory. I see this as potentially a counter to the destructive excesses of the "technological fix" frame of mind.

If it gains strength, it will have consequences for American education, since schools inevitably are influenced by dominant values of the economic institutions. Educators who seek more humane alternatives to "vulgar efficiency" emphases may find an interesting new source of support from those in labor and industry who are moving in the socio-technical direction. When the excesses of vulgar efficiency in the classrooms are brought under criticism once again with the charge of "mindlessness," it would be a relief if educators would be prepared to make responses that could avoid the dreary pendulum swing from "disciplined efficiency" to "child centered freedom."

Educators might profitably study the hyphenated concept of socio-technical theory which aims to establish integral efficiency in industry. They may note that the hyphen implies that both the socio and technical aspects of human reality in our time have to be taken seriously.

Ours is a technological era in which survival depends on insightful problem-solving, requiring mastery of conceptual-technical skills. Schools as "good work" places will have to embody a caring concern for rigorous intellectual effort as well as provision for individual creativity and supportive community.

I hold that the socio-technical idea may help us get back in touch with the strength of our democratic roots in a way appropriate for meeting the challenge of turbulent technological and social change. We turn next, therefore, to an initial exploration of the socio-technical idea.

NOTES

1. Ervin Laszlo, The Inner Limits of Mankind. (New York: The Pergamon Press, 1978), pp. 3-4.

2. E.F. Schumacher, Small is Beautiful: Economics As If People Mattered. (New York: Harper Torch Books, 1973), pp. 51-52. See also Schumacher's Good Work. (New York: Harper and Row, 1979).

3. Laszlo, op. cit., pp. 5-6.

4. Raymond E. Callahan, Education and the Cult of Efficiency. (Chicago: University of Chicago Press, 1962), p. 40. (In the account of Taylorism I have borrowed freely from Callahan's chapter 2, "Reform Conscious America Discovers the Efficiency Expert" and have used also Taylor's own The Principles of Scientific Management. For a recent perceptive analysis of Taylorism and its ideology see Judith A. Merkle, Management and Ideology. (Berkeley: University of California Press., 1980).)

5. Ibid., pp. 31-32.

6. Ibid., pp. 27-29.

7. Harry Braverman, Labor and Monopoly Capital: The Degradation of Work in the Twentieth Century. (New York: Monthly Review Press, 1974).

8. C.A. Bowers, "Emergent Ideological Characteristics of Educational Policy," Teachers College Record, (September 1977, vol. 79, No. 1).

9. Renée Dubos, The God Within. (New York: Charles Scribner's Sons, 1972), p. 4.

10. In Louis Rubin, ed., The Future of America: Perspectives on Tomorrow's Schooling. (Boston: Allyn and Bacon, 1975), p. 44.

11. Karl R. Popper, "Of Clouds and Clocks: An Approach to the Problem of Rationality and the Freedom of Man," in Popper, Objective Knowledge: An Evolutionary Approach. (Oxford: Clarendon Press, 1972), pp. 228-229; 231-232 (Italics mine).

12. Denis Goulet, The Uncertain Promise. (New York: IDOC/North America, 1977).

13. Ibid., p. 18.

14. Ibid.

15. Ibid., p. 28.

16. Ibid., p. 30.

17. Ibid.

CHAPTER III

DEMOCRATIC SOCIO-TECHNICAL THEORY:
AN ALTERNATIVE PARADIGM FOR "GOOD WORK"

A democratic political-economy must begin and
end with the person-in-society, seeing him as
both end and means, and combining his reason
and his actions in empowered participation.[1]
Kalmar H. Silvert.

We have been hypnotized so long by the ideology of economic and technological progress
that we have scarcely noticed that politically
we have become a retrogressive society,
evolving from a more to a less democratic
polity and from a less to a more authoritarian
society.[2]   Sheldon Wolin.

I don't believe our authoritarian corporations
can continue to coexist with democratic
institutions in a democratic society, and the
reverse is true, too. In Poland, I can't
imagine that a free labor movement will
continue to exist in their authoritarian
society....Either the Polish government will
change as their labor movement becomes more
democratic, or the unions will be crushed. In
this country, we must democratize our corporations.[3]   Delmar L. Landen

In this chapter we shall present the theory and
practice of democratic socio-technical theory as an
emerging paradigm for "good work". We shall concentrate on events taking place in work redesign in
industry. We assume that people interested in education who are becoming aware that schools also are work
places, will find an account of changes in the larger
work world instructive for their own purposes. Later
we shall examine issues that affect education more
directly.
Before getting into a substantive account of
socio-technical or industrial democracy trends, a note
of warning is useful. The thesis I am arguing holds
that a basic issue at stake is whether the values of
our democratic traditions can be made operative in our
economic institutions as a means of renewal. In order
to clarify the idea I shall be presenting examples of
such moves which have been relatively successful. If
the trend would develop into a major movement, educa-

23

tors concerned with countering the blight of bureaucratic "rational efficiency" in schooling might find
interesting and important new allies from the ranks of
management and labor.

There is, however, no guarantee that expansion
of socio-technical practice with its support of
democracy as a form of social living at work will
remain authentically democratic. The temptation to
co-opt worker "collaboration," as alternative to
"confrontation," in the interests of narrow "productivity" remains ever present.

American unionists are aware that earlier
efforts at "worker involvement" repeatedly have been
turned into forms of manipulation. One can sense the
possibility of new reverberations of this type in a
manifesto for "re-industrialization" in Business Week
(June 30, 1980). The authors speak of a "new social
contract,"[4] to replace "the politics of conflict" by a
"collaborative relationship" among leaders of labor,
management, government and academia.

While the "re-industrialization" concept is not
completely clear, there is an emphasis on giving
priority to acceptance by all social groups of the
idea that "their common interest in returning their
country to a strong economic growth overrides other
conflicting interests." Past adversarial relationships
and concerns about aspirations of the poor, the
minorities and the environmentalists must be downgrad-
ed because they centered on how to distribute an
expanding output of goods and services. Since economic
growth, upon which the other social goals were dependent, is now problematic, the restoration of it by
giving "re-industrialization" unquestioned priority is
the call of the new manifesto. Americans need little
reminder that there is legitimate concern about
securing improved productivity. "Re-industrialization", however, may be interpreted as the end to which
all else must be subordinated. Citizens of the new
social contract would be asked to dedicate themselves
to "revitalization" - not of the body politic - but
"revitalization of economic growth." As Sheldon
Woldin, editor of Democracy sees it, the call is for
citizen absorption in "the real work of modernizing
American industry," not in reclaiming his or her
political self or recreating a common life.[5]

For some advocates of re-industrialization like
George Gilder, the end requires that rational modes of
work organization and control must be extended into
the upper reaches of private and public employment so
that these tasks emulate "the cognitive style of the

24

industrialists instead of the humanists."[6] Collaboration in this context may mean simply surrender to the will and expertise of the bureaucratic engineers who claim to possess the know-how that will increase the size of the material pie.

There are other leaders in industry and labor, however, who see this dependence on rational control by expert elites and the promise of passive consumer payoff as a major source of industrial malaise. They are exploring a socio-technical philosophy of organizational design that would involve us in a reclaiming of our democratic heritage at work - an approach which might even involve us in the task of creating what Lynn White called "a high democratic culture" under technology.[7] It is to that possibility that we turn next.

A. The Scandinavian Experience

The socio-technical concept of work design has emerged from a number of international sources over the past several decades. Later in this chapter we shall turn to the contributions of American leaders in the field. Some of the most important pioneering work, however, was done at the Tavistock Institute of Human Relations in England, and the Work Research Institutes in Norway. Since important beginnings were made in Norway and Sweden we shall begin with comments on the Scandinavian experience.

In Scandinavia a motivation for creating a new philosophy of work was the break-down in the sixties of the Methods Time Management model which had been imported from the U.S.A. A young, more highly educated Scandinavian work force was responding to the engineering model by absenteeism, sloppy work, alcoholism and malicious mischief. The list transfers easily, of course, to large numbers of our school youth.

Socio-technical theory holds that the fundamental flaw of the cost efficiency model is that it insists on seeking purely technical solutions to systems which, in fact, are socio-technical.[8] "Socio" refers to the personal-social creative aspects of human reality.

It is to the credit of Pehr Gyllenhammar, President of Volvo, that he saw that the mechanistic U.S. management model was harming productivity because it was leading to irrational decisions in the name of rationality. In People at Work (1977), Gyllenhammar describes the factors which led to far-reaching redesign of work.

25

It was worker unrest in 1969 which spurred major organizational changes. Volvo had begun automobile construction in 1927 when it shared the assumption of the time that Taylorist efficiency principles were the means to successful competition. Management was tightly centralized, controlled by the President and a three man executive committee and a large hierarchically organized administrative staff. Its production system was technically oriented and planned in detail, using the American system of Methods Time Management. But at the end of the sixties, however, this orderly system was coming unstuck. The new element was a change in the nature and attitudes of young men and women entering the work force. In Gyllenhammar's words:

> Like other good things, economy of scale turned out to have subtle limits. We begin to find today the symptoms of a new type of industrial illness. We invent machines to eliminate some of the physical stress of work, and then find psychological stress causing even more health and behavior problems. People don't want to be subservient to machines and systems. They react to inhuman working conditions in very human ways: by job-hopping, absenteeism, apathetic attitudes, antagonism ....The younger the worker is, the stronger his or her reactions are likely to be. People entering the workforce today have received more education than ever before in history. We have educated them to regard themselves as mature adults, capable of making their own choices. Then we offer them virtually no choice in our overorganized industrial units. For eight hours a day they are regarded as children, ciphers, or potential problems and managed or controlled accordingly.[9]

Volvo planners began to see that major problems were coming from the more highly educated young workers. They began to consider the idea of retaining the old rules and hiring less educated Finnish and Turkish workers. The logic of staying with what purported to be a rational organization of work was leading them to reject the finest educated youth their country had produced - and it probably would invite social unrest. A second possibility would be to engage in a bold critique of the hierarchical industrial tradition. Volvo made the choice to join an accelerating Scandinavian move toward industrial

26

democracy. The opening sentence in People at Work
sets the tone of the alternative: "People, not
machines, are the real basis for the spectacular
growth of industry during the twentieth century."[10]
Behind this statement is the recognition that
in advanced stages of technology education is the
invisible asset for new approaches to economic and
social development. By the middle eighties 90 percent
of Sweden's young people will complete high school and
70 percent will continue into higher education. In
Gyllenhammar's words, "Among these increasingly
well-educated people Volvo will have to find its
future work force." [11] A democratic society invests
heavily in education to produce people who regard
themselves as mature adults, capable of taking initiative and making intelligent choices. To neglect these
new expectations and capacities is to invite trouble.
To accept them as assets to be nurtured, forces one
into paths beyond the framework of traditional economic thinking. The basic switch in attitudes is from
viewing employees as "hired hands" to seeing and
treating them as adult persons. It says a lot about
what the MTM model has done to people at work, that
the idea of treating them as adults would be considered a momentous innovation.
Puzzling new questions have to be faced if old
habits of management are questioned: What kind of
thinking do you do if you view workers as persons who
want a chance to live and learn as mature adults in
the work place? Is the production process a given to
which humans must adjust, or can technology be redesigned to place it under the control of workers'
intelligence and initiative? What qualities of
leadership are needed to balance the claims of workers, stockholders, customers and general public?
The answer to these questions is dependent on
one's conception of the basic goal of economic enterprise. The President of Volvo frames his answer as
follows: "the purpose of business is to help achieve
and maintain the public good" and the logical extension is the obligation "to administer the resources
with which the company is entrusted and use them to
create economic growth, taking into consideration all
the interest groups involved with the company. This
objective carried with it the demand to provide
meaningful employment." [12] The goal is to view every
worker as entitled to a dignified work place, with
opportunity for personal development and a chance to
influence the work commensurate with his or her
abilities and to do it so that the enterprise "stays

27

in the black." In order to portray the means to realize these objectives we may look briefly at developments in one of the pioneering plants, the Kalmar auto assembly plant. Kalmar was in trouble. Wild cat strikes were erupting, employee turnover was 52 percent and absenteeism was rising. Volvo leaders finally decided that the old technical solutions themselves were part of the problem.

Instead of more time and motion studies, or more automation, the decision was made to create a work process which would increase worker autonomy, initiative and collegial collaboration. Operationally it meant relinquishing the long, straight lines of traditional assembly. The aim of new construction was to build an atmosphere of small workshops, healthful and aesthetic, into the larger plant. A key change in thinking was that technology could be created to give people the flexibility to reorganize themselves at work. Instead of attaching workers to a moving line, materials were to be brought to work stations where autonomous groups of 15-20 persons could do their own organizing. The heart of the Kalmar technology became moveable carriers, low self-propelling platforms, subject to a variety of controls by workers, on which assembly takes place. Work teams could design their own work and rest rhythms, job rotation, collaborative plans for trouble shooting, etc. Responsibility for quality control was assigned to the units by asking each to conduct its own inspections.

From this description we get a sense of the meaning of socio-technical design. At Kalmar the aim became to overcome low morale by involving people in collaborative human groups. But they could not realistically move toward such goals if they stayed with traditionally engineered technology. Gyllenhammar's conclusion was, "Technology can strangle people. On the other hand if it is designed for people, technology can also be a liberator.... It is possible to devise new solutions to combine rational technological systems with greater freedom for human choice." [13]

The Scandinavians are assuming that their decision to develop a society of highly educated persons will increasingly lead to a growing demand for "good work." It will lead to rejection of a concept of work where "hired hands" are managed by authoritarian leadership with a status gulf separating them.

Clarification of the possibilities of a different future for the work place has been carried forward over the past several decades in the Industrial

Democracy Project and the Work Research Institutes in Oslo, Norway. [14] In Norway in the early sixties there was awareness that the introduction of scientific management after World War II had strengthened industry's influence, but there was an unusual agreement among both employer and union organizations that it was showing its limitations in restricting cherished Norwegian qualities, like individual freedom, creativity and social life in the work place. There was sufficient concern so that in 1961-2 the Trade Unions Council and the National Confederation of Employers set up a joint committee to study problems of industrial democracy. From that emerged joint action-research programs involving redesigns of work in industries, shipping, and more recently in education. After years of experience the investigators decided that the heart of the problem is the hierarchically organized bureaucracy itself.

They moved to the position that while classic bureaucratic forms historically emerged to fill real needs, they increasingly are becoming dysfunctional in societies with democratic traditions and with secondary, higher, and continuing education available to the citizenry at large. The general task was to create the theory and techniques for alternatives to hierarchies. [15]

According to the theory generated in the Industrial Democracy Project, the new concern for the quality of life is not merely an aberrant wish of impractical humanitarians. It is rooted in fundamental changes in man's relationship to his environment. The bureaucratic model worked when man's fundamental relation to his world was the physical environment and the technology he developed to act on it. The environment could be conceptualized as an aggregate or cluster of elements which could be manipulated for human gain. Classical science built its theories of universal, deterministic laws on just such an aggregate model. Classical economic and management theory incorporated humans as constituent elements of the aggregate.

The socio-technical theorists maintain that we are entering a new stage marked by the emergence of a turbulent environment.

A turbulent environment is one in which directive correlations established with the environment, on which the survival of an organism depends, unexpectedly break down. Actions that are initiated become attenuated or build up uncontrollably, and goal-directed strategies can lead to the opposite of the intended result. [16]

The source of the turbulence lies in the shift from a situation where the physical environment and technology functioned as the medium for the relation of man to things, to an emerging stage where the predominant relation is man to man. "The turbulent environment is man himself and efforts to solve turbulent type problems with procedures based on principles of the mechanistic, aggregate model increasingly break down."

New types of technology are now emerging designed as integrated systems that can be operated by small staff teams. The rate of change in technological design increases so that "it has now become necessary to build learning capacities into the organization of industrial work teams. This can be achieved only by creating relatively autonomous matrix organizations in which neither task roles nor work relationships are fixed." Within this framework, work teams of persons engaged in on-going learning, become capable of doing research both to find ways to improve production and to develop strategies for coping with changes in tasks. Linkages are established with university and other research units.

The machine model progressively is replaced by developments toward:

A society in which there will be relatively little difference in the educational level and status of those who work in industrial, educational, research, and service organizations. Persons will differ more as regards their focus of orientation than as regards the nature of their work. The leading elements in the transitional stage of development are the rapid increase and diffusion of complex technologies which can be operated by a small number of persons, and the rapid increase and diffusion of higher education. In terms of their operational requirements these will up to a point be mutually supportive. As development continues, the traditional hierarchical type of organization based on the separation of doing, planning and deciding will be replaced by primary work groups in which these functions are integrated. The members of these groups will to an increasing degree be able to participate in policy decisions and be capable of using specialists as consultants. [17]

30

1. Norwegian Ship Life: A Shift from Vulgar to Integral Efficiency.

Reference to a concrete case may illustrate some evolutions in the Norwegian effort to create the new kind of work - "alternatives to hierarchy." In 1980 I had an opportunity to interview Ragnar Johansen of the Ship Research Group at the Work Research Institutes in Oslo.[18]

In 1969, in part to maintain leadership and initiative in world shipping (of which Norway is fourth) representatives from ship owners, seamen's unions, government authorities, and researchers from the Work Research Institutes began experiments aimed at developing more democratic forms of work organization on ships. Johansen described for me at length experiences he had had in working for seven years with the crew of the MS Balao in experiments to create alternatives to traditional ship organization.

Johansen pointed out that the conventional organization of ships is marked by highly compartmentalized departments such as deck, engine room and catering; extremely differentiated jobs based on fixed ratings (e.g. greaser, motor man, third - second - first engineers etc.); strict separatism of work planning by senior officers from control of work by junior and petty officers, and execution of work by the crew. These hierarchical distinctions are reflected in separate messrooms for the captain and senior officers, for the junior and petty officers, and for the crew; in separate day room and recreational facilities; and in great differences between the cabins of the officers and crew members.

The conventional structure is hierarchical with the captain's role almost god-like in character, based on an assumption that crew members need someone to manage and control them. Fragmented specific job ratings assume that individuals can be shifted from one ship to another like machine parts without concern for crew continuity or morale. Barriers between ranks reflected in physical separation of quarters reduced communication to limited, formal exchanges.

By 1970 Norwegian leaders had concluded that this bureaucratic-authoritarian ship tradition was inadequate to preserve the strength and vitality of the crucially important merchant fleet. Several factors pointed to this conclusion.

There was concern about a disturbing number of psychological, social, safety, and operational problems such as psychosomatic illnesses, interpersonal

31

and inter-group conflicts, work related injuries, excessive physical damages, high turnover and the resistance of young, more highly educated Norwegians to hire in.

Secondly, there was a growing recognition that the sophisticated computerized technology of new ships was not amenable to old style organization of ship personnel. There is a steady flow of newness in equipment and operations which requires crews capable of ongoing learning, and of collaborative trouble shooting. It cannot be met by organizational systems where relations are unstable, impersonal and inflexible.

To try to retain the old organizational forms seemed irrational, and Norwegian leaders also were increasingly dissatisfied with the disjunctions between the democratic values and relations in community life, and the authoritarian traditions aboard ships. The basic decision was to experiment with alternatives to hierarchy so that Norwegian ships would become more democratic places in which to live and work. Hopefully this could be done so crews would be prepared to deal more effectively with the new complex technology.

The Norwegians decided it would not be easy to make a sharp break with centuries of ship traditions; therefore, they decided to make starts where people were willing to try change. They provided them with the services of research scholar-consultants like Ragnar Johansen. For example, experiments with horizontal work integration which maintained deck and engine room distinctions but which permitted more flexible work planning were studied on two ships before the launching of the Balao. On the basis of that experience it was decided that work planning was to be the main tool in efforts to try for a more meaningful and democratic organization on the Balao.

A skeleton sketch will have to suffice to convey the idea. The general format which emerged experimentally between 1973 and 1977 includes a Friday meeting by ship's officers in which they discuss their own matters, and sketch a list of ship tasks for the coming week based on a long-term maintenance program.

The final work list and how to accomplish it is decided at Saturday meetings with participation of the full crew. The Saturday meetings evolved into two types of planning: a) a plenary meeting to take the work list and decide who should do which jobs when, and b) small task groups which decide how they will do the work for each assignment. Gradually the Saturday meetings are taking over some of the functions of the senior officers' Friday preliminary meetings.

Under the new procedures, temporary autonomous groups are formed for one week and are changed in succeeding weeks as task definitions change. Duties and functions are no longer divided according to deck or engine crew, or between officers and seamen. Traditional status lines are crossed over. Decisions about who should be in a work group are made on the basis of work load, safety, skill, and training considerations. A matrix organization, in fact, has evolved.

Philip Herbst, who pioneered ideas for alternatives to hierarchies, points out that a matrix organization does not mean that everyone does everything. The assumption is that each person has a special duty based on special qualifications, but in addition learns skills which qualify him or her for a wider range of duties. Within this framework every qualified crew member is capable of becoming a manager, or worker depending on the nature of the tasks, and is qualified to teach skills to others in training.[19]

This non bureaucratic work model evolved on the Balao as follows:

1) The formerly separated deck and engine crews are integrated so that the whole ship becomes a shared area for work and a site for training.

2) Officers and crew engage in weekly meetings to plan and control both the work and training programs.

3) Officers and crew members are formed into relatively autonomous work groups which shift according to tasks at hand.

4) The whole crew has common dining and living rooms and relatively equal cabins with desks and bookshelves for study.

5) The crew's connection to the ship is stabilized by yearly wages and flexible manning requirements.

Johansen told me that they are beginning to think of new titles that will take the place of officer vs. crew distinctions. These might include titles like Sea Engineers, Ship Mechanics or Engineers. Different skill ratings within these could be acquired by on-board training and study as well as by years of higher education on shore. The trend is toward thinking of all officer crews who will engage in continued study and learning throughout their work careers. They will share manual and technical tasks on ship through the autonomous matrix work group arrangements.

An example of autonomous work group procedure is found in the approach taken to cleaning the engine room. In the old days the task would be given to a new recruit with a mop. That won't work when the engine room consists of expensive, complex, sensitive equipment. Engine room cleaning now becomes a task for an autonomous work group of crew and officers who understand the technology, the problems at hand and develop their own work strategies.

Under the new ship organization there are extensive changes in the duties and work assignments of officers and crew members. A decisive condition for these changes is extensive training and the acquisition of new competencies. When competencies are more widely shared the people involved have more options in deciding who should do what work when and how.

Johansen says that one condition is most central for the success of the new procedures:

Constant discussion and exchange of experience about the ship's operating policy is formed by continuous learning in which everyone is involved in reviewing, evaluating and testing new arrangements.

This continuous learning, Johansen says, goes on at three levels simultaneously:

1. For each person there is extensive learning about:

   a. more professional knowledge

   b. how work and training can be planned, executed, and controlled as integrated activities within the work situation.

   c. how such training can guide personal occupational development over time (for example crew members can learn ship mechanics skills within the Balao work/training format).

   d. how such learning can add meaning to life in work and in free time. (The results show up in high stability among the crew, decrease in injuries and illnesses and more satisfaction with ship work.)

2. Organizational learning includes

   a. continuous surveying of problems by members of the ship.

   b. systematic search for alternatives about how to solve problems.

   c. follow-up and evaluation of self-initiated experiments.

   This organizational learning is made possible

by a different organizational structure with agreements that: (1) work planning is the key to goals of greater autonomy, (2) continuous training is essential for the new organization to function and (3) the ship must have a strong voice in selecting and holding well-qualified personnel.

3. Ship-wide social learning includes more interpersonal communication and dialogue as compared to the former isolation by rank, and participation in collaborative study and training. The move has been toward mutual help and tolerance. (Studies have shown that better ship-board social life has also had a positive effect on family relations and has led to increased participation in on-shore community activities.)

Johansen said that increased ship effectiveness under the new procedures had improved the competitive position of the merchant fleet. Officials from multinational corporations and other countries are coming to the Oslo Work Research Institutes to inquire about what is going on.

4. The ethical concern. Scandinavian sociotechnical theorists are recognizing that their approach involves them in issues involving ethical choices. Key problems center not only on how to produce but on what to produce. Adequate thinking about institutional planning requires conscious confrontation of questions of ethical goals. In the technical-bureaucratic stage thinking was limited to how to get material and monetary results. As we become more aware that we have control over the means and methods we apply we are less able to shirk the responsibility of assessing the consequences of our choices. Gyllenhammar reports his thoughts, for example, on consequences of deciding to choose alternatives to hierarchical bureaucratic control. He became aware, he says, that the most effective changes made were those in which the workers themselves had the largest voice. And he adds:

It is almost alarming to realize how much know-how and capability had been locked up in the work force, unavailable to managers who simply didn't realize what an important resource it was. Our experience at Volvo has changed my views of management somewhat. Unlocking working potential has become as important as any display of brilliance in technical terms.[20]

It is an existential choice whether to utilize or to ignore that potential. As we have seen, the

Norwegians made their choice. They committed themselves to years of experimentation to create work life consistent with their cultural allegiance to democratic values, and to meet their need to respond to technological change. Alternatives to the single hierarchical stucture of tasks and roles, and to the old superior-subordinate relationship were developed. Organizational options were designed for different purposes: for emergency situations, for example, relations are of the traditional military type, but for ordinary operation and maintenance, skilled work teams function without any formal officer in charge; other persons assume leadership roles for planning educational and leisure programs for on-board and ashore. As we have seen the trend is toward personnel receiving training for multiple roles so that in many work situations people in superior roles switch to subordinate roles and vice versa to form structures appropriate for the tasks at hand. People retain primary professional identities but the former status isolation of officers from crew is reduced.

In reflecting on features of socio-technical work changes Einar Thorsrud and colleagues summarized some key ideas workers and management need if their goal is to create "good work" for themselves. They need to create:

1. Adequate elbow room. The sense that they are their own bosses and that except in exceptional circumstances they do not have some boss breathing down their necks. Not so much elbow room that they just don't know what to do next.

2. Chances of learning on the job and going on learning. We accept that such learning is possible only when men are able to set goals that are reasonable challenges for them and get a feedback of results in time for them to correct their behavior.

3. An optimal level of variety, i.e. they can vary the work so as to avoid boredom and fatigue and so as to gain the best advantages from settling into a satisfying rhythm of work.

4. Conditions where they can and do get help and respect from their work-mates. Avoiding conditions where it is in no man's interest to lift a finger to help another: where men are pitted against each other so that one man's gain is another's loss; where the group interest denies the individual's capabilities

or inabilities.

5. A sense of one's own work meaningfully contributing to social welfare. That is, not something that could as well be done by a trained monkey or an industrial robot machine. Nor something that the society could probably be better served by not having it done, or at least not having it done so shoddily.

6. A desirable future. Quite simply, not a dead-end job; hopefully one that will continue to allow personal growth. [21]

All participants in socio-technical design agree that one of the hardest challenges is to develop a style of leadership appropriate to work places where employees are treated as adults.

As Gyllenhammar puts it participation does not mean permissiveness. It demands better leadership as well as more self-discipline from everyone. The key quality in the new leader is that he work from awareness of other people's dignity and their wish to do their best. Volvo now looks for managers with enough self-confidence to engage in real give and take, including the capacity to admit mistakes. Managers now need training to see themselves as information gatherers, as aides to workers, as teachers and consultants instead of as bosses. They need to help people develop attitudes and skills of problem solving and self-discipline. [22]

A crucial point in developing leadership to produce "good work" is to sharpen awareness of the difference between this goal and traditional job enrichment, which may include items like flex time, and T group or sensitivity training for workers. The difference stems from the answer given to the underlying question of "What is the essential obligation of economic activity in a democratic society?" If it simply is to increase GNP then all items in the system are viewed in terms of their efficiency toward that end. Job enrichment is a means of manipulating the human variable (psychic dimension included) to increase productivity.

A new perspective is introduced when we say that the purpose of economic activity is "to help achieve and maintain the public good." Socio-technical design of work theory assumes that its approach will be effective with material productivity, but it does not accept the proposition that any technical or psychological change that increases productivity is sufficient evidence of "good work."

This point of view coincides with the premise

stated by Kalman H. Silvert in The Reason for Demo-cracy: "a democratic political-economy must begin and end with the person-in-society, seeing him as both end and means, and combining his reason and his actions in empowered participation."[23] Taken seriously, this requires as Willard Wirtz has said, "...a new econom-ics that takes (the) human potential as its starting point...(This) new economics would start from a commitment to make the fullest practicable use of the most highly developed form of whatever talents are inside people instead of starting from a consideration of the most profitable use or misuse of the elements inside the thin and fragile crust of the planet. Such a policy would measure all major enterprises in terms of their comparative drain on dwindling natural resources and their comparative use of the highly developed -- meaning educated -- human resource." We might then, Wirtz suggests, start evaluating our economic activity in terms of its contribution to Net National Strength (NNS) rather than to Gross National Product (GNP).[24]

B. Socio-technical theory in the U.S.A.: The Process of Change at Harman International Industries, Bolivar, Tennessee

It is fair enough to say, "all of that may sound interesting but Scandinavia isn't the United States so what does it have to do with us?"

The truth is that American thinkers made impor-tant contributions to work redesign theory (often referred to in the U.S. as Quality of Work Life, QWL) in the sixties and seventies. As we entered the eighties some major corporations were translating the theory into practice. Several leading thinkers were Louis Davis (UCLA), Eric Trist (University of Pennsylvania) and Michael Maccoby (Director of the Harvard Project on Technology, Work and Character, and author of The Gamesman).

Prior to the early seventies their writings were winning a significant readership, but trials with the practice they advocated were limited to a few fre-quently cited companies which failed to produce contagious effects.[25] In the section which follows I will describe one of the early influential projects at Harman International Industries, Bolivar, Tennessee guided by the philosophical principles of Michael Maccoby. Then I shall describe the response of General Motors which, under the thrust of Japanese competition, decided to make a major commitment to the

Quality of Work Life orientation in the eighties.

1. The Underlying Philosophy: Michael Maccoby/Erich Fromm.

There are interesting informal and formal international linkages between Scandinavian, English, American and Australian pioneers of work redesign which we cannot describe at length. Some glimpses, however, may be caught in comments on the process of change at the Harman Plant in Bolivar, Tennessee. The work at Bolivar, influenced by the thought of Michael Maccoby, is close to the orientation of the Norwegian socio-technical pioneers.

The work improvement program began at the Harman auto-mirror making plant in 1972 when Sidney Harman, then President of Harman International Industries (later Undersecretary of Commerce in the Carter administration) and Irving Bluestone, Vice President of the United Auto Workers Union attended seminars sponsored by the Department of Labor where Michael Maccoby and others discussed ways of improving work. Harman and Bluestone discovered that they shared aspirations that management and labor could learn to collaborate to stimulate human development in the work place. They facilitated an agreement between the company and the union which opened with this statement:

> The purpose of the joint Management - Labor Work Improvement Program is to make work better and more satisfying for all employees, salaried and hourly, while maintaining the necessary productivity for job security. The purpose is not to increase productivity. If increased productivity is a by-product, ways of rewarding the employees for increased productivity will become legitimate matters for inclusion in the program. [26]

Maccoby was asked to head a third party project to help the program get started. The program was guided from the beginning by four principles developed by Maccoby in an article, "Humanizing Work: Priority Goal of the 1970's." [27]

> Security: as far as possible work should be free of hazards to life and limb, and employees should be secure from loss of their jobs.
> Equity: The distribution of work, the organization of work, the rewards of work, and the rules under which employees work should be as fair as they can be.

Democracy: Each worker should have an opportunity to have a say in the decisions that
affect his life at work.
Individuation: It is recognized that people
have different interests and needs, and efforts
should be made to give people opportunities to
develop in their own way.
The principles did not provide a detailed blue-
print for action, but one of the creative features of
Bolivar was the development of a structure to put the
principles into practice. Before turning to the
operational structure it is appropriate to look at the
philosophical rationale from which these principles
emerged. For a number of years Michael Maccoby was a
colleague of Erich Fromm's in Cuernavaca, Mexico.
They collaborated in writing, Social Character in a
Mexican Village in which they analyzed the relations
between the emotional attitudes in the character of
Mexican peasants and the socio-economic conditions in
which they lived. Maccoby later combined the psycho-
analytic skills of his work with Fromm with observational interview techniques to complete his best
selling study of the character types of American
executives in The Gamesman.
One can detect the influence of Erich Fromm's
philosophical orientation in the style of thought
Maccoby brought to ideas about the quality of working
life. Before turning to the structural practice of
socio-technical theory we can add depth to our understanding by referring to basic concepts in one of
Fromm's major works, The Sane Society.
In The Sane Society Fromm identified basic
human needs by starting from an assumption about the
nature of man's existence. Man alone, through his
special capacity for using language, has developed his
reasoning to the point where he is aware of his own
existence and his own mortality. Through scientific
inquiry he has become aware of his perilous place on
planet earth in the vastness of the universe. Other
organisms are "lived by nature." Man alone has
transcended nature through reason. As a result he has
opened up tremendous possibilities for growth in
experience, but he also experiences the fear, anxiety,
and sense of homelessness that come with detaching
himself from the determinism of nature. He can
tolerate his new freedom in a way that will be productive for his growth only if he creates new bonds of
relatedness with nature, his fellow men and with
himself. The contemporary problem is that men in
industrial societies not only have failed to establish

nurturing bonds, but have created ways of living that are inimical to "needs stemming from the nature of their existence." Men in industrial societies, both capitalist and communist, are creating conditions which run counter to their basic human needs. This results in wide-spread psychic distress and social break-down which led Fromm to conclude that present arrangements in technological societies are not conducive to our sanity.

After reviewing critiques of the modern condition by Owen and Proudhon, Tolstoy and Bakunin, Durkheim and Marx, Einstein and Schweitzer, he summarized what they found is happening to man under technology: Man has lost his central place and has become an instrument for economic aims, he has been estranged from and has lost his concrete relatedness to his fellows and to nature, and has ceased to have a meaningful life. In a condition of alienation he has regressed to a "marketing orientation" which in turn leads to a loss of sense of self so that he becomes dissatisfied, bored, and anxious. He remains intelligent with a welter of information and technical skills, but his reason, which could lead to personally won insights about his condition, has deteriorated so that he becomes a threat to his own civilization and possibly to his own existence. [28]

Fromm holds, that modern man to escape his destructive tendencies, needs to create productive orientations which will enable him to realize more of his creative potential. The new productive relatedness must manifest itself in three areas of basic human needs:

(1) In a relation of community which is the experience of solidarity with other persons. "In the realm of feeling the productive orientation is expressed in love, which is the experience of union with another person, with all men, and with nature, under the condition of retaining one's sense of integrity and independence." [29] More specifically the task is consciously to create conditions which counter the manipulative, depersonalizing tendencies which lead to inauthentic relations. The decisive factor as antidote is decentralization; concrete face-to-face groups, active responsible participation. [30]

(2) In the realm of action the productive orientation is expressed in productive work the prototype of which is art and craftmanship. [31] In meaningful or productive work the person's

goals or purposes are involved. He commits himself as a thinking, feeling, acting person to bring work to consummation, alone or with others.

(3) In the realm of thought the productive orientation is expressed in the grasp of the world by reason. Fromm makes a specific point of distinguishing reason from intelligence. He defines intelligence as the capacity to acquire information and to use it for manipulation of the world.

Reason, on the other hand, aims at understanding; it tries to find out what is behind the surface, to recognize the kernel, the essence of the reality which surrounds us. Reason is not without a function, but its function is not to further physical as much as mental and spiritual existence.... Reason requires relatedness and a sense of self. If I am only the passive receptor of impressions, thoughts, opinions, I can compare them, manipulate them - but I cannot penetrate them. [32]

To reason in Fromm's sense is to gain new meanings about the world or oneself through a personal appropriation of meanings.

If men move in these directions they will have a chance to restore sanity or health to their societies. Fromm believes it is possible to develop criteria for marking features of sane societies.

A sane society is one

in which no man is a means toward another's ends, but always...an end in himself; hence, where nobody is used, nor uses himself for purposes which are not those of the unfolding of his own powers; where man is the center, and where economic and political activities are subordinated to the aim of his growth.... (It) is one which permits man to operate within manageable and observable dimensions, and to be an active and responsible member in the life of society...It is one which furthers human solidarity and not only permits but stimulates its members to relate themselves to each other lovingly; a sane society furthers the productive activity of everybody in his work, stimulates the unfolding of reason and enables man to give expression to his inner needs in collective art and rituals. [33]

To formulate such goals is one thing. To attempt to realize them is another. Maccoby, Harman, Bluestone and colleagues made a serious effort to make moves in that direction through the work improvement program at Bolivar, Tennessee.

Michael Maccoby was the theorist and we can see reflection of Fromm's social philosophy in Maccoby's way of defining "productivity," a concept pivotal to the design of work at Bolivar.

In 1979 when the concern about productivity decline was growing the Associated Press interviewed Irving Bluestone, Director of the U.A.W. General Motors Department, regarding his ideas for making productivity more attractive to labor. He recommended that Michael Maccoby be consulted and Maccoby responded in an article "What is Productivity?" [34]

Maccoby began by making a distinction between what he called the economist's "limited definition of productivity" as measurement of output per man hour resulting in a decrease in the cost per unit, and a broader concept he called social productivity. Social productivity means greater efficiency in the use of available resources (material, technical, human) and may refer to qualities of generativity or creativity as in "productive human beings." Maccoby argued it was important to distinguish the two concepts of productivity, and to recognize that they implied different policies.

He felt that American workers would respond positively to the social productivity idea. There are, however, two general approaches to social productivity: one involving less government intervention about economic decisions, the other more.

Type A might be labelled "free market productivity with constraints." Under it means are sought to improve effectiveness in use of resources to produce goods and services wanted by the American people, but constrained by four conditions; Productivity with restraints:

(1) must not endanger physical health through pollution, unsafe working conditions, or unsafe products harmful to consumers,

(2) must not damage the mental health of workers by dehumanized conditions which deny them dignity, democratic rights, and opportunities for learning and personal development.

(3) must not unduly increase social inequity, injustice, and resentment by inordinately increasing the personal power of a few, or discriminate on the basis of race, sex, age, beliefs.

(4) must not lead to the inability of people to

43

find useful work. "Without job security, economic productivity may inevitablly be socially unproductive."

Type B social productivity accepts as legitimate only the processes of production and the products that positively enhance the lives and strengthen the health of workers, managers, and consumers and, therefore, American society as a whole. While attractive at first glance Maccoby described his personal uneasiness about Type B. In essence it requires that a judgment be made for each product or process in terms of whether it can be justified in positive terms. And who would make this definition? "There are clear risks that arbitrary controls would dampen the willingness of producers to take risks and invest the capital and energy necessary to develop new products."

On the other hand, Type A, "productivity with constraints," does not define what should be produced, which permits more initiatives while also permitting unions and management to work together to improve technology and work relations. A problem is that methods must be employed to evaluate violations of the four areas of constraints. Enforcement may be guilty of nitpicking, or of laxity which does not protect public interest.

"The creative task of government will be to develop means which protect people without destroying initiative. The creative task of consumers will be to demand the positive development of those goods and services which enhance their lives."

Maccoby concluded that what is needed is the creation of a National Commission on Productivity - and felt that progressive unions might take the lead in developing the new definition of "Social Productivity" and the policies it implies.

This brief account of Maccoby's concept of productivity leaves many questions unanswered, for example, how to deal with the power of advertising. But it does provide a background for the operating structure of work improvement at Bolivar.

2. The Philosophy at Work at Bolivar.

In an article "The Quality of Working Life - Lessons from Bolivar"[35] Maccoby said that his assumption was that new technology and products assure that work in our time will change constantly. The issue is how will it change? Will it change to meet social-human as well as technical-economic criteria? The

44

effort at Bolivar was not to promise a formula for sure-fire answers but to get a process going that would attempt to meet both criteria .

A basic fact was that the Harman auto mirror plant was part of a highly competitive auto parts industry where price squeezing by the four major companies and fluctuating demand for cars intensified insecurity and dehumanizing work conditions. The Harman plant had followed the mainline management tradition of trying to increase productivity by increasing controls. There was hostility, resistance and open conflict when the project began.

Under the leadership of Harman and Bluestone there was a management/union agreement to establish a work improvement project based on Maccoby's principles of security, equity, individuation and democracy.

The security principle was employed for example when work experiments led to improved productivity in a recession time. It was decided to take the gains in time off rather than to lose jobs because of increased production. And safety was improved by listening to worker complaints and acting on them. Equity was followed in agreeing that if productivity increased, financial gains should be shared equitably.

Individuation meant respect for differing needs of people. Not all work can be made interesting. But committees explored how opportunities could be created to learn new things and to enlarge understanding of work and participation. It included recognizing, too, that some people wanted simply to finish work earlier so they could get home to their gardens and families.

Democracy was interpreted as establishing the right of individuals to have a say in decisions affecting them. No pretense was made that the factory would be a "pure democracy." A serious effort, however, was made to seek out and listen to proposals from the shop floor. The goal was to move in the direction of creating new areas of democracy and participation in analysis and decision making. A survey showed 70% of workers had had ideas for improving work which they had kept to themselves. Committee meetings at all levels opened opportunities to propose and evaluate ideas, and a plant newspaper, The Harman Mirror, presented articles critical of plant practice by members of unions and management.

There remained, however, the need to develop operating procedures. As Maccoby put it, "Ultimately, the spirit of an organization is determined by the psychological traits that are stimulated and reinforced by total work experience. A spirit cannot survive

45

based on ideology and good intentions. It must be
rooted in human experience...For a new spirit (of
mutuality) to be realized, new organizational structures and decision making processes must be created."
     To facilitate improved communication and
cooperation a ladder type structure was created
(Traditional union/management relations are indicated
by solid lines and new relations by dotted lines).

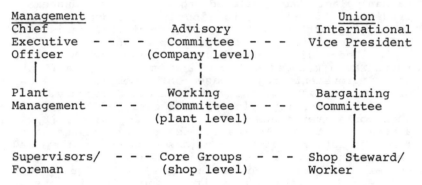

```
Management                                          Union
Chief                  Advisory            International
Executive  - - - -     Committee    - - -  Vice President
Officer               (company level)
   |                        |                     |
   |                        |                     |
Plant                   Working             Bargaining
Management  - - -       Committee   - - -   Committee
                       (plant level)
   |                        |                     |
   |                        |                     |
Supervisors/  - - - Core Groups  - - -   Shop Steward/
Foreman             (shop level)         Worker
```

     At the Bolivar plant much of this structure
evolved as the program developed. A key item for
successful work redesign is support from the top
because supervisory and union personnel take risks
when changes are made. At the company level, Sidney
Harman and Irving Bluestone had made the original
agreement. They were supported by an advisory group
of academics like Maccoby and Einar Thorsrud of
Norway. The chart also shows union involvement at all
levels. It is critically important that regular
bargaining procedures function to handle standard
union/management issues, and that the union has the
right to approve any new changes at work.
     At the company and shop levels the project
required new styles of leadership by both management
and the union. Managers needed to learn how to
analyze problems cooperatively and stimulate participation in decision making. Union leaders needed to
learn how to bargain cooperatively (with win/win
results) without weakening their position in adversary
collective bargaining.
     At the beginning, a Working Committee was
created at the plant level (with five union and five
management members) to consider how to handle problems
of heat, cold, ventilation and safety hazards; and it
began weekly meetings to consider employee suggestions

46

about how to alleviate parking problems, the need for a credit union, etc. Members of the Working Committee also began to read and discuss articles on work restructuring provided by the academic project staff. Eventually Core groups were created at the shop level in every department usually composed of a foreman, shop steward and an elected worker who conducted their own departmental meetings and funneled ideas to the plant Working Committee.

We cannot elaborate on details here but the Bolivar experience showed that it is important that all aspects of the ladder structure be actively functioning. Difficulties in other work design situations have developed when this principle was not followed.

Another assumption of the project was that an adequate response to a changing work world requires that the process of change itself be made a part of on-going learning for all involved. The academic advisors acted as researcher-educators with the task of providing knowledge and teaching new methods of analysis and evaluation. For example, Einar Thorsrud, a pioneer of the Norwegian Industrial Democracy Project, was brought in at the early stages to suggest how to initiate change through experimentation. Thorsrud did not give directions as the outside expert but explained methods used in Norway in which participants analyzed alternatives to standard work organizations and communication procedures; and how they evaluated alternatives according to "socio" as well as "technical" criteria. Maccoby commented that Thorsrud's ideas seemed "to represent the kind of active learning described by J. Piaget where the role of the educator is to help define the problem and to criticize solutions according to agreed on criteria...In so doing, the educator is teaching critical thinking according to new criteria."[36] It should be evident that moves in the socio-technical direction are not easy. To change established relations and habits is threatening. Conflicts and crises emerge, and failures happen. But accomplishments and satisfaction can also come from taking the risks.

I talked with one woman in Bolivar, with fifteen years of experience on the line, who said:

> We are the real experts on production problems. They used to think we were just a bunch of dumb hill-billies. They would bring in an industrial engineer from Detroit who would inspect and recommend. We all kept silent. He couldn't get it changed by him-

self. Now they ask us - and try our ideas. We know how to do it. We would never choose to go back to the old days.

She showed me a copy of the employee run <u>Harman Mirror</u> which listed courses in "The Harman School" conducted by both workers and supervisors, open to all: courses ranging from technical courses to upgrade skills like engine repair or computer techniques to courses in dulcimer playing, quilting, poetry writing, current events and seminars on better parenting. The issue also reported on activites of a shop level core group in the electric mirror plant:

An active core group meets every Thursday to guide the program and deal with any problems in the plant. Workers are learning to interpret the daily operating statements, to understand and be concerned about the figures on efficiency, supplies, and downtime. When workers finish their initial job assignment, they help those on slower jobs until everyone's production is met. They do the necessary inspection on the lines and perform any rework operations needed in order to get the parts right before they are counted. Indirect workers are included in the plan and when production is met, all may leave the plant and be awarded credit for the full day's work.[37]

There have been changes, too, for managers and union leaders. A supervisor received permission to teach workers in his group the functions of scheduling, record keeping, etc. and in several months workers were carrying out most of these functions. When an executive was asked at the Working Committee if managers weren't afraid of losing authority, the answer was "I've never had so much authority since I started giving it away."[38]

Union officials began with deep suspicions about "the work improvement" idea. Maccoby reports that through involvement changes began to occur: "Members of the bargaining committee are learning about pricing, controllable costs, how to read the daily, monthly and yearly statements. With new confidence, they are able to cooperate with management in order to cut costs and save jobs. At the same time they have a better understanding of what the company can afford to pay them."[39]

Beyond such changes among people in the plant there is the larger question, still essentially unexplored, of whether changes like these in work life might not point to possibilities of social and cultur-

48

al change in the community outside the plant.

We have elaborated on the Bolivar situation because it illustrates a conscious effort to implement work changes consistent with the principles of Maccoby's socio-technical philosophy of work redesign. The structural design, at least, has had a continuing influence as the Quality of Work Life idea has begun to move into corporate giants like General Motors.

C. Socio-technical theory in the U.S.A.:
Quality of Work Life at General Motors

In 1977-78 the Los Angeles Times [40] made an extensive survey of the state of the new industrial reorganization around the world and found it flourishing in many industrialized nations. But the idea was still in an experimental stage in the United States with most industry and union leaders saying that it was too soon to expect changes in the traditional relationship between management and labor. In fact, though, the concept of work-place democracy was primed for a take-off in a number of major corporations. By 1980, when Japanese competition put survival of American industries at stake, all of the auto companies had signed contracts with the United Auto Workers Union to press ahead with worker involvement programs. The Communications Workers of America included worker participation concepts in its contract with American Telephone and Telegraph Company, and the United Steel Workers signed contracts with agreements to promote on-the-job democracy for over a half-million steel workers.

For our purposes it is enough to establish that as we entered the eighties important industries were making significant departures from the classical scientific management tradition. General Motors is an important case in point and we limit our comments to trends emerging there. Delmar E. Landen, director of organization research and development and a pioneer in Quality of Work Life (QWL) philosophy at GM, said that the majority of QWL plans had been launched since 1979 and they are expanding rapidly. General Motors has committed $43 billion for new plants and re-tooling for 1980-85. In every new plant being designed a socio-technical planning approach is being used. [41]

While there is no doubt that a significant new momentum developed at the tail end of the seventies, it is also true that forerunners had been underway for decades. Elton Mayo's famous "Hawthorne experiment" at Western Electric was an early effort to break from

the narrower version of Taylorist scientific management. A notable example consisted of wide-spread
joint labor-management committees in World War II
under the War Production Board which contributed to
the production miracle of the war years. In 1940
Philip Murray, President of the Steel Workers, said
that labor and management should cooperate on the shop
floor by "tapping the brains of labor" - seeking
workers' advice on how to improve production purposes.[42] Such ideas were permitted to lapse in the
rush to "get back to normal" after the war. In the
1950s studies of job satisfaction helped sharpen
awareness of attitudes in the work place. In the 50s
and 60s job enrichment and "humanizing work" schemes
got some attention as responses to "blue collar
blues." Present work theorists, however, tend to
dismiss these latter developments as management
prescribed innovations designed to manipulate worker
speed-ups. They contributed, in fact, to a skeptical
attitude of union members toward "work reform" ideas
in general.

General Motors made its first serious moves in
the direction of work place democracy in the early
seventies. A GM executive acknowledged that the
worker participation program would never have gotten
to first base without Irving Bluestone, "who helped
convince his own union people but most of us in
management, too."[43]

Disruptions at the Lordstown, Ohio plant had
been but a dramatic example of growing worker malaise
which could no longer be ignored and it was part of
changes in the general social climate. Landen said
that the move toward worker participation must be seen
in the context of changes in the social scene of the
60s and 70s. The ground work was being laid by the
Civil Rights Movement, the Women's Movement, the
legislating of affirmative action programs, the draft
resistance of the Vietnam years, and the emergence of
a younger, better educated work force skeptical of
established authority and less willing "to take crap".
Beneath the protests was a growing demand to be able
to experience one's humanity more fully - and to
resist arrangements that violated personal dignity.

On the other hand changes in the social climate
were slow in penetrating established leadership of
management and unions. It took repeated, sobering
shocks of the energy shortage and the threat of
Japanese competition to create the readiness required
for serious change.

50

1. Quality of Work Life at Tarrytown, New York.

If Bolivar is recognized as an early landmark of work place democracy in the United States, Tarrytown is a landmark of change within General Motors. We shall limit our comments to observations which demonstrate how the orientation of Bolivar was incorporated into a major corporate giant, and indicate something of the spirit which has been emerging and gathering momentum as we entered the eighties.

In 1970 the car assembly plant at Tarrytown had one of the poorest labor relations and production records at G.M. Absenteeism, labor turnover, waste and operating costs were high. Frustration, fear, and mistrust characterized the relationship between management and labor, with as many as 2000 labor grievances on the docket. As one manager put it, "Management was always in a defensive posture. We were instructed to go by the book, and we played by the book. The way we solved problems was to use our authority and to impose discipline." A union officer described the embattled relation with management: "The company's attitude was to employ a stupid robot with hands and no face. When I walked in each morning I was out to get the personnel director, the committeeman was shooting for the foreman, and the zone committeeman was shooting for the general foreman." [44]

Workers disliked the job and were mad at everyone. They viewed the company as an impersonal bureaucratic machine. "They number the parts, and they number you." They disliked the inexorable movement of the line - 56 cars per hour - "a minute and a half per operation, per defined space." Foremen were viewed as enemy controllers whose guiding principle was, "If you can't do the job like I tell you, get out." They were angry with harrassed union committeemen for not handling grievances effectively or speedily enough. [45]

By 1971 the situation had become more threatening. Because of high labor turnover the plant was hiring a larger number of young people who resisted dictatorial management and over whom the union had little control. The plant manager saw the need for a different philosophical orientation. He began seeking support from the union at different levels. In time he got it, from Irving Bluestone on down.

At the plant level, basic production line renovation for the Hard and Soft Trim department was being introduced. "At first the changes were introduced in the usual way. Manufacturing and industrial engineers and technical specialists designed the new layout, developed the charts and blue prints, and planned every move." They then presented them to the supervisors who ordinarily would have begun the process that would have led to new directives and control procedures over the work force. But the plant manager had gone to the union officers and grievance committee saying that he wanted to try a different philosophy of management in which union officials and workers would be consulted.

A production supervisor aware of this shift suggested to the industrial engineers, "Why not ask the workers themselves to get involved in the production redesign? They are experts in their own right. They know as much about trim operations as anyone else."[46]

At about the same time, in 1972, Irving Bluestone, vice president of the U.A.W. for the G.M. Department, made what is considered a kickoff speech for the quality of work life movement:

Traditionally management has called upon labor to cooperate in increasing the productivity and improving the quality of the product. My view of the other side of the coin is more appropriate; namely, that management should cooperate with the worker to find ways to enhance the dignity of labor and to tap the creative resources in each human being in developing a more satisfying work life, with emphasis on worker participation in the decision making process.[47]

In 1973 GM and the U.A.W. negotiated a national agreement. Included was a "letter of agreement" signed by Bluestone and George Morris, GM head of industrial relations, in which both parties committed themselves to establishing formal mechanisms for exploring new ways of dealing with the quality of work life. This was the first time QWL was explicitly addressed in any major U.S. labor-management contract.

The following year management, following the Bolivar model, proposed that a professional consultant be brought in to involve supervisors and workers in training programs for problem solving. Local Union leaders, suspecting a trick, turned to UAW's Solidarity House Headquarters which recommended participation. Management and the union selected coordinators to work with the consultant, and thirty-four volunteers from the Soft Trim Department agreed to enter training sessions in September 1974.

Layoffs and dislocations flowing from the OPEC oil crisis led to a number of set-backs beginning in

November 1974. But a core of union/management
personnel kept the idea alive through several discouraging years. In 1977 Tarrytown, once again under
full production, made the "big commitment." A series
of steps were taken with strong support from Bluestone
and Charles Katko, vice president of the GM division,
which led to plant-wide QWL training programs involving 3000 people. Workers and supervisors in groups of
25 began a series of Tuesday, Wednesday and Thursday
nine hour a day training programs.

Substitutes had to be hired to fill their
places and 250 worker volunteers were trained to be
QWL trainers in the training programs. Such trainers
now became teachers of their supervisors as well as of
their fellow workers.

The training sessions had three emphases:

1) Learning about the QWL concept: a union
officer presented ideas from Bluestone's speeches, and
a management representative referred to writings of
GM's "Dutch" Landen.

2) Learning about the plant and the function
of management and the union.

3) Learning problem-solving skills important
for effective participation and involvement in decision making.[48]

There was encouragement from early results.
The glass installation area had been in trouble.
Scrap and repairs were at an intolerable rate. Half
the workers had received disciplinary measures within
the past six months. Absenteeism and labor turnover
were very high. The training led to a plan to let the
workers with a foreman figure out how they wanted the
work done. In a period of seven or eight months
scrap, repairs, absenteeism and turnover were markedly
down, and no one had been disciplined.[49]

The principle enunciated by Maccoby at Bolivar
has been accepted in GM's QWL programs, i.e., the
purpose is not to increase productivity, but if
productivity results, ways of rewarding workers became
legitimate matters for inclusion in the program.[50]
The writing of both management and union spokesmen
repeatedly affirm that while the direct goal is
improvement in the quality of work life, they are
convinced that ideas for QWL and better productivity
tend to go hand in hand. There is general agreement
that efficiency and cost of production improved
significantly at Tarrytown as well as plant morale.
The union claims without confirmation from management,
that Tarrytown went from one of the poorest plants in
its quality performance to one of the best among the

eighteen plants in the division.

2. Union and Management Spokesmen on QWL Principles.

We may now summarize some of the principles emerging in the G.M. experience. Since Irving Bluestone was a key figure at both the Harman Company and at G.M. we shall let him be a spokesman.

In an interview in The Harvard Crimson (February 21, 1979) Bluestone was asked a number of questions about the why and what of QWL programs. Bluestone admitted that through most of the seventies he had been part of a small minority of union leaders to support the idea; and he acknowledged that there had been failures as well as successes. Bluestone, however, had taken the lead in the GM section of the union and there is now solid commitment to the idea by both management and the union at General Motors.

Bluestone said that there is one fundamental change now necessary for work improvement:

> Management must come to the realization that what it has been doing for the past seven decades, adhering to the scientific management espoused by Frederick Taylor, is no longer as applicable as it used to be. Workers are not willing to accept the authoritarianism of the workplace as was true a generation or two ago. They're much better educated by at least four years of education coming into the plant.... Management must certainly come to the realization that they don't own all of the brains in the world in deciding how a plant should be operated. I distinguish between participation in decision-making by workers in managing the enterprise and managing the job. We're a long way in this country from workers participating in managing the enterprise per se, but I think we're getting closer to the other aspect of it - managing the job. [51]

He made a sharp distinction between QWL and job enlargement (which he dismissed as an imposition by management and industrial engineers to get workers to perform more operations over a longer time period.) Work Life Improvement, he said, is a much broader idea, the core ingredient of which is mutual respect between the union and management which can make possible a joint resolution of problems "instead of finding out how to screw each other, so to speak."

With this as the essential condition, QWL programs may be introduced with worker participation at every stage. It is wrong to think that a set formula can be followed, but in general, QWL must emanate from the bottom up. It has "got to come from the workers and the line foremen rather than being imposed from the top down." At G.M., he said, there is not a program that has been mandated by G.M. national headquarters or the national office of the union. (I can testify to that personally. A vice president at G.M. had told me who to talk to at Tarrytown to arrange interviews about the QWL programs. When I called Tarrytown the local spokesmen said "What are they up to in Detroit anyway? Our plant Working Committee made a decision to admit no more inter-viewers because we are overrun with them. Sorry, that's the decision and we are sticking with it.")

Bluestone's own words about the effective way to proceed are as follows:

First we must convince the local management and local union that they ought to try some-thing then we let representatives get together to see what they can dream up, and begin involving workers on only a voluntary basis. At that point there is no end to the ingenuity of people to decide what they want to do -- all the way from deciding what color they want their machinery painted, to laying out a plant, to laying out an operation, to devel-oping the methods, means and processes of manufacturing.

The key is the goal of management cooperation with the workers in order to see to it that the workers have input and have more to say about what goes on in the shop rather than being an adjunct of the tools as workers on assembly lines are, or workers on automated equipment are....Too often QWL is written up as the workers cooperating with management to do something for management. It's quite the contrary. It's the management moving toward the workers and surrendering certain preroga-tives which management historically has enjoyed.[52]

Yet the model, within the new work climate, has to combine traditional union/management practice with the QWL approach. Bluestone described three basic paths collective bargaining is following: (1) the normal hard boiled adversarial bargaining over wages and benefits. Both sides bargain like tigers to see how the pie of profits will be divided - and there may be strikes over these issues; (2) once the basic contract is in place there are joint cooperative means for implementing them, such as health and safety, and alcoholism programs also based on hard bargaining; (3) finally, there are the newer QWL approaches which can't be written with specific contract provisions because they have to evolve through give and take at the work place. But three basic principles have to be agreed on at G.M.: (a) the introduction of any program will not increase the work pace; (b) the program will not be the source of layoffs; and (c) the agreements reached with the corporation are inviolate.

In reading statements by G.M. spokesmen like Delmar L. Landen and Howard C. Carlson, Director and Assistant Director of organizational research and development at G.M, one finds much congruence with Bluestone's perspective and finds parallels with the Scandinavian and Bolivar orientations.

For example Carlson echoes Gyllenhammar of Volvo in saying that a key idea for affecting the quality of life in organizations is, "the notion that we have to begin to treat all people, whether in a company or in a school or in any other institution, as adult human beings and not as children, and involve them in decisions that affect their lives." An incident involving Alfred S. Warren, Jr., Director of Personnel, Fisher Body Division, was cited in which he acknowledged discussions with workers about their participation on community school boards, and in political activities including friendship with congressmen which led him to realize, "these workers are responsible citizens, and treating them as anything less is ridiculous."[53]

I personally find it ridiculous that this should come as such a revelation and it points to the gulf separating management and labor. Yet the shift in perspective seems to be making significant differences not only with blue collar but also salaried employees.

Bluestone himself sees a trend developing which management may not be aware of. "Little by little," he says, "we are attacking the double standards which have established first and second class citizenship in both large and small corporations, in this country. And eventually, workers who are currently on hourly rate will be treated as salaried workers are treated and be placed on salary."[54] (The elimination of separate parking lots and dining halls at a few plants may be symptomatic.)

Another theme repeatedly enumerated by management and labor is that "quality of work life is not a

56

program, it is a concept and a way of life, a very broad and flexible philosophy."[55] Thus when Carlson was asked what advice GM could give other companies he said:

> I wouldn't presume to give them advice, and I think there is a very great danger in 'programs'...The principle that we use is to start with the organization where it is, not where we are. So I would want them to start where they are, understanding their own organization and listening to it and becoming aware of it, and let whatever flows happen....Our notion of what a change process is about says that you first need to become aware that you're hurting. We start where G.M. units are hurting instead of suggesting to them what they should be doing. So I would hesitate to advise others to try what General Motors is doing.[56]

Another principle emphasized is that "quality of work life should be viewed as an on-going process in which people and organizations are always at transitional stages of development." Within the process, efforts can be made to reach specific goals but this is different from carrying out "programs" with a beginning and an end. As a UAW official put it "It is a never-ending process. You'll finish one problem and then you'll have others."[57]

For example, people have been much impressed with Japanese Quality Control circles. Howard Weisenbaum, a Manager at Delco Products, reported how the idea has evolved there.[58] Since the term "Quality Control Circles" implied more of an emphasis on production than was wanted they used the term "employee participation circles" and emphasized they wanted basic philosophy rather than a program - with an emphasis on more involvement by people. Entry into the groups was voluntary with weekly one hour meetings in which ways of solving and implementing work related problems were discussed.

When things went well in this effort a decision was made to extend the goals and scope by creating Participative Work Groups which would involve workers daily in assuming supervisory tasks and quality control on elements like: safety - housekeeping, maintenance schedule compliance, how to handle overtime, inspection/quality etc. Salaried supervisors were assured that their jobs were not under threat but were being redefined. They became an integral part of quality and inspection functions that were assumed by hourly production workers. As supervisors they could advise, facilitate and have final authority in some areas.

This organic development toward autonomous work groups illustrates another trend Bluestone sees as possible. In a speech to G.M. executives he said "... I'm convinced the time will come (I haven't convinced you fellows to do it yet) when you will recognize the wisdom at model change time of saying to the workers: 'instead of the foremen and the engineers balancing the line, you sit down and work it out. Now here are the functions that have to be performed. Here are the parts that have to be assembled. You figure out how to do it and balance the line so that everyone is treated approximately equal.' And I'll bet you they do as good a job or a better job, than your foremen and engineers." [59]

There is a growing recognition, too by theorists like Carlson and Landen, that quality of work life cannot be isolated. It has effects on qualities of individuals and on the quality of life of a whole society. Landen says there is a growing recognition that work has a direct effect on people's attitudes, upon their perspective of life and upon their feelings about themselves. [60]

Carlson notes that the move toward autonomous work groups, like the one at Delco, cannot take place until preliminary changes in the work climate have been experienced. But developments at each stage provide the individual employee with "a qualitatively different kind of life in the organization that he or she may not have experienced, known, or cared about previously. Setting up an autonomous work team in the organization, for example, means a new self-management experience for employees; this experience, in turn, teaches the employees new skills, such as planning, budgeting, setting overtime schedules, and so on. Thus, each individual employee is also viewed as a learning system. It is assumed that each successive stage of transition releases new energy for each individual and can encourage trial-and-error or creative behavior, goal achievement, satisfaction, and self-development at all levels not typically experienced in the past." [61]

That the ideas about work we have been describing have broader implications for society as a whole is indicated in a statement by Carlson that "QWL is a social movement" - a movement related to, but with somewhat different emphases from West European industrial democracy. We shall return to the larger issues

58

of social philosophy raised by QWL in the last chapter. For the moment, though, we may end with another observation by Bluestone to G.M. executives on possible long term trends.

Bluestone said that all of them were aware of a subsurface issue which goes beyond work place management, i.e. the question about workers managing the enterprise. He noted that when Chrysler was in trouble the corporation presented the name of Douglas Fraser, President of the International U.A.W. as a member of the Board of Directors. He noted also the condition of co-determination in Germany, and described his discovery that in Egypt there must be, by law, four elected worker representatives on Boards of Directors of all corporations.

> The fact is that we are a long way off from an agreement on worker representation on the Board of Directors. But I've said this in the past, and I think it's true. Workers ask their union to take care of their immediate problems ....So when we have a problem involving pensions, we work at it and negotiate it. Or when we have problems involving health and safety, we finally get the corporation to agree to establish joint committees. But we know that decisions relative to where the product will be produced, even your accounting procedures, your marketing analysis, all have an impact on worker security. At some point down the road, you may as well face it, workers are going to be saying, 'Look those decisions are important to us and, therefore, we want to have input.' Well I don't think it's going to come in the 1982 negotiations, but I think that at some point in time, the wisdom of seeing to it that this mutuality of concern is shared with the worker will be recognized. I'll be long gone by then.[62]

When notions like these are raised shudders go through large sections of the corporate system. Socio-technical or quality of work life theory can no longer be dismissed as a backwater aberration when General Motors has made a major commitment to it, but it is far from clear what its fate will be, or what turning it will take in the coming years. The bedrock issue is whether the democratic values of American society will be taken seriously in corporate life - this time on the grounds that the re-vitalization of American productive effort requires new ways of tapping the creative energies of the work force, but also for the reason given by Irving Bluestone:

We are currently in a period of grave uncertainty in our industry. We are deeply worried
about what is happening. Some managements
might say "Now is the time to get involved in
QWL, because when things are lousy, everybody
gets worried....Everybody is concerned, and
this is the time to get people involved"....
But let me say that improving the quality of
work life is not a sometime thing. It is not
a concept which lives only in periods of
recession or depression or uncertainty, but it
should be embraced simply because it is the
right thing to do. It is the moral, human way
to treat people. It proves to be of advantage
to everybody.[63]

D. The Future of Work in America

Bluestone may be satisfied with trends he sees
emerging, but those who come out of a tradition of
management as hierarchical prescription, supervision
and control can feel deeply threatened.

Rather than a stampede toward the socio-
technical prespective it is more likely that we shall
find deep divisions at the corporate level about
philosophies of management. Hackman and Oldham in
Work Redesign describe two possible scenarios for the
future of work in the years ahead which probably
describe the forces that will be in contention.[64]

The first scenario is one based on socio-
technical principles. It will be marked by efforts to
humanize work by "fitting jobs to people," so that
workers will feel a stake in the operation. As often
as possible responsibility for ways of planning and
executing work will be located at the level where the
work is actually done. Those who do the work will
have a voice in the technical design; they will be
included in problem solving, and they will be involved
in quality control of their efforts. As more initiative is shifted to persons at the work site, organizations will be leaner with fewer hierarchical levels of
management. Information required to do the work will
be given directly to the people at work. Deliberate
efforts will be made to break with the Taylorist
tradition which separated thinking from execution.
The question will be asked, "How can work be organized
so as to treat people as adults and responsible
members of the community?" This with full awareness
that consequences must be accepted when responsibili-

ties are not met. There will be a relinquishing of the assumption that there are single answer formulas for getting work done. Initiatives when possible, will be shifted to individuals or groups. Organizations will assume obligations to become places where people can learn and grow because it is necessary for adaptation to change, and because the need to continue to learn is strong in many or most people.

The second scenario represents an extension of the dominant present model of "fitting people to jobs," with emphasis on maximizing technological and engineering efficiency. External controls will be used to shape desired behavior with financial rewards attached to correct performance. Techniques for engineering tasks into minute trainable steps will create more and more "people proof" jobs. Psychological tests will facilitate closer fit between people and work tasks. Work performance and productivity will be closely monitored by managers using highly sophisticated information systems. Integrated circuit microprocessors will facilitate gathering performance data that presently defy cost-efficient measurements. More sophisticated information systems will provide managers with reliable data about job performance and costs, which may be used to control production processes efficiently. Experts who think about the design of production will be separated sharply from people who do the work. In spite of generous material rewards for desired behavior, self-esteem levels will tend to drop and symptoms of alienation will increase. Statements will be heard like, "The harder I work the more pay and praise I get and the more headaches I get." To counter the problems of alcohol and drug abuse, absenteeism and apathy, management may introduce drug and alcohol abuse programs for those who "slip into bad habits;" and "counseling" for the depressed and resentful. Such firms may publicly congratulate themselves for their progressive employee maintenance programs. Hackman and Oldham suggest that choices between scenario 1 and scenario 2 will be made by many seemingly insignificant decisions in far-scattered sites of white and blue collar work across America.

We now move strongly on the road toward scenario 2. We know how to operate it. It fits the style and values of the main-line economic - engineering model of work we have created; the majority of workers and managers have route 2 habits and inclinations and are not comfortable with the idea of change. But there is also unease. The counter force derives from a sense that the costs of route 2 are too high; that it is dysfunctional as evidenced by material and human breakdowns, that it represents a betrayal of cultural values that go beyond the "get mine Jack" ethic - and, perhaps most notably, that it is a source of our economic crisis. When I asked a G.M. manager why they were choosing the trauma of uprooting old habits, he answered with one word: Pain.

Behind all this, of, course, is the question of what kind of people we want to be under technology. As the century has unfolded we have, as Sheldon Wolin pointed out, "evolved from a more to a less democratic polity." We have surrendered ourselves to authoritarian rational-positivist controls at work in return for the brutally simple goal of M O R E . We have let spin-offs from this orientation strongly affect the education of our children.

But it is also patently false that the United States has become nothing more than a self-indulgent corporate-engineer controlled society. Americans in this century have also fought for gains in civil rights for minorities and women, and in a crunch like the Vietnam - Watergate era have shown commitment to civil liberties. Presently we are creating alternative work designs that tap the strength of our democratic values.

We are, in fact, still in the process of making decisions about what identity we want to assume for entering the twenty-first century. Whatever it is, it will be getting into the education of our children.

In America as a Civilization (1957), at the end of our first decade as a dominant world power, Max Lerner caught nicely the divided soul of the American people: America as the "Business Civilization" with an over-riding commitment to pursue material prosperity and world economic pre-eminence, and that other America Paul Goodman referred to as the libertarian, pluralist, democratic, populist experiment.

> It is hard not to feel that while America is still on the rising arc of its world power it is on the descending arc of its inner social and moral origin; that it has allowed itself to be switched off from the main path of its development into the futile dead ends of the fear of ideas and the tenacious cult of property. Toynbee has suggested how frequently a civilization has been weakened by its "pathological insistence upon pushing to extremes its master institution...If the master institution of America is property,

62

there is evidence of the beginning of a pathological insistence in pushing it to extremes. Linked with it is a fear of subversive movements which may threaten or overthrow the institution - a fear that therefore induces a...loss of belief in the inherent efficacy of democracy. The result is a negativism of outlook which puts stress on the defense of the master institution rather than upon the affirmation of its linkage with democratic human values....

One may guess that America will lead the world in technology and power for at least several generations to come. But it is one thing to fill a power vacuum in the world with transitional leadership, and quite another to offer to the world the qualities of leadership which it requires, attuned at once to the life of nature and life of the spirit.[65]

Max Lerner writing these words in 1957 was concerned about the corrosive effect of McCarthyism but could still write that the American people had not yet "suffered decisive defeat in a war, nor the agony of internal revolutionary violence."[66] All of that was to change in the two decades to follow as we experienced the sobering traumas of the burning of the cities in the Civil Rights struggle, the humiliations of Vietnam and Watergate, the oil crisis of the 70s and the spectacle of being surpassed economically by a defeated island nation of Asiatics.

It was difficult indeed to admit we had lost overwhelming world pre-eminence and were locked into the mutual interdependencies of the shrunken planet. In neither the stage of pre-eminence nor the stage of interdependence have we given a clear indication of our capacity to provide "the qualities of leadership ...attuned at once to the life of nature and the life of the spirit."

The issue that Max Lerner set forth remains unresolved. In the eyes of much of the world, struggling to rise from degrading poverty and repression, America has taken on the image of the conservative defender of property - the ally of entrenched privileged elites opposing aspirations of human dignity for the majority. Time is running out on our chance to demonstrate that we can marshal the qualities of leadership "which a beleaguered humanity requires", a leadership which would demonstrate the possibility of linkage between our economic life and democratic human values appropriate for a technological era.

The values of the work world of adults exert powerful influences on the quality of life of children in our schools. We should not be surprised to find that American education throughout the twentieth century has experienced an ongoing tension between Taylorist scientific management principles and the impulses toward school environments congruent with values of our democratic traditions. We turn next to tracing manifestations of this tension in the history of American schools in this century.

NOTES

1.   Kalman H. Silvert, The Reason for Democracy. (New York: The Viking Press, 1977), p. 117.

2.   Sheldon S. Wolin, "Why Democracy?" Democracy (January 1981, Vol. I., No. 1.), p. 4.

3.   Delmar L. Landen, in Los Angeles Times, October 23, 1980.

4.   Business Week, June 30, 1980 (See "A Solution: A New Social Contract," pp. 86-88 et passim).

5.   Sheldon S. Wolin, "The People's Two Bodies," Democracy (January 1981, Vol. I, No. 1), p. 23.

6.   George Gilder, Wealth and Poverty. (New York: Basic Books, 1980), p. 211.

7.   Lynn White, Jr., Dynamo and Virgin Reconsidered. (Boston: M.I.T. Press, 1968), p. 29.

8.   See Philip G. Herbst, Socio-Technical Design. (London: Tavistock Publications, 1974).

9.   Pehr G. Gyllenhammar, People at Work. (Reading, MA: Addison Wesley, 1977), p. 4.

10.   Ibid., p. 2.

11.   Ibid., p. 21.

12.   Ibid., p. 29.

13.   Ibid., p. 68 and 159.

14.   See, for example, E.F. Emery and Einar Thorsrud, Form

and Content in Industrial Democracy: Some Experiences from Norway and Other European Countries. (London: Tavistock Publishing, Ltd., 1969).

15. Philip G. Herbst, Alternatives to Hierarchies. (Leiden: Martinus Nijhoff: Social Science Division, 1976), p. 17.

16. Herbst, Socio-Technical Design, pp. 204-205.

17. Ibid., pp. 207-208.

18. The account which follows is based on an interview with Ragnar Johansen (May 14, 1980) and on a report of his: "Democratizing work and social life on ships: A Report from the experiment on board M.S. Balao," (Ship Research Group, Work Research Institutes, Oslo). For a more available account see Einar Thorsrud, "Breaking Down Bureaucracy," in Dyckman W. Vermilye, ed., Relating Work and Education. (San Francisco: Jossey-Bass Publishers, 1977).

19. See Herbst, Alternatives to Hierarchies.

20. Gyllenhammar, op. cit., pp. 123-124.

21. Fred Emery and Einar Thorsrud, Democracy at Work. (Leiden: Martinus Nijhoff, 1976), p. 159.

22. Gyllenhammar, op. cit., pp. 17-19.

23. Silvert, op. cit., p. 117.

24. Willard Wirtz, "Education for What?" in Dyckman W. Vermilye, ed., Relating Work and Education. (San Francisco: Jossey-Bass Publishers, 1977).

25. See Daniel Zwerdling, Democracy at Work. (Washington, D.C.: Association for Self Management, 1978).

26. Margaret Molinari Duckles, et al., "The Process of Change at Bolivar," (Available from The Harvard Project on Technology, Work and Character, 1710 Connecticut Ave., N. W.; Washington, DC 20009.).

27. In Louis E. Davis and A.B. Cherns, eds., The Quality of Working Life, Vol. I. (New York: Free Press, 1975).

28. Erich Fromm, The Sane Society. (New York: Rinehart and Winston, Inc., 1955), pp. 270-271.

29. Ibid., p. 32.

30. Ibid., p. 350.

31. Ibid., p. 32.

32. Ibid., pp. 169-170.

33. Ibid., p. 276.

34. See Michael Maccoby "What is Productivity?" (Available from The Harvard Project on Technology, Work and Character, copyrighted, Michael Maccoby, 1979), pp. 7-8 et passim.

35. Michael Maccoby, "The Quality of Working Life - Lessons from Bolivar." (September 13, 1964), pp. 1-14 et passim. (Available from The Harvard Project on Technology, Work and Character).

36. See Jean Piaget, To Understand Is to Invent. (New York: The Viking Press, 1973).

37. The Harman Mirror, June 1977, pp. 4-5.

38. Maccoby, op. cit., p. 9. (It is important to recognize, however, that the change in style can be threatening to managers and foremen. In an auto plant in Detroit I was told, "Some old-time managers who have been used to exercising authority by direct orders, can't take it. Some have just quit, or asked for other assignments." (Interviews, November, 1981).)

39. Ibid., pp. 9-10.

40. Harry Bernstein, "Democracy Moves into the Work Place," Los Angeles Times, October 23, 1980.

41. Ernest C. Miller, "GM's Quality of Work Life Efforts ...An Interview with Howard C. Carlson," Reprint from Personnel (July - August, 1980). (Available from Organizational Research and Development Department, General Motors Corporation, 8-206 GM Building, Detroit, MI, 48202)

42. Business Week, August 18, 1980, p. 98.

43. Bernstein, op. cit.

44. Robert H. Guest, "Quality of Work Life - Learning from Tarrytown," Harvard Business Review, (Vol. 57, No. 4, July-August, 1979), p. 77. (The account of Tarrytown is based on this article pp. 76-87 et passim).

45. Ibid.

46. Ibid., pp. 78-79.

47. Irving Bluestone, "A Changing View of Union-Management Relationships," Vital Speeches, December 11, 1976. (The speech has been repeated a number of times with variations.)

48. Ibid., p. 83.

49. Interview with Irving Bluestone, "UAW-Loosening the Chains," The Harvard Crimson, February 21, 1979, p. 3.

50. Delmar L. Landen, "Labor-Management Cooperation in Productivity," April 21, 1980, p. 12, (available from Organizational Research and Development Division, General Motors).

51. Bluestone, Harvard Crimson.

52. Ibid.

53. Miller, op. cit., p. 16.

54. Irving Bluestone, "Quality of Work Life: Its Status and Its Future," Proceedings of the 1980 Executive Conference on Quality of Work Life (General Motors), p. 32.

55. Miller, op. cit.

56. Ibid.

57. Bill Horner, "UAW Involvement," Proceedings of the 1980 Executive Conference, op. cit., p. 81.

58. Howard Weisenborn, "The Next Step," Proceedings, op. cit., pp. 94-98 et passim.

59. Bluestone, op. cit., p. 32.

60. Delmar L. Landen, "The Real Issue: Human Dignity," Survey of Business, (Vol. 12, No. 5, May/August, 1977), p. 15.

61. Howard C. Carlson, "A Model of Quality of Work Life as a Developmental Process," in W. Warner Burke and Leonard D. Goodstein, eds., Trends and Issues in OD: Current Theory and Practice. (San Diego: University Associates, 1980), p. 95.

62. Bluestone, op. cit., pp. 33-34.

63. Ibid., p. 35.

64. J. Richard Hackman and Greg R. Oldham, Work Redesign.

(Reading, Mass: Addison-Wesley Publishing Company, 1980), pp. 259-271 et passim.

65. Max Lerner, America As a Civilization. (New York: Simon and Schuster, 1957), p. 947.

66. Ibid., p. 948.

CHAPTER IV

JOB AND WORK -- TWO MODELS FOR SOCIETY AND EDUCATION:
VOCATIONALISM AND THE SCHOOLS IN THE EARLY
TWENTIETH CENTURY

Max Lerner's statement about our conflict over
"which America" shows that the issue is not a new one.
If we use Lerner's language, the current choice is
whether we organize our work and school life according
to the efficiency traditions attached to "the tena-
cious cult of property," or whether we seek institutional renewal through an "affirmation of democratic
human values."

In this chapter I wish to argue that the issue
has been there since the opening of the century when
we were becoming a corporate-industrial, bureaucratic
society and were attempting to create mass public
education. The issue showed up with stark clarity in
the debate over vocationalism between: (1) social
efficiency philosophers like David Snedden of Teachers
College, Columbia University and Charles Prosser,
executive secretary of The National Society for the
Promotion of Industrial Education and (2) John Dewey
and a democratic reform wing of progressivism. By
looking at that early struggle we can sharpen our
awareness of value conflicts that we confront as we
end the century.

Before getting into substantive aspects of that
earlier history, it is useful to note a distinction
between job and work which Thomas Green identified in
Work, Leisure, and the American Schools.[1] I shall
maintain that the social efficiency philosophers and
progressive reformers like John Dewey divided sharply
between job and work orientations. The split showed
up in different ideas about what the good society is
and how to get it, and in different images of what
good schools should be. Green maintains that it is
useful to distinguish job and labor from work along
lines such as the following. Having a job in the most
basic sense is to have a way of making a living. If
the living is made by labor alone it includes features
like doing tasks separated from a sense of completion
or fullfillment in some object. Labor is separate
from the personal purposes of the laborer. And it
involves production of items primarily to be consumed
rather than to be put to use in people's lives. It
involves low engagement of self. Its goal is for
income you can consume with.

Work, as he uses it, is a different phenomenon.

It includes dimensions like production of persistent stable products which enrich or sustain life, and in which the worker's purposes and meanings are involved. A person's quest for work is related to the human quest for potency in which the person may explore his potential, test the limits of himself, be in touch with his powers and in the process discover his human dignity and worth. Green maintains that in the modern world the sphere of labor has been enlarged and the sphere of work diminished. As we shall see the social efficiency philosophers could view that development with equanimity or favor. Dewey viewed it with dismay.

First, some comments on the social efficiency approach to education. Among the early proponents for vocational education in the nineties were representatives of the business community. The National Association of Manufacturers (N.A.M.), for example, was founded in 1895. Its leaders were motivated in part by the need to increase their share in foreign markets to overcome the woes of the depression of 1893. As they came to see it this meant that they needed to increase the efficiency of their modes of production. They found difficulty in meeting the challenge of their chief competitor, Imperial Germany. When they investigated the source of German achievement, they found it in the existence of the highly differentiated vocational training programs geared precisely to the hierarchical skill needs of German industry. This was a system separate from the general schools and administered by "practical men" from the Ministry of Commerce rather than by "fuzzy-minded educators." Hence, a dual system.

Impressed by what they found in Germany, the manufacturers set up their own N.A.M. Committee on Industrial Education. Its chairman, H.E. Miles, in 1911 reported a dismal contrast in American public education. His committee rolled out statistics of cost against performance of American schools, and was dismayed at "the low yield of school products." What, Miles asked, were the people getting for an outlay of $450 million and a school investment plant of $1 billion? Only fifty percent of children in school finished the sixth grade; one in three completed grammar school, and only one out of thirty finished high school. The problem, he said, was that the work of the schools rested on "theories instead of reality."[2] The schools, said Miles, offered a literary education which satisfied the one student in thirty who was abstract minded. They were guilty of inexcusable neglect of the other twenty-nine.

Mile's Committee became convinced that the German system not only offered an answer to the drop-out tendency of the non-literary oriented students but it also provided the German nation with a reliable labor force motivated by a positive work ethic. The words of a leading German philosopher of vocational education impressed the manufacturers:

The first aim of education for those leaving the elementary school is training for trade efficiency, and joy and love of work. With these is connected the training of those elementary virtues which efficiency and love of work have in their train - conscientiousness, industry, perseverence, responsibility, self-restraint, and devotion to an active life. [3]

What a difference such attitudes could make in American factories, where, as Miles said, "...our factory children look upon a shop too much as upon a jail. There has developed among a considerable part of the adult factory workers a dislike, almost a hate of work." [4]

The Association became convinced that American manufacturers could compete successfully in international markets only if the American school system introduced a set of separate vocational schools, guided by men of industry, patterned after the German model. These American business men shared the ethic of rugged individualism held by international capitalist entrepreneurs. N.A.M. members in their speeches at national conventions repeated their belief that the Social Darwinist philosophy of William Graham Sumner expressed the source of human progress. This ideology assumed that society consists of isolated individuals of varying abilities and capacities. When left to pursue self advantage in rugged competition they will bring forth the promise of ever increasing material plenty for all. From this well-spring of increased consumption flow all other goods: a home of one's own; more education for the kids; support for religion, philanthropies, and the arts.

Perceptive leaders operating from these premises were aware that new corporate-technological economic conditions were emerging based on increased rationalization of production and specialization of job functions. A critical contribution from American schooling would be required to meet the challenge of European competition. The logic of Social Darwinism for vocational education was quite clear. Its task

was to increase material productivity as had vocationalism in Germany, to give priority to meeting hierarchical skill needs, and to instill attitudes and
training to preserve the dominant values of Social
Darwinist ideology. Ideally the logic called for a
set of separate vocational schools, guided by men of
industry, patterned after the German model.

The movement in the direction of adding a vocational component to American education had been under
way for three or four decades before the turn of the
century. The Civil War, like other major wars, had
revolutionary consequences for American society. It
generated the conditions for a new America marked by
corporate capitalism and urbanism. The expansion of
railways, heavy industries, mining, machine-centered
agriculture, and business and government bureaucracies
broke the mold of traditional ways of producing and
distributing goods. Apprenticeship systems and
on-the-job learning were no longer adequate for the
new situation.

Before the war, a bright young man might pick
up principles and skills of engineering by working
with those who were pushing through the railroads on
the frontier. But as engine plants produced larger
locomotives, as steel mills produced the components
for heavier bridges and equipment, seat-of-the-pants
training no longer sufficed. In retrospect we can see
that the earliest innovations for formal technical
training were designed to train leaders who could
handle the complexities of science and industry. In
1860 there were perhaps only five schools of engineering. By 1880, as the shortage of engineers became
painfully apparent, the number had increased to
eighty-five. This development was accompanied by the
creation of other professional schools in American
universities: colleges of business administration,
mining, agriculture and horticulture, forestry,
veterinary medicine, and education. At lower levels
commercial courses were introduced to train the white
collar secretariat of the new corporations; for the
work shops, beginning efforts were made in industrial
drawing and the manual training movement was launched
for pre-engineering in the high schools and for the
cultivation of leadership within the labor force.

In spite of these moves only a tiny percentage
of the population was involved. By the end of the
nineties, a watershed decade, discontents about urban
schooling were sharply on the rise. Interest groups
as divergent as business and industry, organized
labor, farm organizations, social workers and women's

72

rights groups began to call for some version of industrial education as an antidote to the sterility and ineffectiveness of the public schools. This broad move culminated in 1906 with the publication of the Douglas Commission's Report of the Massachusetts Commission on Industrial and Technical Education, and the founding of the National Society for the Promotion of Industrial Education (NSPIE), committed to moving American schools in the direction of the German model.

If America was to make such a radical innovation in its public school system, new legislation and funding eventually would be required. The ground work for that would have to be prepared by thoughtful and persuasive argumentation. Two educators within the vocational education movement, David Snedden and Charles Prosser, became prominent articulators of a social efficiency philosophy to support the German type idea. David Snedden left a professorship at Teachers College, Columbia University, to become Commissioner of Education in 1909 under Governor Douglas in Massachusetts. He appointed his colleague, Charles Prosser, as his deputy to create and administer the new vocational programs. Snedden was a voluminous writer and was listed by Norman Woelfel as one of the seventeen leaders in American education who were "Molders of the American Mind." He was the first editor of The American Vocational Journal. Charles Prosser became Executive Secretary of the National Society for the Promotion of Industrial Education (NSPIE) in 1912 and had the organizational genius to bring together the coalition of groups to make possible the enactment of the Smith-Hughes Act. He was, in fact, the effective author of the Act. The rationale they developed to support the technocratic model was marked by a conservative social philosophy, a methodology of specific training operations based on principles of stimulus-response psychology and a curriculum designed according to the job needs of industry. The doctrine of social efficiency they espoused contained an image of man, a vision of the good society and a set of recommendations for school practice, not only for vocational education but for education in general.

Snedden shared the basic faith of Herbert Spencer and the conservative social Darwinists that the emergence of scientific-corporate capitalism was the cosmic instrument for progress. He accepted the basic proposition of the manufacturers that what was good for business was good for America. In order to help more Americans enjoy progress, the task of education was to aid the economy to function as efficiently as possible. He called those who bemoaned the mechanization and depersonalization of work "simple-lifers" or "romantic impracticalists" who yearned for times that were gone forever. Modern men might be subjected to fragmented, routine job tasks; but production specialization and differentiation enabled them to live longer, more comfortably, and with the leisure to consume the arts. Moreover, the application of mass production methods to school life could help to forward still newer advances. As he put it "Quantity production methods applied in education speedily give us school grades, uniform textbooks, promotional examinations...strictly scheduled programs, mechanical discipline and hundreds of other mechanisms most of which are unavoidably necessary if our ideals of universal education are to be realized."[5]

Snedden, furthermore, was convinced that the new science of sociology showed that characteristics of the population fitted neatly the needs of the corporate economy. He quoted his sociology teacher Franklin Giddings, "The process of selection is based upon the differences growing out of the unequal conditions of both heredity and nurture to which man is born. Inequality -- physical, mental, and moral -- is an inevitable characteristic of the social population."[6]

Snedden likened the good society to a winning "team group." A team was made stronger by specialization of functions. Some, like the officers on a submarine crew, would be trained to lead and coordinate; others would be trained for their special functions in the ranks.[7]

As Snedden saw it scientific testing instruments combined with vocational guidance would make it possible for schools to do what Charles Eliot had suggested in 1907 - differentiate children into programs according to their "probable destinies" based on heredity plus economic and social factors. The new junior high schools would perform the task of sorting students into differentiated courses: pre-vocational offerings in commercial subjects, industrial arts, and agricultural or household arts for those "who most incline to them or have need of them."[8]

Seen properly the condition of inequality was not something to be deplored but a fact which would help us all more toward a common goal. Men of industry and labor might have their conflicts but they were in agreement about the proper motivation and goal of progress. Samuel Gompers, after all, was willing to boil down the goal of his wing of the labor movement to that single potent word - "More."

Snedden shared that sentiment and felt that new insights into the rationalization of labor could now be applied to schooling in ways that would enable all Americans, at all levels, to advance in the common quest for More. It was a clear example of what Green tells us has been a basic expectation of Americans - the function of the schools is to help you to get ahead in the system. The model which emerged from this motivation was a Social Darwinist job efficiency approach. The nature of the jobs to be planned for children in schools was roughly to parallel the design of jobs in the work world. Application of the rationalization of labor could increase the efficiency and productivity in both realms. The question of whether or not such arrangements were instrumental in helping children or grown-ups to "find a work" in Green's sense, could not be seen as a serious question, or could be dismissed as the talk you might expect of those "easy lifers."

The job efficiency approach was projected as the proper model for the whole school effort. This shows up in Snedden's way of defining the relation of vocational and liberal studies. As Snedden saw it, "Man stands to the world about him in a two-fold relationship. He is a producer of utilities...and he must utilize utilities." That education which trains him to be a good utilizer or consumer is liberal education. [9]

Snedden clarified his new proposals for liberal studies in an address to the New England History Teacher's Association in 1914. He characterized the old chronological approach to history as "cold storage" education and said that for "the rank and file", at least, history should be taught to satisfy specific aims drawn from functional social needs." History was for citizenship. "Having once conceived of the citizen as we should like to have him, we can work back and by analysis find the numberless specific forms of training by which we can produce this type." On the question of which social values the teacher should advocate, Snedden said the teacher should remember that he was a public servant and as such had the obligation to teach the "opinions and valuation of the controlling majority."[10] A teacher interested in minority views should either surrender them to majority opinion or leave. When the U.S. Commissioner of Education, Philander P. Claxton admitted to feeling a "shudder of abhorrence" at the "brutal efficiency" implied by this new and more effective education,

Snedden replied that he, too, stood for cultural education. But the proper definition of both cultural and vocational education had to be derived from an analysis of the social functions each should perform. These functions were to be revealed by insights from educational sociology, a new discipline of which Snedden was the foremost practitioner.

Snedden's philosophy sets before us in stark outlines a concept of society and of schooling based on a job efficiency model. The task of schooling was "to make the child a better socius, a more fit member of an efficiently functioning society." The school in both its vocational and liberal aspects is modeled on the job as archtype. Schooling will sort us out according to our various capacities. As we all become more efficient we all help increase the size of the pie to be consumed. This perspective fits Samuel Hayes' comments on life in the United States in 1914. "The American people subordinated religion, education, and politics to the process of getting wealth. Increasing production, employment, and income became the measure of community success, and personal riches the mark of individual achievement."[11]

Frederick Fish, President of A.T. and T. and Chairman of the Massachusetts Board of Education, was impressed by the vision of his Commissioner of Education and called on the schools to revise their values by providing training to meet "the practical needs of life" for "the rank and file."[12] The Snedden-Fish regime was prepared to act as well as talk. Snedden appointed his Teachers College colleague, Charles Prosser, to develop a system of vocational schools for the major industrial centers of the state. By 1912, when Prosser became Executive Secretary of the National Society for the Promotion of Industrial Education, he had clarified his goal: to reject the impractical manual training of the general educators and replace it with "real vocational education," by which he meant training for useful employment - train the person to get a job, train him so he could hold it and advance to a better job.

Prosser insisted that all of vocational content must be specific and that its source was to be found "in the experience of those who have mastered the occupation." A prototype of the plan favored by Prosser was established in the short unit courses which he developed while Director of the Dunwoody Institute in Minneapolis. At the Dunwoody Institute, units were programmed in great detail to lead students step-by-step through the skill development cycle.

Students punched in on time-clocks and instructors behaved like shop foremen rather than public school teachers. A no-nonsense attitude prevailed. If students were not punctual, orderly, and efficient, they were asked to leave.

The manufacturers were alert and vocal in their statements about the kind of training the schools should incorporate for their skill needs. Prosser and Snedden spoke their language, and they became enamored with H.E. Miles' cost accounting way of thinking about learning. These social efficiency oriented men saw themselves as progressive reformers. They would bring to new large-scale organizations the rationality, objectivity and measurement methods of the new scientific management. The model of "the perfect clock" provided the standard, with minute parts working flawlessly under the watchful eye of qualified system designers and controllers. The groundwork was laid for the expert controlled society.

But there were other reformers uneasy and unhappy with these trends. Robert Wiebe noted that tensions within progressive reform were quick to show themselves. "By 1905 urban progressives were already separating along two paths. While one group used the language of the budget, boosterism, and social control, the other talked of economic justice, human opportunities, and rehabilitated democracy. Efficiency as economy diverged further and further from efficiency as social service." [13]

On the subject of industrial education both groups were lamenting "the waste in education." A closer look though reveals that "the social efficiency progressives" were alarmed most by financial waste as they measured "school output" against efficiency criteria - the new rage of the era. The "humanitarians", however, were bothered about the human waste - the entry of young school leavers into dead-end child labor jobs and the irrelevance of classroom recitations. Thus Dewey in a chapter on "Waste in Education" [14] charged that out-of-school experiences were not drawn on in classes and recitations had little relevance for children when they fled at the end of the day. The schools, he said, were "isolated from life."

The humanitarian wing of progressivism had powerful spokesmen to confront the kind of talk coming from the N.A.M. and the vocationalists. In 1913, for example, at a joint meeting of the National Vocational Guidance Association (NVGA) and the National Society for the Promotion of Industrial Education (NSPIE), a

77

group of "progressives" led the Guidance Association
to a refusal of the invitation of Charles Prosser to
join NSPIE. The "humanitarians" were represented by
speakers like Ida Tarbell, queen of the muckrackers,
arguing for the inclusion of girls in industrial
education; Owen R. Lovejoy, Secretary of the National
Child Labor Committee; and representatives of a
Chicago reform group like George H. Mead and Frank
Leavitt of the University of Chicago who joined John
Dewey in opposing pressures to establish separate
vocational schools.

Owen R. Lovejoy enunciated the point of view
represented by this wing. Lovejoy told the convention
that both industries and schools needed to be reformed
before children could experience the "Promise of
America." He said that schools needed to introduce
programs of vocational guidance which would "analyze"
our industries and train our youth to distinguish
between a 'vocation' and a 'job'. He criticized "the
captains of industry" who said, "Here are the jobs:
what kind of children do you have to offer?" Educators and guidance personnel must reverse the inquiry,
said Lovejoy, and ask, "Here are your children: what
kind of industry have you to offer?"[15]

His position was supported by Frank Leavitt,
who was to become the first President of NVGA.
Leavitt said guidance workers needed to study industries from the point of view of whether they were
"good for children." Such studies, "if carried out in
a comprehensive, purposeful and scientific way, may
force upon industry many modifications which will be
good not only for the children but equally for the
industry." Vocational guidance will not hesitate to
make such demands just because an industry is rich and
powerful, Leavitt added. "Why should we hesitate to
lay hands on industry in the name of education, when
we already laid hands on the school in the name of
industry."[16]

While attending the 1913 convention John Dewey
was at work on the thinking which would emerge in
Democracy and Education (1916). In it Dewey said "At
the present time the conflict of philosophical theories focuses on discussion of the proper place and
function of vocational factors in education....
Significant differences in fundamental philosophical
conceptions find their chief issue in connection with
this point..."[17] As we shall see in the next chapter,
Dewey felt that the mode of learning, represented in
science, which was changing human work contained
important lessons for education. Experiences with

78

emerging technologies and vocations and the underlying thought processes transforming them could provide significant active learnings for twentieth century children. So he gave careful attention to the question of the relation of vocations to education. But Dewey, the philosopher of democracy, was bringing a very different frame of reference to bear on the topic. We find a clear articulation of his position in Reconstruction in Philosophy:

> All social institutions have a meaning, a purpose. That purpose is to set free and to develop the capacities of human individuals without respect to race, sex, class or economic status...(The) test of their value is the extent to which they educate every individual into full stature of his possibility. Democracy has many meanings, but if it has a moral meaning, it is found in resolving that the supreme test of all political institutions and industrial arrangements shall be the contribution they make to the all-around growth of every member of society. [18]

To Snedden this kind of talk sounded like the language of the "romantic impractialists," and he confessed to a difficulty in understanding Dewey's position. He thought Dewey was an ally in condemming "sterile, bookish education" and he was hurt when he found Dewey opposing the German type dualism. He expressed his sense of betrayal in a letter to The New Republic "...to find Dr. Dewey apparently giving aid and comfort to opponents of a broader, richer, and more effective program of education...is discouraging." Dewey replied sharply that his differences with Snedden were profoundly social and political as well as educational:

> The kind of vocational education in which I am interested in is not one which will "adapt" workers to the existing industrial regime; I am not sufficently in love with the regime for that. It seems to me that the business of all who would not be educational time servers is to resist every move in this direction, and to strive for a kind of vocational education which will first alter the existing industrial system and ultimately transform it. [19]

The differences were indeed profoundly social and political. Dewey's aspiration was to redesign industrial and educational institutions so they would be supportive of democratic values. Furthermore, Dewey charged that Snedden had failed to meet the heart of his argument on pedagogical matters. "I argued that a separation of trade education and general education of youth has the inevitable tendency to make both kinds of training narrower and less significant than the schooling in which the traditional education is reorganized to utilize the subject matter -- active, scientific, and social of the present day environment."[20]

Dewey's central concern was with the problems of persons and of democratic traditions in the technological society. He rejected the image of isolated individuals moved by the play of natural forces in the market place. He operated from the social psychology position of his colleague George H. Mead - with its self-other concept of personality. The self was seen as emerging from both the patterning of culture plus the value choices of the individual. The premise held that if you wanted persons with qualities capable of sustaining democratic values they had to be nourished in communities marked by such values. As Dewey saw it people were beginning to repeat the rhetoric of democratic values while living in contradiction of them in their daily work life.

The task of overcoming the contradictions, as Dewey defined it, was to develop strategies for bringing qualities of the democratic ethos into institutions being transformed by science, technology and corporatism. His general strategy was to seek means by which the qualities of mind, required to reform institutions, could be made available across the entire population. The schools were assigned a critical role; they could teach the hypothetical mode of thought required to handle complex problems; the schools themselves could be turned into communities, where the young in living and learning would experience the life qualities exemplified in the creative work of scientists and artists. By spending the years of childhood and youth in such learning communities the young might become the kind of persons who could change institutional life-styles so they would serve to liberate persons rather than manipulate them as functionaries. While Dewey in the early 1900s shared the faith of the progressives that the schools could be in the vanguard of social reform he later realized that democratic social reform had to go on simultaneously in industry and education. We are ready then to examine in more detail the connections Dewey saw between the possibility of industrial democracy and a reform of public schools.

NOTES

1. Thomas F. Green, <u>Work, Leisure and the American Schools</u>. (New York: Random House, 1978), Chapter 2, "Work and Leisure."

2. National Association of Manufacturers <u>Proceedings</u>, 1911, pp. 187–188.

3. Diane Simons, <u>George Kerschensteiner</u>. (London: Methuen, 1966), p. 30.

4. National Association of Manufacturers <u>Proceedings</u>, 1912, p. 154.

5. David Snedden, <u>Toward Better Educations</u>. (New York: Bureau of Publications, Teachers College, Columbia University, 1931), pp. 330–331.

6. Franklin Giddings, <u>Principles of Sociology</u>. (New York: MacMillan, 1896), p. 9.

7. David Snedden, "Education for a World of Teamplayers," <u>School and Society</u>, (Vol. 20, Nov. 1, 1924), p. 554.

8. Charles W. Eliot, National Society for the Promotion of Education. <u>Bulletin</u>, (No. 5, 1908), pp. 9–14.

9. David Snedden, "Fundamental Distinctions Between Liberal and Vocational Education," N.E.A. <u>Proceedings</u>, 1914, pp. 154–155.

10. David Snedden, "Teaching History in Secondary Schools," <u>History Teachers Magazine</u>, (Vol. 5, November 1914), pp. 227–282.

11. Samuel P. Hays, <u>The Response to Industrialism</u>. (Chicago: University of Chicago Press, 1957), p. 12.

12. Frederick P. Fisch, N.E.A. <u>Proceedings</u>, 1910, pp. 367–368.

13. Robert Wiebe, <u>The Search for Order</u>. (New York: Hill and Wang, 1967), p. 176.

14. John Dewey, <u>School and Society</u>. (Chicago: University of Chicago Press, rev. ed., 1923), Chapter 3.

15. Owen R. Lovejoy, "Vocational Guidance and Child Labor," U.S. Bureau of Education <u>Bulletin</u>, No. 14, U.S.

Government Printing Office, 1914, p. 13.

16. Frank M. Leavitt, "How Shall We Study the Industries for the Purpose of Vocational Guidance," U.S. Bureau of Education, _Bulletin_, No. 14, U.S. Government Printing Office, 1914, pp. 79-81.

17. John Dewey, _Democracy and Education_. (New York: MacMillan, 1916), p. 358.

18. John Dewey, _Reconstruction in Philosophy_. (New York: The American Library, 1950), p. 147, (italics mine).

19. Letters in _The New Republic_, (Vol. 3, 1915), pp. 40-42.

20. Ibid.

CHAPTER V

JOHN DEWEY'S PHILOSOPHY ON THE RELATION OF
EDUCATION AND INDUSTRIAL DEMOCRACY

> The dominant vocation of all human beings at
> all times is living -- intellectual and moral
> growth.[1]   John Dewey

> The moral function of...institutions is in the
> last analysis educative. [2]   John Dewey

John Dewey stated in the Preface to Democracy
and Education (1916) that his goal was to show how his
philosophy of education was related to the experimentalist and evolutionary features of science, the
growth of democracy, and the need for industrial
reorganization. Even though he was forthright about
his convictions regarding the connections of education, science, democracy and industrialism, the
linkage he saw between education and "industrial
reorganization" has been among the least explored
features of his work.

In this chapter I shall (1) indicate the nature
of Dewey's discontents with American industrialism and
education, (2) point to his distinctive view of
science as an emergent model of creative learning that
is linked to values of democratic community, and (3)
show how his way of thinking about science caused him
to hold that a basic twentieth century task was to
create parallel reorganizations of industry and
education.

A. Dualisms: Social and Intellectual as Sources of Repression

Dewey was sensitive to cultural reproduction in
the schools which reflected social class and related
philosophical dualisms, but he rejected economic
determinism. His faith was that forceful analysis of
the human costs of institutional dualisms, combined
with action through democratic processes, could lead
us toward a social democracy. A distinctive conviction was that by clarifying the human possibilities
inherent in the values of science, we could identify a
forming ideal of democratic community to guide the
reconstruction of institutions.

Lewis Feuer's insightful essay, "John Dewey and
the Back to the People Movement in American Thought"
shows how the emergence of Dewey's social concerns

about class division in the late eighties and nineties
left enduring marks on the development of his general
philosophy.[3]

Dewey came to Chicago from the University of
Michigan in 1894, during the administration of the
reform governor, John P. Altgeld, when Chicago was a
center of radical political thought. His departure
from Michigan (1894) coincided with the end of an
abortive effort to start a new kind of newspaper, The
Thought News, in collaboration with the journalist
Franklin Ford, an eccentric syndicalist socialist.
The general idea had been to help advance a new
industrial order to be administered by the emerging
labor unions. Ideas for guiding the movement in "the
interest of all classes, the whole" would come from
intellectuals, "men of letters," such as Dewey, who
would awaken the awareness of the American people to
economic facts by "the socializing of intelligence."
The complex plan never got under way.

When Dewey arrived in Chicago, however, he soon
gravitated to activities of Jane Addam's Hull House,
which was becoming a center for those working on "the
side of the underdogs." Dewey joined other intellectuals like Henry Demarest Lloyd and Prince Kropotkin
in lecturing to the Working People's Social Science
Club. His encounters with anarchists, single-taxers
and socialists coincided with his statement in 1894,
"that economic needs and struggles have been the
determining force in the evolution of all institutions
...is too important as theory and...in practice to be
overlooked."[4]

The publication of Veblen's Theory of the
Leisure Class (1899) gave Dewey the language for
stating the socio-political basis of his philosophy.
Shortly after reading Veblen, he wrote that philosophical dualisms are "a survival from a dualistic past--
from a society which was dualistic practically and
politically, drawing fixed lines between classes, and
dualistic intellectually."[5] "Our culture," he said,
"is still tainted with an inheritance from the period
of the aristocratic seclusion of the leisure class --
leisure meaning relief from participation in the work
of a work-a-day world."[6]

As a philosopher of the back to the people
movement, Dewey held that social democracy means an
abandonment of this dualist heritage. "It means a
common heritage, a common work, and a common destiny.
It is flat hostility to the ethics of modern life to
suppose that there are two different ends of life
located on different planes; that the few who are

educated are to live on a plane of exclusive and isolated culture, while the many toil below on the level of practical endeavor directed at material commodity."[7] The task he chose for himself was to define the grounds for a social and an educational alternative to a class divided society. But, as we shall see, he chose to distinguish his analysis from Marxist-Leninist philosophy.

In founding the University of Chicago Laboratory School in 1894, Dewey created a micro arena in which to combat dualisms. The school, in addition to being a laboratory for pedagogical innovation, was also dedicated to a philosophy of social democracy to counter "the competitive, anti-social spirit and dominant selfishness in society as it is."[8]

B. Science and Social Reform

1. A Missed Opportunity.

As we enter the twentieth century, Dewey identified the inventiveness of science and technology as the underlying source of an industrial, corporate, enormously productive economic order. He also saw science as an exemplar of the capacity of all humans to tap levels of creativity that had been repressed by the social and intellectual features of feudalism. Science and technology, by lifting the ancient curse of scarcity, for the first time could provide a realistic opportunity to realize the promise of the democratic vision: to open to the people at large, the possibility of personal and social fulfillment.

But the facts showed a betrayal of the hope. Dewey came to argue that the key to understanding the betrayal lay in realizing that the genie of science could point in two directions. Veblen's insights helped him see that science could either be turned into a servant of the materialist impulses of the leisure classes, with competitive emulation by the middle and working classes, or with proper analysis, it could be seen as the source of philosophy and practice which could serve the values of a social democracy. Dewey repeatedly analyzed the nature of the missed opportunity and its consequences.

In his Ethics, Dewey lamented the perversion of science to the crass aims of the leisured classes: "...its generic social usefulness is limited by consideration of private profit. Applied science works powerfully upon society, but not so much as application of science as of the mechanism of pecuniary profit, to which science itself is subordinated."[9]

On the eve of the depression, in The Public and Its Problems (1927), Dewey stated that a science attached to the greed and power motive of the industrial revolution, instead of making a contribution to people's ability to control affairs for their own growth, has often contributed to the weakening of community and to an increase of human oppression. It has "played its part in generating enslavement of men, women, and children in factories in which they are animated machines to tend inanimate machines. It has maintained sordid slums, flurried and discontented careers, grinding poverty and luxurious wealth, brutal exploitation of nature and man in times of peace, and high explosives and noxious gases in times of war. Man, a child in understanding of himself, has placed in his hands physical tools of incalculable power. He plays with them like a child, and whether they work harm or good is largely a matter of accident."[10] To glorify the idea of "pure" science under such conditions, Dewey said, is an escapist rationalization.

In Individualism Old and New, Dewey spoke about a value cleavage in American life. The democratic theory teaches that self-respecting people can design machines for their own human and moral purposes, and religious teachings frown on a creed of self indulgence. But "anthropologically speaking we are living in a money culture,"[11] where worth is measured by ability to get ahead materially in a competitive race which pits all against all.

The corrosive effects of materialism were being felt in all institutions including the schools. The aim of schooling, said Dewey, was being narrowed to "getting on" in the world, with growing pressure to teach utilitarian skills of making a living to suit the hierarchical skill needs of industry. Furthermore, the new "science of education," co-opted by an industrial philosophy of social efficiency, was reducing learning to the measurable content of "expert designed tests." "The school, like other agencies has been laid hold of by strong minorities and used to subserve their own ends."[12]

Thus Dewey was identifying the predatory compulsions of Veblen's "leisured class," and its corrosive influences in the culture at large, as the source of the failure to realize the democratic promise. Dewey responded by assuming the obligation of demonstrating that the perversion of science was not inherent in science itself. On the contrary, science, when properly understood, could be seen as an ally of democratic humanism.

2. "Scientific Temper": An Informing Image of Democratic Humanism.

Our disillusionment with science is now so deep that we can scarcely consider Dewey's thesis that a more fundamental meaning of science transcends its technical aspects: that science may be seen as a moral ideal and a liberating form of social relationships. Nevertheless, his position regarding the reorganization of industry and education makes no sense unless we face this distinctive feature of his philosophy.

It is useful to recognize that Dewey referred to science in the broad sense, as "the scientific temper" - a general mode of inquiry and learning; while he used the term "the scientific technique" for science in its functionings in specific disciplines and in technological applications.[13]

In its broad sense, Dewey saw the evolutionary emergence of man's capacity to do science as exemplifying our most effective mode of learning to date. As a tool in inquiry, "the scientific temper" demonstrates the creative potential in all persons. It exemplified our capacity to free our intelligence; to extend our perceptions of the world and our condition. It demonstrates, as method, that mind is not an entity, but a form of acting in the world. It shows our capacity to get in touch with confused, problematic, unsatisfying situations and to create ideas as plans of action that can be tested, tried and evaluated as instruments for effecting change. Beyond that, science reveals to us the kind of collaborative relations required to support our capacity for creative learning - and these coincided with values of democratic community.

Dewey saw the social relations represented in science as supporting the primary human needs for individuality and community. In Lewis Feuer's words, "He was the first philosopher who dared to read democracy into the ultimate nature of things and social reform into the meaning of knowledge."[14] By looking at science as an evolutionary development in human experience, it could be seen as providing an organic union between the needs of freedom and individuality, and collective authority and community. "Science has made its way by releasing...the elements of variation, of invention and innovation, of novel creation in individuals...who freed themselves from the bonds of tradition." But while honoring the freedom of individual inquirers, the warranty or authority of scientific findings is based upon collective activity, cooperatively organized. "The contribution the scientific inquirer makes is collectively tested and developed and, in the measure that it is cooperatively confirmed, becomes a part of the common fund of the intellectual commonwealth."[15] The inquiry modes of scientific learning depend on critical, collaborative community.

From the evolutionary perspective science demonstrated the emerging human capacity to create conditions supportive of liberating learning. There was a fit with democratic values of individuality and community. Dewey felt that the openness of American society and its departure from European traditions had supported a variety of democratic impulses. The question for the twentieth century was whether meaningful democratic community could be sustained or created under corporate, bureaucratic, industrial conditions. The test of excellence of a scientific/ democratic society, if it could be created, was nothing less than whether it would support the learning of all its members in all its institutions.

C.   Features of a Liberating Society: Industrial Reorganization

In The Public and Its Problems, while struggling with twentieth century challenges to democracy, Dewey identified two essential requirements if democracy were to have a chance: (1) the need for free and full communication, like that needed by the community of science, and (2) the need to counter emerging depersonalization by nurturing the vitality of face-to-face community within corporate bigness.

On the first point, Dewey said the needed shift from The Great Society to a Great Community can begin to happen only when "a subtle, delicate, vivid and responsive art of communication" will take the place of manipulative public relations, to provide the public with a sense of the full consequences of associated activity. Only then can democracy come into its own because "democracy is a name for a life of free and enriching communion."[16]

His second point underscored his conviction that "democracy is more than a form of government, it is primarily a mode of associated living, of conjoint communicated living."[17] This way of reaching for the core of democracy as social rather than political helps explain his two essential criteria of democratic community: "How numerous and varied are the interests or goals which are consciously shared? How full and free is the interplay with other forms of association?" [18] The two are illustrated, said Dewey, in the good family where all participate in a variety of intellectual, aesthetic and material interests; where the progress of one is seen as enriching the experience of the others; and where the limitations of parochialism are overcome by free interactions with a variety of external groups with alternative perspectives. These criteria set forth the conditions supportive of on-going learning or "the reconstruction of experience." They are congruent with the social relations of a scientific community when it honors the canons of its practice. If, in reality, scientists cling to discredited paradigms or engage in petty rivalries, they simply are betraying the conditions required to do science - to be effective learners. The underlying "inherent promise" of the movement of science, said Dewey, "looks forward to a time when all individuals may share in the discoveries and thoughts of others, to the liberation and enrichment of their own experience." [19]

But Dewey pushed for a special emphasis, basic to the practical reformation of institutions in an age of corporatism: "In its deepest and richest sense a community must always remain a matter of face-to-face intercourse." It is conceivable, he said, to imagine the possibility of The Great Community marked by free and full intercommunication replacing the deceptions of the Great Society. This is indispensible, said Dewey, but it is inadequate, for it can never substitute for the qualities of face-to-face community. Ultimately institutions of the larger society must be judged by whether they have met their responsibility for "enriching the experience of local associations." In fact, the source of much of the instability and disintegration that mark twentieth century living comes from the invasion and weakening of primary human communities. "There is no substitute for the vitality and depth of close and direct intercourse and attachment."[20]

The forces against restoration of community are forbiddingly large, e.g., corporate aggregated wealth, and the growth of giant hierarchially structured bureaucracies. But, Dewey said, we should not underestimate the depth of the need, which is reflected in the mania for superficial excitement and the "frantic search for something to fill the void." Inner calm and order "can be found only in the vital, steady and deep relationships which are present only in immediate community."[21] In the final analysis, institutions like industries and schools cannot become "good work" places until they support the powers of persons to learn and communicate at the work site itself. That means having the chance to be engaged in authentic interpersonal relations. It requires taking seriously the need to create smallness within bigness.

> The final actuality is accomplished in face-to-face relationships by means of direct give and take. Logic in its fulfillment recurs to the primitive sense of the word: dialogue. Ideas which are not communicated, shared, and reborn in expression are but soliloqui, and soliloqui is but broken and imperfect thought.[22]

With Dewey's insistence on the core of democracy as social democracy - "conjoint communicated living" it is not surprising to find that he gave the experience of dialogue a central role in human liberation. There are different nuances in the uses of dialogue by Dewey and Paulo Freire but the importance they both attached to the concept helps explain why both men resisted accepting any specific political forms as adequate in themselves. Specific political or economic practices always had to be weighed as means. In Dewey's case, the moral test always must be: Do the means support authentic, supportive, liberating communication? Do the means help all people get in touch with their powers for creative learning, and for experiencing the twin needs for individuality and community? Attempts to reduce democracy to simplistic forms of "let everyone vote on everything," or "state ownership" can impede the primary moral obligations - as many doctrinaire "progressive" teachers and other social ideologues learned to their sorrow. With this conception of science/democracy as furnishing the moral directive, we may turn to the implications Dewey drew for industrial and educational reorganization.

In attempting to understand why life in industrial society was so disappointing, Dewey resorted to his favorite genetic method, i.e., the way to get insight into any complex phenomenon "is to trace the process of its making - then follow it through the successive stages of its growth."[23] Following this method, Dewey reviewed the fact that modern science and the philosophy of economic liberalism had been partners in attacking the oppressive restrictions of feudalism, i.e., its entrenched orders of economic and political privilege, and its dogmatic authoritarian restrictions on inquiry. The conjoint victory of the two was spoiled, however, when the collaborative inquiry values of science were co-opted by the self-serving values of capitalism. While essentially a critic of the corrosive effects of laissez-faire philosophy on industrial life, Dewey in his genetic analysis also chose to weigh the virtues as well as the defects of its doctrine of "freedom."

Dewey argued that ideas for institutional redesign had to work from the premise that the real issue is not to demarcate separate spheres for "authority and freedom," as laissez-faire philosophy did, by championing unlimited economic freedom and minimal public authority. But, we had to effect an organic connection "between conservative factors in the very make-up of individuals" - factors which provide strength derived from enduring custom and tradition, together with liberating factors deriving from "the variable and innovating" potential of individuals. The necessity for harmonizing the two "is inherent in, or part of, the very texture of life." [24]

Weighing liberalism from this perspective, Dewey held that liberalism's assertion of the value of the variable tendencies of human beings - "those that mark off one person from another and that are expressed in initiative, invention, and energetic enterprise - is something that should be permanently embodied in any future social order." And, yet, he declared, it is also clear that liberalism had run its socially justified course. The positive values of liberalism had been perverted so that in Carlyle's terms all had been reduced to a "cash nexus." By now it was, in fact, "engaged in justifying the activities of a new form of concentrated power - the economic which... has consistently...denied effective freedom to economically underpowered and underprivileged." And, Dewey added, it has now become an organized institution which resists all further social change and basic criticism. [25]

Liberalism's betrayal of its own principle of freedom of mind was due to a fatal flaw. Corporate capitalism, successor to classical economic liberalism, failed to recognize that the industrial development of which it was so proud was primarily the fruit of the collective, cooperative intelligence of science and its technological applications. [26] Instead of considering whether this mode of human relations could be extended more widely, the proponents of laissez-faire put the new science to work "in the interests of old ends of human exploitation." Historically, feudalism was brought down, but capitalism rather than "a social humanism" took its place. Production and commerce were carried on as if the new science had no moral lesson, but only "technical lessons as to economies in production and utilization of savings in self- interest....It left a void as to man's distinctively human interests which go beyond making, saving, and expending money...." [27]

Dewey noted that Americans under industrialism had available more power over nature and intellectual resources than were available to classical Athenians or to the people of the Renaissance. Why, he asked, has this collective enrichment not operated more to elevate the quality of our lives? The reason, he said, was that we live in a culture where our technique and technology are controlled too exclusively by "the notion sedulously cultivated by the class in power, that the creative capacities of individuals can be evoked and developed only in a struggle for material power."[28]

> Economic associations are fixed in ways which exclude most of the workers in them from taking part in their management. The subordination of the enterprises to pecuniary profit reacts to make the workers "hands" only, their hearts and brains are not engaged. They execute plans which they do not form, and of whose meaning they are ignorant -- beyond the fact that these plans make profits for others and secure wages for themselves. [29]

As long as priority is focused primarily on economic gain rather than human dignity, he said, the intellectual and moral development of both workers and management will be one-sided and warped.

The alternative, Dewey said, is to know how the power of science, industry and technology can be directed toward "making a different sort of world and society," one designed to assure "an ordered expression of individual capacity and for the satisfaction of the needs of man..." [30] And where industry itself can become an educative and cultural force for those engaged in it. [31]

At the end of the great depression, Dewey supplemented his critique in Individualism Old and New with a barebones outline of his priorities for "The Economic Basis of the New Society" (1939):

> 1. Remove debilitating unemployment, with the state as agency of last resort, providing "some kind of productive work in which a self-

respecting person may engage."

2. Use the kind of cooperative and administrative intelligence employed in wars to attain large social goals, e.g., to attack poverty with its vitiating human effects.

3. Make better use of society's human power by giving workers a greater voice in the control of industry, instead of having them experience external control "where they have no interest, no insight into what they are doing, and no social outlook upon its consequences.... This means an increasing share given to the wage-earner in controlling the conditions of his own activity." [32] Again Dewey was echoing a Veblen type complaint about a dualist separation, which led machine workers to become mechanized in their habits of thought, while managers could work with ideas and knowledge.

4. Require scientists to acknowledge intellectual responsibilities for the social effects of their work. "Such a science would be at the opposite pole to science conceived as merely a means to industrial ends." It would contribute toward building a humane society in which there would be "a demand for a science that is humanistic, and not just physical and technical." Such a science would replace, too, the dualism which sees man pitted against nature with "...a naturalism which perceives that man with his habits, institutions, desires, thoughts, aspirations, ideals, and struggles is within nature, an integral part of it - willing to employ nature as an ally of human ideals and goals." [33]

Thus Dewey saw the machine age as a challenge to extend the promise of democratic values to the entire population. The solution to the crisis in culture he saw as dependent on nurturing creative individuality within collaborative community. The search for such tensional balance had to be explored experimentally in an open, never-finished way. The reader of Dewey waits in vain for a commitment to a final economic position. He voted for the Socialist Party on several occasions, and was active in a long list of organizations on the political left. He was both supporter and critic of New Deal reforms. His criticism of capitalism became more strident in the decade of the great depression. He never wavered, however, in his insistence on the priority of democratic values, in any economic-political program. Dewey noted that his indictment of economic liberalism might seem to commit him to support a collective planned economy as alternative. But, he said, his argument about the twin human needs for freedom and community applied here also: "...while movements in the direction of collective, planned economy may cure evils from which we are now suffering, it will in the end go the way of all past attempts at organization of authoritative power." Unless we come up with fresh ways of effecting an "organic condition" of organization and freedom, we are doomed to witness the dreary historical replay of oscillation from one principle to the other that has "so characteristically marked the past." [34]

Marxist oriented scholars have despaired over Dewey's unwillingness to join the Marxist critique of capitalism. It is argued that his unwillingness to accept the centrality of class conflict reduced him to an apologist for the status quo. But there is nothing surprising in Dewey's refusal to move beyond a democratic planning society which included defense of civil liberties rooted in the liberal tradition. In the 1930's, Marxist-Leninism was insisting on the necessity of the dictatorship of the proletariat. Dewey could not follow. Dictatorial means cannot be separated from dictatorial consequences which destroy the conditions for experimental learning and growth. Dewey's fundamental quarrel with Marxist-Leninism was with its inadequate resolution of means/ends issues. [35] By the end of the thirties with the potent example of the economic depression in the U.S. and the powerful surges of fascism and stateism in Europe, Dewey said:
    The urgent...question...is whether the needed
    economic-social changes...can be effected in
    ways which preserve and develop what was
    fundamental in earlier liberalism, or whether
    social control is to be instituted by means of
    coercive governmental control from above in
    ways which destroy...all that was best con-
    serving in older democratic ideas and ideals;
    intellectual and moral freedom; freedom of
    inquiry and expression; freedom of association
    in work, recreation, and for religious pur-
    poses. [36]

D. Educational Reconstruction

If Dewey saw waste in industry, deriving from social dualisms which cut working people off from the

94

intellectual underpinning of their work, and which kept them from exercising their capacities for collaborative thought and action, he also saw waste in the schools of industrial age children and teachers. School learning was isolated from daily experience; conceptual learning was isolated from the holistic impulses of children to inquire, manipulate, and interact socially; "cost efficiency" compulsions turned learning into competitive rivalry for quantitative scores; teachers were reduced to processing packaged content designed by remote experts; and administrators, diverted from collaborative communication with staffs, were turned into social control agents who "kept book" on test scores results and "noise levels."

Philosophically, Dewey fought the dualisms in the nineties in his efforts to create an "experimentalist" alternative to empiricism and idealism. His philosophical interests led him to found the Laboratory School aimed at creating practice consistent with values of social democracy and experimental inquiry. In his original 1895 Plan of Organization, he stated that he saw the central problem of education as one of "...harmonizing of individual traits with social ends and values. Education is a difficult process... precisely because it is so extremely difficult to achieve an effective coordination of the factors which proceed from...the psychological constitution of human beings with the demands and opportunities of the social environment."[37]

His comments on the school reflect his efforts to avoid the isolation of "science as technique" from its humanizing possibilities, and to create a reenforcing unity between the general methods of science and democratic social life. In reflecting on the school's approach, Dewey remarked that the goal was to help students to:

> realize that scientific method is not something purely technical, remote and apart, but is the instrumentality of socially controlled development. As their studies move on from year to year, the subjects labeled scientific and those labeled social and historical are kept in vital unity, so that each side deepens the meaning of the other.[38]

The democratic process of the school, based on the model of science, emphasized the emergent quality of community. A guiding hypothesis was that when individuals are given the leeway to experiment and to seek out and develop their own powers, then the emergent community will have healthy qualities of both spontaneity and social control. The hope was that when members of the community learned to assess a situation before framing a plan of action, and to weigh the consequences with regard to its social value, then spontaneous activity would not become disruptive and uncontrolled.

In 1903, as Dewey prepared to leave Chicago, he pulled together ideas for an alternative to the emerging bureaucratic urban school system. In "Democracy In Education" he said that the fundamental flaw of the public school system was its failure to recognize that its primary educative responsibility lay in "the freeing of intelligence" of students and teachers. The result was that "the teacher has not the power of initiation and constructive endeavor which is necessary to the fulfillment of the function of teaching. The learner finds conditions antagonistic...to the development of individual mental power and to responsibility for its use."[39] In turning his attention to the experience of teachers and students, he contrasted the industrial concept of social efficiency as reflected in the dominant school system with the concept of efficiency based on the science/democracy ethic he sought for his own school.

In the work places of industry and in schools influenced by them, social control and social efficiency, he said, are concerned with subordinating individuals to class authority and to acceptance of the status quo. In the economic model, rational division of labor reduces jobs to mechanical routines and defines ends in terms of material output and dollar return. This reflects a "depreciatory estimate of the masses" as the managing elites assume that the common man can be bought off by material rewards. These are said to be the marks of "scientific management," but a more perceptive view of the moral end of science provides a different image of efficiency.

> ...ultimately social efficiency means neither more nor less than capacity to share in give and take of experience. It covers all that makes one's own experience more worthwhile to others, and all that enables one to participate more richly in the worthwhile experiences of others....In the broadest sense, social efficiency is nothing less than socialization of mind which is actively concerned in making experiences more communicable; in breaking down the barriers of social stratification which make individuals impervious to the

interests of others.

In short, the moral meaning of defensible social efficiency in a democracy is when "a social return is demanded from all and the opportunity for development of distinctive capacities is provided for all."[40]

Dewey then set about identifying features which distinguish schools as "good work" places: the criteria being whether they support the freeing of intelligence for all who work there.

Where teachers were concerned, his first attack was on emerging bureaucratic centralism which, for example, located authority for text selection in hands of people outside the system; or which gave superintendents the power to appoint experts to dictate subject matter and educational methods to a body of passive, recipient teachers. These efforts at reform by scientific experts are by their nature doomed to fail, said Dewey. When teachers are denied access to "their intellectual and spiritual individuality" they can only follow the prescriptions of outside experts in a mechanical, capricious manner. The prevalence of external dictation only perpetuates conditions of inefficiency; lack of interest; and inability to assume self direction; and works to retain incompetents because the best minds will not "submit to conditions which no self-respecting intelligence likes to put up with."[41]

The only lasting remedy is for work design that gives all opportunity for "free and full play of their own vigor;" that permits every member of the school system "from the first grade teacher to the principal of the high school some share in the exercise of educational power."

All other reforms are conditioned upon reform in the quality and character of those who engage in the teaching profession. Just because education is the most personal, the most intimate of all human affairs there, more than anywhere else, the sole ultimate reliance and final source of power is in the training, character, and intelligence of the individual teacher ....But as long as school organization ...tends to repel all those of independent force, of intellectual ability, or tends to hamper them in their work... so long all other reforms are compromised at their start... [42]

There is evidence that the Dewey School made moves in that direction. The teacher historians of

97

the school reported that "association and exchange among teachers was our substitute for what is called supervision, critic teaching, and technical training." [43] The lure of the values of the school is illustrated, too, by the decision of Ella Flagg Young, a vigorous educational statesperson of her time. She resigned her position as Assistant Superintendent of Chicago Schools, as a protest against the policies of a superintendent who proposed to reduce "school work to the lines of a business corporation" and to make "mere tools and clerks of the teachers." She joined the Laboratory School where she collaborated with Dewey on six monographs in education.

The undemocratic suppression of the individuality of teachers, Dewey said, is linked to a suppression of the intelligence of students. The limiting of mind to mastery of ready-made material is a violation of a principle of moral self-directing individuality. Dewey warned, however, that statements like that, often lead to misguided swings to exaggerated "freedom." Educators need to know that the heart of educational reform lies in securing the degree of freedom and social direction necessary to support the freeing of intelligence. For an understanding of what "freedom as freeing of intelligence" means, Dewey once again turned to the work of scientific investigators as the instructive model. "In that freed activity of mind which we term 'science' there is always a certain problem which focuses effort, controls the collecting of facts and observations, and the calling into play of imagination as a source of fertile suggestions for formulating possible solutions..." [44] On-going experiences of thinking and acting are accompanied by reflection on their meanings which leads to the reconstruction of experience - the seeing of new meaning which can lead to further ideas and tries. This way of defining education, Dewey said, does not depend on expert engineering of instruction, but on creating conditions which make it necessary for students to take an active share in building questions and participating in means for resolving them.

A distinctive attempt to move learning in this direction in Dewey's elementary school was the use of "the occupations" such as weaving, gardening, cooking and construction, as centers around which study in the physical sciences, mathematics, history, geography, humanities and the arts could be integrated. The main function of the occupations, said Dewey, should be first to give children examples of the types of processes men utilize to create the primal necessities of life; second to reveal how changes in techniques have enabled men to advance from primitive to civilized stages; and finally, to provide opportunities for children to feel a sense of personal involvement, to engage in manipulative and expressive, as well as mental activities, and to grow in social insight. Through historical study, students can see the pervasive influence of modes of production on all other phases of life including social class and other dualisms, and they can perceive the revolutionary changes wrought by science and technology. [45]

He tried to link his ideas for the pedagogical uses of the occupations to the missed opportunity of industry to use the scientific-technological base of new industrial processes to create a "social humanism." Industry, said Dewey, has become technological, based on discoveries in mathematics and the physical sciences. As such, industrial occupations have infinitely greater intellectual and cultural potential than ever before. But unless workers come to learn the scientific and social meanings of their work they inevitably sink to the role of appendages to the machines they operate. The intellectual <u>possibilities</u> of industry have multiplied, but actual industrial conditions have made work less educative for the masses than in pre-industrial times. Dewey concluded, that under these conditions the burden of realizing the intellectual possibilities inhering in work is thus thrown back on the school. [46]

The schools, however, instead of seizing the opportunities, tended to introduce a narrow vocational training aimed at teaching specific salable skills. In a passage in <u>Democracy and Education</u>, Dewey indicated how the schools missed an opportunity for fulfilling their primary obligation of freeing intelligence by failing to make educative use of "the occupations."

Both practically and philosophically the key to the present educational situation lies in a gradual reconstruction of school materials and methods so as to utilize various forms of occupations typifying social callings, <u>and to bring out their intellectual and moral content</u>,....This educational reorganization cannot be accomplished by merely trying to give a technical preparation for industries and professions as they now operate, <u>much less by reproducing industrial conditions</u> in the school. The problem is not that of making the schools an adjunct to manufacture and com-

merce, but of utilizing the factors of industry to make school life more active, more full
of immediate meaning, more connected with
out-of-school experience. The problem, is not
easy of solution. There is a standing danger
that education will perpetuate the older
traditions for a select few, and effect its
adjustment to the new economic conditions more
or less on the basis of acquiescence in the
untransformed...unsocialized phases of our
defective industrial regime. Put in concrete
terms, there is danger that vocational education will be interpreted in theory and practice as trade education; as a means of securing technical efficiency in specialized future
pursuits....
Education would then become an instrument of
perpetuating unchanged the existing industrial
order of society, instead of operating as a
means of its transformation. [47]

This way of thinking about education reflected
Dewey's own life experience in two American communities. He was born in pre-Civil War, Burlington
Vermont (1859) where participation by children in the
active, manipulative pursuits of daily living, and
direct experience with the democratic values of
individuality and community were the significant
'teachers.' His professional maturity took place in
metropolitan Chicago, in the nineties, where both the
community and his philosophy were being transformed by
the dramatic change of science. The problem for Dewey
became how to bring the two together, so democratic
values could be presumed and extended in the emerging
age of technology.

In the University Laboratory School, Dewey and
staff tried to work the magic that would combine Old
Vermont with new science. They created the rather
exotic idea of the occupations as a hypothesis which
could turn the school into an embryonic community in
which children would learn the old virtues of responsibility, self-initiative and cooperation together
with what he called the "reflective attention" habits
of science: The school as an "embryonic community"
would provide a setting where students and teachers
could identify questions, formulate ideas, report and
criticize results, and generate new questions, which
would help everyone "to grow in experience." It was a
way of living that should be available to all human
beings.

As educators periodically react against the

de-spiriting blandness of standardized instructional programs they often turn for ideas to the activity oriented approaches of Dewey's Lab School. The discouraging number of failures of such efforts are due, in part, to a neglect to confront Dewey's own qualifications about the "active learning" idea. This term has become a progressive slogan which is always in danger of sliding into "anti-intellectuality" or "permissiveness."

For Dewey those Lab School "occupations" were justified only if they could be made into "active centers of scientific insight...points of departure which could lead children into realization of the historic development of man," including artistic and cultural accomplishments. If permeated with the "reflective attention" habits of science, they could foster the skills needed for "free and active participation in social life."[48]

In an often overlooked statement in School and Society, Dewey said it was also important to take advantage of the occupations to teach the skills of reading, calculation and composition in a "systematic and progressive way." There must be a periodic alternation, he said, between learning in the occupations and skill learning, with one or the other alternatively being brought to the foreground. Without the skills, children would be frustrated in higher levels of learning.[49] But he failed to emphasize the point, and in the public mind today his name is often associated with "permissive freedom."

This charge was hurled at him early and he made one of his important efforts to clarify his position on the freedom-discipline, structure-unstructure issue in The Child and the Curriculum (1902). He said that the history of education reveals two educational sects, the one with the slogan of "the child and freedom" on its banner, the other marching under the flag of "subject matter and discipline." His conclusion was that this long-standing division points to the dilemma that legitimate values are represented in both camps.

Dewey defined education as a matter of helping learners to reconstruct experience so they will see their world and themselves with new meanings; learning is primarily a meaning-seeking affair, therefore, both the subject matter and the experience of individuals had to be taken seriously. The studies require careful respect because they contain meanings that have grown out of human inquiry. In How We Think (1910) Dewey said that the teacher had to be steeped

101

in his subject: "Unless he has mastered the subject matter...and is thoroughly at home in it he will not be able to attend to the pupils' intellectual reactions"[50] and to open new insights to them. In "Progressive Education and the Science of Education" (1927) he said that the teacher as the person with "the riper and fuller experience and the greater insight into the possibilities of continuous development found in any project, has not only the right but the duty to suggest lines of (educative) activity."[51]

On the other hand he emphasized, over and over again, that the locus of reconstructing experience was always in the life of the individual learner. This led him to assert in Democracy and Education that, "How one person's abilities compare in quantity with those of another is none of the teacher's business. It is irrelevant to his work. What is required is that every individual shall have opportunities to employ his own powers in activities that have meaning."[52] Dewey's position tells us that we are in trouble whenever we fail to win students to the life of the mind; but we are in trouble, too, when we get lost in complicated measurement games instead of helping each person find his or her own power to learn.

It is specious to claim that some magic answer to our educational problems can come from a return to the writings of John Dewey. Educators won't find detailed guidance from Dewey on such important matters as skill training, or curriculum content or how to handle behavior problems. But they will find in him a concept of the teacher in marked contrast to the teacher in the efficiency model. He favored teachers as persons of freed intelligence. There was no need to provide them with minute details about "what to do on Monday morning." In the Source of a Science of Education (1922),[53] Dewey said, that the function of the scientific planning of education was not to supply teachers with fixed objectives or ready-made rules, but to provide whatever "enables the educator, whether administrator or teacher, to see and to think more clearly and deeply about whatever he is doing." "Education," he insisted, "is a mode of life and action" - not an antiseptic delivery system. From this viewpoint there is no way to get children to experience education as a meaning seeking way of life unless teachers are experiencing that themselves. There is no way you can combine this concept of education with teacher-proof packages - nor with

102

equating teacher efficiency with student performance on standardized test scores.

In both teacher-student relations and collegial relations this concept of teaching requires open communication and treating ideas about teaching as working hypotheses. If learning is to have an inquiry emphasis for students, then teachers need freedom to be inquirers into the processes of their own work.

It will help to be candid about several consequences that follow from this conception:

1)   It is a lot more complex than romantic "freedom."

2)   It is a style that does not lend itself to mass educational engineering. Any such effort will only pervert it. It is risky to make tries along these lines unless one is willing to create smaller learning communities, within larger systems, that assure teachers initiative and integrity.

3)   It is an educational point of view with consequences for social philosophy. It does not seem far-fetched to hold that the Deweyan conception of schools as "good work" places is compatible with the philosophy of industrial democracy and the working principles of sociotechnical work design theory.

E.   Summary

I have explored Dewey's idea that we need a parallel reorganization of industry and education to realize the values of democracy in an era of science and technology. This position is rooted in aspects of his general philosophy. As we entered the twentieth century, Dewey argued that the issue was whether we would limit our conception of science to a technical phenomenon, to be put at the service of mindless material gain or, whether we would see science intrinsically as a mode of learning - a mode of inquiry, problem solving, reconstructing of experience including reflection on value choices which could be open to all persons - and which encompasses basic human needs for individuality and collaborative community. The moral obligation of a democratic society becomes then to reconstruct itself so that it reduces the waste of natural and human resources and explores ways to support the learning of all its members in their daily living. The kind of efficiency in which a democracy can put its final trust to meet pervasive, rapid change is one in which "a social return is

103

demanded from all and opportunity for development of distinctive capacities is provided for all."[54]

In the next two chapters we shall show that Dewey's criticism of social efficiency philosophy failed to weaken its influence. In fact, sophisticated versions of it have made powerful advances in recent years. We are confronted with the questions of whether we wish social efficiency orientation and values to provide the defining conception of American education.

NOTES

1. John Dewey, Democracy and Education. (New York: MacMillan, 1916), p. 362.

2. John Dewey, Ethics. (New York: Henry Holt, 1908), p. 405.

3. Lewis Feuer, "John Dewey and the Back to the People Movement," Journal of History of Ideas, Vol. 20, 1959, pp. 545-568.

4. Ibid., p. 558.

5. Ibid., p. 567.

6. John Dewey, Education Today. (New York: Putnam, 1949), p. 48.

7. Ibid., pp. 48-49.

8. Feuer, op. cit., p. 559.

9. Dewey, Ethics, p. 408.

10. John Dewey, The Public and Its Problems. (Chicago: Swallow Press, 1954), p. 175.

11. John Dewey, Individualism Old and New. (New York: Capricorn Books, 1962), p. 9.

12. Dewey, Ethics, p. 406.

13. John Dewey, Problems of Men. (New York: Philosophical Library, 1946), pp. 170-175.

14. Feuer, op. cit., p. 568.

15. John Dewey, <u>Intelligence in the Modern World</u>, ed.,
Joseph Ratner. (New York: Modern Library, 1939), p. 358.

16. Dewey, <u>The Public and Its Problems</u>, p. 184.

17. Dewey, <u>Democracy and Education</u>, p. 101.

18. Ibid., p. 96 (Prof. J. Burnett has underscored the
significance of Dewey's emphasis on democracy as social rather
than political in "John Dewey and the Ploys of Revisionism,"
<u>Educational Considerations</u>, (<u>7</u>, No. 2, 1980), pp. 2-8.

19. Dewey, <u>Individualism Old and New</u>, p. 154.

20. Dewey, <u>The Public and Its Problems</u>, p. 211.

21. Ibid., p. 214.

22. Ibid., p. 218.

23. Dewey, <u>Democracy and Education</u>, p. 251.

24. Dewey, <u>Intelligence in the Modern World</u>, p. 347.

25. Ibid., pp. 351-352.

26. Ibid., pp. 360-361.

27. Dewey, <u>Democracy and Education</u>, p. 331.

28. John Dewey, <u>Liberalism and Social Action</u>. (New York:
Capricorn Books, 1963), p. 89.

29. Dewey, <u>Individualism Old and New</u>, pp. 131-132.

30. Dewey, <u>Liberalism and Social Action</u>, p. 188.

31. Dewey, <u>Individualism Old and New</u>, p. 133.

32. Dewey, <u>Intelligence in the Modern World</u>, pp. 417-424.

33. Dewey, <u>Individualism Old and New</u>, p. 153.

34. Dewey, <u>Intelligence in the Modern World</u>, pp. 356-357.

35. See Jim Cork, "John Dewey, Karl Marx and Democratic
Socialism," <u>Antioch Review</u>, (Vol. IX, No. 4, December 1949), pp.
435-453.

36. Dewey, <u>Intelligence in the Modern World</u>, p. 425.

37. John Dewey, "Plan of Organization of the University Primary School" (unpublished, University of Chicago, 1895).

38. Katherine C. Mayhew and Anna C. Edwards, The Dewey School. (New York: Appleton-Century-Crofts, 1936), p. 431.

39. Dewey, Education Today, pp. 62-63.

40. Dewey, Democracy and Education, pp. 141-142.

41. Dewey, Education Today, pp. 64-68.

42. Ibid., p. 68.

43. Boyd Morros, "The Concept of Community in John Dewey's Educational Philosophy" (Ph.D. dissertation, Washington University, 1978), p. 39. See also Joan K. Smith, Ella Flagg Young: Portrait of a Leader (Ames, Iowa: Educational Studies Press, 1979).

44. Dewey, Education Today, p. 70.

45. For accounts of "the occupations" in The Dewey School see Arthur G. Wirth, Education in the Technological Society. (Washington D.C.: University Press of America, 1980), pp. 189-192.

46. See Arthur G. Wirth, John Dewey as Educator. (New York: John Wiley and Sons, 1968), Chapter 9, "The Occupations."

47. Dewey, Democracy and Education, pp. 369-370.

48. John Dewey, The Child and the Curriculum and School and Society. (Chicago: University of Chicago Press, 1943 ed.), pp. 19, 23.

49. Ibid., pp. 113-114.

50. John Dewey, How We Think. (Boston: D.C. Heath and Co., 1933 rev. ed.), pp. 274-275.

51. John Dewey, "Progressive Education and the Science of Education," Progressive Education, (July 1928, Vol. V.), p. 203.

52. Dewey, Democracy and Education, p. 203.

53. John Dewey, The Sources of a Science of Education. (New York: Horace Riverwright, 1929).

54. John Dewey, Democracy and Education, p. 142.

CHAPTER VI

TOWARD A NATION OF "NERVOUS RIGHT ANSWER GIVERS":
EMERGENT TECHNOCRATIC IDEOLOGY IN
AMERICAN EDUCATION

It has become fashionable to combine the word "bureaucracy" with the word "technology" to yield "technocracy". Theodore Roszak has dramatically defined the term:

By the technocracy I mean that social form in which an industrial society reaches the peak of its organizational integration. It is the ideal men usually have in mind when they speak of modernizing, up-dating, rationalizing, planning. Drawing upon such unquestioned imperatives as the demand for efficiency, for social security, for large-scale coordination of men and resources, for ever higher levels of affluence and ever more impressive manifestations of collective human power, the technocracy works to knit together the anachronistic gaps and fissures of the industrial society. The meticulous systematization Adam Smith once celebrated in his well-known pin factory now extends to all areas of life, giving us human organization that matches the precision of our mechanistic organization.

The technocratic society strives to rationalize all social institutions, including education. [1]   Arthur Wise.

In the 1960's and 70's we witnessed a transformation of American schooling by technocratic ideology and systems analysis techniques - the sophisticated successor to Taylorist social efficiency practices of the early twentieth century.

We may be grateful that this trend has been documented by a number of scholarly studies. We shall draw heavily on three of these in forming our own account: "Evaluation as Scientific Management in U.S. School Reform" by Ernest House, a historical analysis of the introduction of cost/benefit evaluation procedures into federal education legislation in the 60's; Legislated Learning: The Bureaucratization of the American Classroom by Arthur E. Wise, an elaboration of the "hyperrationalization of American Schooling by legislative and judicial procedures" tying school learning to scientific management concepts like "accountability," and "minimal competency testing"; and "Emergent Ideological Characteristics of Educational Policies" by C.A. Bowers, an analysis showing the relation of the underlying epistemology of technocratic ideology to the assumptions of positivist science.

Before turning to details of the emerging influences of technocratic ideology, we may note the analysis of Peter Berger, et al., in The Homeless Mind about how scientific management concepts have led organizational planners to think in terms of:

> mechanisticity (seeing the work process as tied to a machine process); reproducibility (no action in the work process is unique but must be reproducible), measurability (the individual's activities can be evaluated in quantifiable terms), componentiability (everything is analyzable into constituent components that are seen as interdependent), problem-solving technical inventiveness (a tinkering attitude toward areas of experience that can be dealt with in terms of technological solutions), and the self anonymization of the worker (learning to divide the self into component parts, and to accept the human engineering process that organizes the self in terms of technological functions.)[2]

As C.A. Bowers pointed out, the continuing use of the machine as a model, as in systems analysis, for organizing experience in factories, offices and classrooms indicates the growing pervasiveness of this mode of consciousness. The style and values of this technocratic ideology are becoming the taken-for-granted assumptions of the everyday work of large numbers of scientists, bureaucrats, educators and business people who occupy directive roles in society. We turn now to some dimensions of the impact of the emerging technocratic ideology on education.

A. Scientific Management in Federal Educational Reform Efforts

In recent years, as the techniques of scientific management became more sophisticated and pervasive in business and industry, their influence on educational planning and evaluations increased dramatically. One way of developing awareness of this point is to note the intrusion of the technocratic style in reform efforts of the 60s when an unprecedented amount of federal funding was allocated to American schools.

In the 60s, public attention was focused first on desegregation efforts of the blacks, and then on the criticism of the "mindlessness" of American classrooms by the compassionate or romantic critics: Charles Silberman, Edgar Friedenberg, Jonathan Kozol, George Dennison, Herb Kohl et al. Their criticisms called forth a wide range of responses: outside the system - free schools, street corner academies and "de-schooling"; within the system - "schools without walls," "open education," Black Studies and other ethnic oriented alternatives. While these "humanistic" efforts were in the public eye, another unpublicized set of forces began which would become more potent in transforming American schools - the introduction during the Johnson administration of systems analysis thinking from the Pentagon, into the education component of the Department of Health, Education and Welfare.[3]

The move in this direction was, in part, the result of deliberate policy decisions and, in part, a by-product of efforts to secure greater equity for minority children under the Elementary and Secondary Education Act of 1965 - cornerstone of President Johnson's desire to be known as the "Education President".

President Johnson's proposal to introduce massive federal support for education was a break with the tradition of schooling as a local and state affair. Political support for the legislation was fragile and the backing of the liberal Senator Robert Kennedy was vital. Senator Kennedy's major interest was in Title I provisions for disadvantaged children. He had doubts that the schools could deliver quality education for minority children. His hunch was that the schools operated in ways which excluded effective communication by black parents. More money of itself would not cure that defect. He made his support contingent on inclusion of a legislative provision that school districts be required to report on learning results of federally funded programs. His reasoning was that poor minority parents had a right to know what results schools were obtaining for their children. With test score information available, poor parents could make teachers accountable for results.

While Senator Kennedy was making this "civil rights" type demand for modern educational evaluation, that same demand was receiving strong endorsement from a very different group of educational planners.

In August 1965 President Johnson announced the

introduction of the Planning, Programming, and Budgeting System (PPBS) throughout the federal government. This idea "to develop program goals that could be stated, measured, and evaluated in cost/ benefit terms" received strong support from officials in HEW, including key figures imported from the Department of Defense.[4] HEW Secretary, John Gardner created a new office entitled the Assistant Secretary for Program Evaluation (ASPE), headed by William Gorham, who had worked with PPBS in the Defense Department. One of his deputies was Alice Rivlin, also from Defense, who was to play a key role in charting educational evaluation policies.

The new group, committed to the systems analysis perspective, had evaluation goals quite different from Senator Kennedy's concern about school responsiveness to poor families. The goal of the ASPE group was to measure the economic efficiency of Title I programs in cost/benefit terms. The assumption was that one could define a "production function," as the relative effectiveness of specified inputs in reaching specific objectives. Thus, educational techniques could be compared in terms of test score results. Ideally this would make it possible to prescribe in legislation that only the most effective approaches could be used.

Milbrey W. McLaughlin in Evaluation and Reform, a detailed study of these developments, noted that both the Kennedy and ASPE approaches to evaluation were highly rationalistic. Both assumed that a requirement to evaluate would lead to "objective" measures of program effectiveness, and that planners and educators would act on the data.

He noted further that educators viewed these developments with skepticism and misgivings. They generally agreed that standardized tests were insensitive and inappropriate measures of the effectiveness of Title I. They argued that prescriptions for detailed testing procedures would make the schools less responsive to children, would be a waste of resources, and would lead to federal prescription of curricula which would violate teachers' professionalism.[5] The level of evaluation prescription in Title I legislation was reduced as a result of these protests. But a general formal evaluation requirement was stipulated which the Office of Education was asked to implement. Educators were being brought under the influence of the new idea requiring an "evaluation stipulation for all social legislation" - even though at the time no one knew exactly what the idea meant.

Local reports from the field during the first
two years of Title I were highly positive and enthusiastic. But many of them were not quantitative and
they were not uniform in format. This was highly
frustrating to the ASPE staff in that without uniform
quantitative data, they could not do cost/benefit
analyses to determine which programs were most efficient. ASPE moved to tighten evaluation and to mount
several special studies of its own along cost/ benefit
lines.

Alice Rivlin, who took a leadership role, said
the purpose was "to see how much of a resource gives
how much increment in a specified outcome." She saw
the problem as securing the efficient allocation of
resources in "the production of social services."[6]
Since social service practitioners lacked the social
science skills to produce more effective services, the
function of the systems analyst was to establish a
"production function" - a functional relationship
between the types of resources and the results produced. The approach assumed a "regular and discover-
able" relationship between educational inputs and
outputs.

Ernest House commented that:
Rivlin's thinking was striking in its use of
physical analogies. She perceived education
techniques and children the same as raw
materials in a manufacturing process. They
could be put into various combinations to
determine the most efficient single grouping
which would consistently give the best output
- products in factories, test scores in
education. The analysis methodologies were
lifted straight from manufacturing. This was
the essence of the systems analysis approach.
Relate input to output and determine the most
efficient combination. This would save on
scarce resources. 'Biggest bang for the buck'
in manufacturing, in weapons systems, and in
social services."[7]

One staff member said, "the model was
McNamara."[8] McLaughlin adds that in 1966 McNamarism
was "almost a religion" and that ASPE never questioned
that it could define the evaluation problem according
to the model.

Operating with this rational economic model
Rivlin accepted that the analyst must identify objectives before comparing benefits. Little attention was
paid, however, to the deep differences over educational goals in American culture. When educational

111

objectives eluded the precision that the model required, Rivlin pushed aside the complicated problems of specification and measurement and assumed a social consensus on the subject. As she put it, "Despite appearances, however, I believe there is a wide measure of agreement in the nation about desirable directions of change."[9] This statement reflects the fact that technocrats are not comfortable with weighing the claims of competing goals and values. They prefer a neutral role which permits them to say, "you give us the goal and we will use our expertise to produce and measure the results." When a community is divided over educational goals, technocrats find it convenient to discover some consensus on minimal goals such as reading and arithmetic. (Even here the consensus may be deceptive because people have honest differences about what is the essence of reading. What the technocrats can measure for some, may miss the point completely regarding what is important about reading for others - as we shall see later).

When repeated efforts failed to yield test score results that correlated neatly with successful programs, Alice Rivlin and her colleagues never questioned the validity of their rationale. They attributed their frustrations to the failure of social services to be organized in ways to answer the evaluators' questions. The ASPE solution was to exert more governmental control over program inputs and design; the aim being to structure educational programs that would be amenable to the tools of the evaluators.

Despite repeated and costly evaluation efforts, little emerged in the way of definitive results. As House put it, "Between 1966 and 1972, $52 million was spent on evaluating Title I, and yet the Office of Education still could not provide data on the impact of Title I."[10] The inconclusive results were used to disparage the work of educators and to curtail funding of educational programs.

Rivlin blamed the failure of the studies on the Title I program itself: the program was not designed to yield information on effectiveness; and there was no experimental design.

As Ernest House put it:
In Rivlin's view the world was not organized properly to yield information about production functions. Variations between school districts were not great enough to discern differences in effects. Therefore, one must resort to systematic experimentation. Assuming that social services were not now effec-

tively organized and that some techniques were better than others, one could find out what the efficient techniques were by systematic experiments using control groups, longitudinal information, and more sophisticated analyses. Systematic experimentation required following plans, common measures of effectiveness, and strong central leadership....

Rivlin's argument for planned experimental variation was unequivocal in its claim for being the only way to knowledge. 'Information necessary to improve the effectiveness of social services is impossible to obtain any other way.' She eliminated all other ways of knowing such as practitioner knowledge. Again her research paradigm was that of physical science. Specify the treatment exactly and control all extraneous factors. By a sufficiently large number of trials one can average out the effects of the uncontrolled elements. Repetition and specification were key ideas.[11]

It is not difficult to understand why Alice Rivlin and her ASPE colleagues felt so correct about the rightness of their approach. Who can quarrel with efforts to find ways to improve the quality of social services through scientific experimentation; or to conduct experiments to improve the efficiency with which tax monies are used? It is in fact a necessary and useful task.

The root of the problem, however, lay at a deeper level than Rivlin and her colleagues were willing to explore. It involves the question of the adequacy of the techniques of the positivist physical science tradition for the study of problems of human affairs - of human existence. The tendency of that tradition is to treat problems of all systems as if they would lend themselves to the "one right way" of the techniques of the physical sciences. But what if there is something about human existence that is violated deeply by such well-intentioned efforts? We shall return to the issue of positivist research and evaluation in educational settings in the next chapter.

For the moment we may note the close affinity of the systems analysis approach to evaluation with Taylorist scientific management concepts. With the general aim of efficient productivity, management would define the job and provide detailed task specifications. Quantitative measurement would reveal "scientific" data which would prescribe work procedures and production standards. Scales of measurement could be used to differentiate efficient from inefficient teachers. With measurement scales that were scientific, and therefore fair, teacher excuses would no longer be acceptable. Supervisory inspection systems could make certain that teachers didn't cheat. To beleaguered tax payers, worried about demands for new school levies while test scores dropped, it could all seem reasonable and appealing. "Let's get on with it."

If Ernest House is correct, however, and I believe he is, there is a flaw in the argument:

> The systems analysis approach to evaluation promises to substitute specific techniques derived from 'science' for the knowledge of craft in teaching. It is a false promise, for such simple techniques cannot substitute for full fledged professional knowledge, much of it tacit rather than explicit, which has been acquired over many years. Such a technological vision of knowledge rests on a confusion of tacit knowledge with generalizations and rules of procedure. In teaching as in speaking, if one relied on the formalized, externalized rules of procedure, one would be mute. The challenge for evaluation then is to arrive at approaches which are complementary to professional craft and which sharpen actual practice rather than those which threaten to replace practice.[12]

As House points out, questions of educational practice are converted into questions of efficiency by systems analysis. When the concern for efficiency is made the overriding consideration, the educational process is distorted.*

---

*(Michael Polanyi, physicist turned philosopher, challenged the empiricist-mechanist theory of learning which holds that knowledge derives from our being passive recipients of impressions from the environment. He argues that human learning includes an important tacit dimension based on the fact that "we can know more than we can tell." Learning marked by understanding and meaning requires a component of active personal engagement and integration. Cruder empiristic notions ignore what is distinctive about us - our capacity to be intentional, reflexive, meaning seeking. See for example, Michael Polanyi's The Tacit Dimension, Meaning, The Study of Man, and Personal Knowledge.)[13]

114

The federal government took the lead in pushing technocratic ideology into education in the 60's. As we came out of that troubled decade, the conservative mood which followed was supportive of the simple demand to get clean-cut, measurable educational results. Back to basics, competency based education, and accountability became educational catchwords of the 70's. Legislative and judicial decisions gave them added authority. "Free the children" gave way to calls to control the children and their teachers.

B. Hyper-Rationalizing the Schools

(The) policy making process has an affinity for a rationalistic conception of teaching and the teacher. The reasons are simple: The will of the policy maker must be implemented; the expectations for what the schools are to accomplish must be translated into action; the workers (teachers) in the factory (school) must perform their assigned tasks; and the bureaucracy must be peopled by bureaucrats who will implement the official goals of the institution. [14]

In this section we shall show the extension of the technocratic ideology at the level of the states in the 70's. We shall present examples of specific ways in which educational policies have been affected. For this part of the story we shall rely heavily on the meticulous research and analysis of Arthur E. Wise in Legislated Learning: The Bureaucratization of the American Classroom. For the unfolding of important details, I urge the reader to turn to Wise. We shall settle for illustrative examples.

Wise's thesis is that we are witnessing the hyper-rationalization of the schools through the application of management ideology.[15] This effort, which is having unfortunate consequences, is rooted in good intentions: the desire to promote equity and to increase productivity in our educational institutions. Hyper-rationalization occurs, however, when policies lead to the strengthening of bureaucratic characteristics without attaining the hoped for educational outcomes. When schools turn to "rational" management strategies, decision-making about the use of people and resources is based on prescribed formal rules and techniques of scientific management to increase efficiency. Since cause and effect relations between rational management strategies and learning outcomes is unproven and dubious, the attempts to improve

115

schools through rational processes often fails. Legislators and bureaucrats respond with new attempts to impose "improved" rational procedures. Hyper-rationalization thus becomes a self-perpetuating phenomenon.

As we saw in the preceding section, the embrace of the rational model at the federal level was one force which moved educational policy in the hyper-rationalization direction. But the temper of the country gave widespread support to efforts to get no-nonsense, tangible educational results. For example between 1963 and 1974 states passed at least seventy-three laws which demonstrated a shift from an emphasis on providing educational opportunity to a concern for ensuring educational achievement.[16] The call was to make schools accountable for results. The means was a turn to the scientific management techniques which legislators from business and industry had faith in, and which bureaucrats increasingly had been trained in. In addition to terms like cost/benefit analysis, systems analysis, planning-programming-budgeting-systems (PPBS) which we already have noted, the lexicon of rational educational management also included concepts like management by objectives (MBO), cost effective analysis, zero-based budgeting, systems engineering and program evaluation and review technique (PERT).

Management ideology focused sharply on measurable educational "outputs" in relation to society "inputs" by introducing educational schemes which fit the terminology of the ideology: competency based education (CBE), performance based education (PBE), competency based teacher education (CBTE), behavioral objectives, mastery learning, learner verification, assessment systems (federal, state and local), and criterion-referenced testing .

Arthur Wise has documented ways in which this lexicon of accountability was utilized in legislation affecting the schools[17] of which we note several examples:

1. In 1971 the Colorado legislature passed an Educational Accountability Act intended "to define and measure quality in education." The general assembly declared that the educational accountability program developed under the legislation "should be designed to measure objectively the adequacy and efficiency of the educational programs offered by the public schools," and to assist patrons to determine the relative value of their program as compared

to cost. The accountability program should develop broad goals and specific performance objectives for the educational process, and identify school activities to advance students toward the goals. Means should then be developed to evaluate student achievement and performance.

2. Florida outdid Colorado in enacting an accountability law in every year between 1969 and 1976. The 1971 Act directed state educational officials "to establish grade by grade standards in the basic skills and to use tests based on specific theories of testing."

3. In 1971, Virginia enacted management by objectives (MBO) type legislation which specified certain objectives of the state board and local school boards. The legislation included, in Wise's words, the ambitious, if enigmatic prescription that "The percentage of the student population achieving at or above grade level norms or the equivalent as measured by approved standardized achievement tests should equal or exceed the mean level ability level of the student population as measured by appropriate scholastic aptitude tests."

4. In 1973, an Oklahoma law imposed a systems analysis procedure on each school district which wished accreditation. The prescription was for "a district wide needs assessment involving all grades under its jurisdiction." A systems analysis process, including goals and objectives, should then be utilized "to plan the instructional program to fit the needs of the students of the said district."

5. A number of states passed laws requiring performance-based teacher education, certification, or evaluation. California's Stull Act, for example, mandated that the evaluation of teachers be based upon their competence. Each district was required to establish specific guidelines which were to include:
The establishment of standards of expected student progress in each area of study and of techniques for the assessment of that progress...The establishment of procedures and techniques for ascertaining that the employee is maintaining proper control and is preserving a suitable environment for learning.

Beyond this, the law stipulated that teachers should be evaluated according to their contribution to

117

their students' performance.

In 1973, Rhode Island passed a law specifying that the Board of Regents approve a master plan for not only public elementary and secondary schools but also colleges and universities and non-public schools. The Regents presumably were to define "what men should know and be able to do" with enough precision to be able to evaluate whether Rhode Island schools were, in fact, producing such persons.

These laws and many others were aimed at making schools accountable for results. As Wise summarized: "The techniques they recommend are directed to the outcome of the educational process. These education specific techniques, together with the techniques of 'pure' scientific management, are designed to promote educational achievement." [18]

Beyond these legislative stipulations that schools be accountable for results, other legislation was written which mandated that learning will occur.

This showed up in a brief flurry of "performance contracting" with corporations who had turned to the educational market with instructional hardware and software. California, for example, passed the Guaranteed Learning Achievement Act (1971) which provided for "performance contracting" between private contractors and public school districts for the teaching of reading and mathematics." Payment to the private contractors was made contingent upon student acquisition of the basic skills. The trend was toward the idea that schools should guarantee that each student attain minimum performance standards. If private contractors could be held to a "payment for results," why not teachers? The idea remained attractive to legislators even though performance contracting with the corporations soon ran into snags when the companies were unable to produce the promised results; and there were charges of 'teaching for the tests' to get the payments. The U.S. Office of Education and the Office of Economic Opportunity, after glowing promises of learning break-throughs in 1969, were hastily dropping the idea when a number of studies were showing that "performance contracting was not responsible for any significant improvement on an overall basis." [19]

Arthur Wise's study showed that the development of minimal competency testing in the basic skills evolved out of the accountability movement.

Earlier versions of accountability held out the promise of accommodating virtually any goal for education so long as that goal was,

118

in principle, measurable. It was assumed that in time the appropriate measures would be developed. Measures were most readily available, however, only in reading and arithmetic. The collapse of the accountability movement occurred because of the decline in certain test scores between the mid-60's and the mid-70's. A call arose for "back to basics" and was immediately translated into minimal competency testing legislation. The schools, of which so much had been asked, were now being directed to concentrate on instructing students in the basic skills.[20]

The blunt fact is that these enactments were efforts to find "technological fix" answers to complex human problems of education. Because partial truths are contained in these approaches, one may find examples of gains in test scores here and there. But the kinds of results intended by the legislation simply have not been realized. In addition, the true believers have chosen to overlook the kinds of unintended consequences documented by Wise: an increase in hyper-rationalization (failures to engineer learning are followed by more elaborate efforts to engineer results) and a simultaneous increase in bureaucratic controls. As we shall see, technocratic ideology leads to an erosion of a sense of ethical purpose and a demoralization of teachers, which leads to further loss of confidence in public education.

Eventually the thought may dawn that this dismal cycle will not be broken by further doses of hyper-rationalization. It is my thesis that it can be broken only by bringing under criticism technocratic ideology itself and by probing for alternatives. The first point we shall explore is that technocratic ideology is out of touch with the complex human reality of schools - the classical problem of the "technical fix" mentality. In the next chapter, we shall bring the technical fix mentality itself under question.

C. Technocratic Ideology - A Divorce from Reality

No matter how educational policy is created, its purpose is to affect (presumably to improve) the practice of education. Inevitably it must be based upon some theories or hypotheses about educational practice. If these assumptions are correct the policy will have its intended consequence... Policies based upon incorrect assumptions probably will not work and may well have unintended (possibly undesirable) consequences. [21]

The argument of this section is not that the techniques of testing and measurement, and concern about competency in basic skills are all wrong. They are necessary. The problem is that the reductionist quality of the rationalistic model puts it out of touch with the complex human reality of school life. As a result it becomes a threat to "good work" of teachers and students.

Believers in the new technocratic ideology hold to a faith that a systems analysis approach which produces airplanes will also produce efficient child learning; and to belief in a crude form of behaviorism which assumes that behaviors will occur if it is specified that they shall occur. They assume that the principles of a mechanical model of production and cost/benefit economic principles can be transferred to education. The intention is to conceive of instruction as a management system. This requires the existence of a science of education analogous to the sciences of mechanical production. Serious problems arise when such a science of education does not exist, yet policy makers create prescriptions for educational practice as if it did. Efficiency advocates who sound like hard-nosed realists may be seen in a different light when they act in ignorance of the message of a major educational researcher like John Goodlad:

> There is not a science of education sufficient to give credence to the scientism necessarily indicated if any model of accountability of the kind described here is to function effectively. It is an idea whose time has not yet come, whatever rhetorical and political support it is able to muster. But it will be back again, probably in new trappings. [22]

To ignore this fact is to risk creating mischief-making fantasies.

To true believers in educational results by "scientific efficiency" and bureaucratic social controls, the rationalistic model of schooling, however, is unquestionably correct. If the schools are given clear, measurable objectives, the objectives will be met. If schools are not producing well, they are instructed to tighten specific operations - a form of bureaucratic rationalization. If teachers are not securing hoped for results with poor children, they are to be precisely instructed on what to teach and how to teach. Teachers will be motivated to be more effective by being held accountable in terms of test score results.

We have had more than a decade of intensive efforts based on these assumptions. We ought to be basking in satisfaction with the results. However, clear evidence of productivity progress which the model promises is hard to locate and, in fact, "the evidence appears to be precisely in the opposite direction." [23]

As John Goodlad put it, there is irony in the common claims that the score declines are due to the "soft and tender" innovations of the 1960's, while evidence amounts that these reforms as major events never occurred at all. They were, for the most part, non-events. "On the other hand, there is all around us evidence that accountability by objectives, PPBS, competency based teacher education, and the like, have dominated the scene for some time. Is it not time to consider seriously the proposition that this cult of efficiency has failed to make our schools more efficient?" [24]

Advocates have little stomach for looking at consequences that fall outside their theoretical frame. But it is time for hard questions to be raised by those who care for the values of humane learning, and for the morale and welfare of the profession of teaching.

As American schools have been shaped by the rationalistic model, many educational policies that emerged in the 60's and 70's were shaped by its assumptions. These include:

1. A belief that limiting the goals of schools will facilitate achieving the goals. The reach for "efficiency" narrows school tasks to teaching the basics and to career adjustment or survival skills.

2. A belief that goals must be stated in forms which make them measurable. In practice the main effort has been given to defining the basic skills of reading and arithmetic for which measurement instruments exist. [25]

3. A belief that the appropriate way to assess performance is to use test scores to compare students, teachers, principals, schools, districts, and states. Such comparions are assumed to facilitate improvement.

4. A belief that educational goals should be pursued in a cost-effective manner with the aid of ever more sophisticated evaluation and accounting systems.

121

5. A belief that rules and procedures are more effective in promoting equal and fair treatment than trusting professional judgment.

Beyond these, legislators have begun to legislate prescriptions about the processes of education. These prescriptions assume the existence of a science of education which yields treatments which teachers can apply to students to get results. Thus, there has been state legislation mandating the use of "objectives- based" education and requiring test-teach-test-reteach-test models of instruction. "Courts are requiring 'thorough and efficient' education, state school boards are requiring competency-based educational outcomes, and legislators are requiring minimum standards of attainment."[26]

A major result of this effort to make the schools accountable is that the tests have come to define the goals of education. As policy makers have come to prefer goals which appear attainable and measurable, they move to a substantially narrower view of the goals of education.

The generalized goal that schools should teach children to read and do arithmetic is transformed into the objective that children should be able to prove their ability to read and to do arithmetic by taking an examination.[27]

As we become fixated on test scores, parents seem to become uncertain that seeing their children reading books really constitutes 'reading'. The consuming question becomes "is she above grade average?" The belief grows that only the technology of testing provides a reliable indicator. It produces a cut-off score which determines the "scientific" level of performance which is adequate. (This in the face of a statement by Dr. Henry Dyer of the Educational Testing Service that grade equivalency scores are "psychological and statistical monstrosities.")[28]

More recently, norm-referenced tests have been supplemented by criterion-referenced testing to measure another goal of the minimalist model of education: relating skill teaching to the "survival needs" of adult life (i.e. how to write checks, how to fill out a job application, how to interpret terms and directions on medicine bottles, how to interpret documents such as menus, ballots etc.)

Preparing children to "function in society", is of course, an ancient goal. What is new in the rationalistic model, however, is the effort to state the goal in terms of precise operational controls. In practice this gets reduced to securing an acceptable level of right answers on criteria referenced tests. When teachers, schools and systems are compared on results, it is not surprising that school study is dominated by study for the tests. While many of these functional goals may be useful, the public has an obligation to ask if it really wants more and more of school study to be devoted to the mastery of narrow specific skills. It is useful to know how to balance a checkbook. (I wish I had success with it more frequently). In a world of turbulent change, however, does the effort to get children to score well on long lists of "life-survival" test items really give them a "functional" education, or is it the illusion of one? It seems moot, at best, that such efforts will foster the intellectual enthusiasm of youngsters so that they will become eager to learn about the fascinating, baffling, challenging world they are entering. The compelling question of the liberal tradition was, "How do we win students to the life of the mind?" The new rationalists seem to have little patience with such questions.

Arthur Wise points out that the narrow instrumental view of the goals of education which policy makers have been prescribing, may be at odds with the view of education they want for their own children.

> Their personal goals for the elementary schools may be not only to teach basic skills, but to instill the desire to learn and to develop the potentials of the child; for the secondary schools, not only to prepare students vocationally but also to develop their critical capacities and to cultivate various interests; for the colleges, not only to produce credit hours but also to preserve, create, and transmit our cultural and scientific heritage. In the real world of policymaking, however, these larger goals are not integral to the process.[29]

If we restrict ourselves to the limits of what our primitive technical tools in education permit, we risk the trivial results of a vulgar efficiency.

While the policies of the rationalistic model appear on the surface to be logical, the model is in trouble when what appears to be logical does not connect with reality. This applies to the working world of teachers. Legislators, impatient to get results, may legislate that learning outcomes should occur while blandly ignoring the possibility that neither the knowledge nor the resources exist to produce that outcome. If high school graduates are

123

incompetent, impose competency based high school graduation requirements. If teachers appear to be incompetent because children from low-income families are "below grade level," create competency based teacher education programs. One may give the appearance of solving a problem by creating a program with the same name as the problem. Pseudo action is easier than confronting the possible facts that the knowledge and/or resources for getting poor children "to grade average" may not exist; or that poverty is the source of handicaps; or that peer group socialization and the informal curriculum are more potent than the school curriculum. It would be a salutary exercise in honesty and humility to admit we don't know many of the answers, and to permit groups of teachers to design a variety of programs to which they are professionally committed. Then to study them in collaboration with researchers to see what can be learned and reported - along the lines suggested by Robert Schaefer in The School as a Center of Inquiry.[30]

Policy makers, who inhibit this from happening by imposing simplistic "competency models," ought themselves to be held accountable; for there is no convincing evidence that engineered education is superior to, or as good as the creative work of committed professionals.

There is, in fact, evidence that the actual world of school life is sharply at odds with the "reality" envisioned by the rationalistic model. Accountability schemes aim, for example, to focus the attention of teachers on test score output; and it assumes that the primary goal of teachers is to maximize aggregate achievement scores. Teachers under the lash of these pressures have taught for the tests, but teachers, in fact, seem to be guided by personal values and satisfactions rather than by the test score goals of the systems makers. Thus Dan Lortie in School Teacher, noted that teachers, when confronted with the formal goals of the system, tend to "reduce such goals into specific objectives they use in their daily work," and in practice, they guide their work by personal convictions and personal values patterned after admired teachers.[31]

Philip Jackson in his insightful Life in Classrooms also found that many teachers did not evaluate their effectiveness in terms of test score results.

In the more global terms, the goal of the schools is to promote learning. Thus, ideally we might expect teachers to derive a major

124

source of their satisfactions from observing growth in achievement of their students. Further, the students' performance on tests of achievement (commercial or teacher made) would seem to provide objective and readily obtainable evidence of this growth. Logically, at least, the conscientious teacher ought to point with pride or disappointment to the gains or losses of students as measured by test performance. But, as is often true in human affairs, the logical did not occur. One of the most interesting features of the interview material was the absence of reference to objective evidence of school learning in contexts in which one might expect it to be discussed. [32]

Teachers rarely mentioned testing and attached minor importance to it in helping them understand how well they had done. Some teachers will conform to the management model of instruction but many flesh and blood teachers, working with flesh and blood children, simply will not confine their work to boundaries of the rationalistic model no matter what form it takes - competency based education, behavior modification, minimal competency, etc.

Those non-educators, business men or social scientists, enamored of rationality for teachers, choose to close their eyes to the reality of the classroom as revealed by Jackson's careful study. By insisting on treating schools as technical systems, they shut children off from the 'non-linear' strengths of creativity and caring of their teachers.

Jackson concludes that a major flaw of the engineering view of teaching is that it begins with an over-simplified view of what goes on in elementary classrooms.

The business of teaching involves much more than defining curricular objectives and moving toward them with dispatch; and even that limited aspect of the teacher's work is far more complicated in reality than an abstract description of the process would have it seem. When it is remembered that the average teacher is in charge of the twenty-five or thirty students of varying abilities and background for 1000 hours a year and that his responsibilities extend over four or five curricular areas, it is difficult to see how he could be very precise about where he is going and how to get there during each instructional moment.

He may have a vague notion of what he hopes to achieve, but it is unreasonable to expect him to sustain an alert awareness of how each of his students is progressing toward each of a dozen or so curricular objectives. [33]

What we need to recognize is that the continual use of the machine as model in educational engineering efforts makes teachers unwittingly carriers of a technological consciousness as described by Berger et al. in The Homeless Mind - a technological consciousness marked by mechanisticity, anonymous social relations, fragmentation of learning and experiencing of selves in a partial and segmented way.

This technological consciousness is communicated in classrooms where features of the engineering model are in practice. In competency based education, teachers are taught to think of classrooms as "management systems," with the goal of increasing the efficiency of the system by constantly evaluating (in behavioral terms) the output (measured learning) in relation to the inputs, by teachers and instructional programs. Teachers are taught to think and talk in terms of performance objectives, sequencing instruction, instructional package, modules, data based decision making. Students, as parts of "the production function," are taught "to view their own learning experiences as something that can be reduced to discrete components and measured objectively, to determine whether it has been efficiently shaped by the delivery system of the classroom."[34]

Michael Apple has analyzed examples of the encroachment of technical control procedures through the use of pre-packaged sets of curricular materials which school systems may purchase. These typically include statements of objectives, curricular material aimed to realize them, minutely prescribed teacher tasks and student responses, and tests coordinated with the materials. [35]

Some brief references to one of the widely used systems for science instruction in the elementary schools may illustrate the style: Module One of Science: A Process Approach. The material is pre-packaged into cardboard boxes with attractive colors, divided into 105 separate modules with sets of pre-specified concepts to teach. The pedagogical steps for the teacher and the responses of students are precisely specified. For example, one module concerns colors. Following are brief excerpts of instructions to teachers:

Put thirty yellow, red, and blue paper squares

in a large bag or small box. Show the children three plates: one marked red, one
yellow, and one blue (All of the plates,
colored paper, etc. are provided in the
module.) Ask the children to come forward, a
few at a time, and let each child take one
square from the bag and place it on the plate
marked with the matching color. As each child
takes a colored square ask him to name the
color of that square. If the child hesitates,
name it for him. (Science ... A Process
Approach, 1974: 3-4).

In the "appraisal" stage, the no-nonsense clarity of
directions for the teacher's behavior is continued:
Ask each of six children to bring a box of
crayons and sit together...ask each child to
point to his red crayon when you say the word
red. Repeat this for all six colors. Ask
each child to match one crayon with one
article of clothing that someone else is
wearing...Ask each child to name and point to
the red, blue, and yellow crayon. (Science
... A Process Approach, 1974: 7).

A final stage of the module has competency measures
built into it, with exact words which the teacher
should use to assure that each child has reached the
appropriate skill level:
Task 1: Show the child a yellow cube and ask,
What is the color of this cube?
(After this is done for each color, cubes are
placed in front of the child.)
Task 4: Say, Put your finger on the orange
cube.
Task 5: Say, Put your finger on the green
cube.
Task 6: Say, Put your finger on the purple
cube.
(Science ... A Process Approach, 1974: 7).

Michael Apple in addition to commenting that
"little is left to chance" in the design of the
"production process" points out also that a process of
de-skilling is happening to teachers.

Regarding the de-skilling, Apple notes that
skills that used to be considered essential to the
craft of teaching - such as curriculum deliberation
and planning; and the design of teaching strategies
for specific children based on personal, intimate
knowledge - are no longer as necessary. With the
influx of pre-packaged materials, planning is done by
people external to the situation; execution under

specific direction is left to the teacher. Meanwhile, teachers are being <u>re-skilled</u> to think of their work in terms of the language, procedures, and ideological visions of "the management of instruction." Unrecognized is the fact that the technology, which presumably is simply "neutral" material aimed to produce greater effectiveness of instruction, has significant impacts on social relations. To the extent that prepackaged systems become the basic curricular form, the need for interaction among teachers about ideas for teaching is no longer necessary. They become detached from each other and from the stuff of their work. Whether or not one approves of the results of such efforts, and it is clear that individual teachers and staffs will react in different ways, it is also clear that technology has effects on social relations. Those effects typically are not considered in the calculations of the planners of the packages of instruction. Nor is their aim to design materials which can be used flexibly and sensitively in terms of the teacher's intimate knowledge about the lives of the children.*

When competency based instruction is complemented by behavior modification, the qualities of technological consciousness are still further accentuated. Teachers are taught that "the reinforcer controls the behavior of the organism." Proper sequencing of positive reinforcers should shape behaviors in the desired pattern. The teacher who acts within the behaviorist frame of reference is taught to view learning activities as correct elicited responses from learners and to see the practice of shaping behavior as <u>the</u> characteristic responsibility of pedagogy.

As C.A. Bowers points out, when these techniques are used, students are learning far more than the facts and skills teachers think they are imparting.
They are also learning that socially legitimated authority (the teacher) sees only those behaviors that conform to institutional expectations, and that these behaviors will be reinforced. Aside from being presented a mechanistic model for interpreting our behaviour (and the behaviour modification teacher will not present other models) the student is

_____
*There are, of course, other kinds of curriculum materials which are not so minutely prescriptive and which suggest activities that can engage the creativity of both students and teachers.

also being socialized in the values of the consumer society. In effect, the use of behaviour modification teaches two important cultural messages: success is a matter of conforming to a technologically controlled environment, and as one accepts external control she/he will enjoy the benefits of the consumer society.[36]

If readers develop a sense that systems efficiency talk and thought seem at odds with the educational ideal of liberalizing human experience, I cannot quarrel with them. Our minds, and our images of ourselves and our society are affected by the language of discourse we use. There are consequences from limiting our language about education to the lexicon of technocratic management ideology. There is little room in that language for thinking of ourselves as persons capable of projecting personal intellectual goals and pursuing them passionately, capable of making value choices and of becoming cultural critics. Most important, perhaps, is that there is no room in the management concept of education for developing awareness of what submission to technological consciousness is doing to ourselves and to the quality of our learning. Nor does it encourage inquiry about the impact of "production function thinking" on our ecology and cultural values. Education becomes simpler, less controversial and more impoverished as we reduce it to imparting particles of knowledge as machine-scored "right" answers. (I may have overdone it. That is justified, however, if it helps us see the tendency of what we are doing.)

NOTES

1. Arthur E. Wise, Legislated Learning: The Bureaucratization of the American Classroom. (Berkeley: University of California Press, 1979), p. 64.

2. Peter Berger, et al., The Homeless Mind. (New York: Vintage Books, 1974). See pp. 26-34. (For application of the concept to education see C.A. Bowers, "Cultural Literacy in Developed Countries," Prospects, Vol. VII, No. 3, 1977).

3. We are guided by Ernest R. House, "Evaluation as Scientific Management in U.S. School Reform," Comparative Education Review, (Vol. 22, No. 3, October, 1978), pp. 388-401.

4. Ibid., p. 389.

5.   Milbrey W. McLaughlin, <u>Evaluation and Modern Reform</u>. (Cambridge, Mass.: Ballinger, 1975), p. 10.

6.   Alice M. Rivlin, <u>Systematic Thinking for Social Action</u>. (Washington, D.C.: Brookings Institution, 1971), p. 46.

7.   House, op. cit., p. 395.

8.   McLaughlin, op. cit., p. 34.

9.   Rivlin, op. cit., p. 46.

10. House, op. cit., p. 393.

11. Ibid., p. 396.

12. Ibid., p. 400.

13. For his major work see Michael Polanyi, <u>Personal Knowledge</u>. (Chicago: University of Chicago Press, 1958)

14. Wise, op. cit., p. 94.

15. See Wise, Ibid., Chapter 2 "Hyperrationalizing The Schools."

16. Ibid., p. 12.

17. Ibid. (See Chapter 1 "Educational Policies: From Opportunity to Achievement," pp. 3-22 et passim.)

18. Ibid., p. 23.

19. See James Mecklenberger, <u>Performance Contracting</u>. (Worthington, Ohio: Charles A. Jones Publishing Co., 1972), p. 85.

20. Wise, op. cit., pp. 26-27.

21. Ibid., pp. 54-55.

22. John Goodlad, "A Perspective on Accountability," <u>Phi Delta Kappan</u>, (Vol. 57, No. 2, October, 1975), p. 10.

23. John Goodlad, "Can Our Schools Get Better," <u>Phi Delta Kappan</u> (Vol. 60, No. 5, January, 1979), p. 343.

24. Ibid.

25. John Goodlad, "A Perspective on Accountability," p.

109.

26. Wise op. cit., pp. 58 and 56-58 et passim.

27. Lee J. Cronbach and Patrick Suppes, eds., Research For Tomorrow's Schools. (Toronto: MacMillan, 1969), p. 73 in Wise, p. 60.

28. Mecklenberg, op. cit., p. 43.

29. Wise, op. cit., p. 61.

30. Robert Schaefer, The School as A Center of Inquiry. (New York: Harper and Row, 1967).

31. Dan C. Lortie, School Teacher. (Chicago: The University of Chicago Press, 1975), p. 208.

32. Philip W. Jackson, Life in Classrooms. (New York: Holt, Rinehart and Winston, 1968).

33. Ibid., p. 165.

34. C.A. Bowers, "Cultural Literacy in Developed Countries," Prospects (Vol. VIII, No. 3, 1977), p. 325.

35. Michael Apple, "Curriculum Form and the Logic of Technical Control," Economic and Industrial Democracy (Vol. 2, No. 3, August, 1981), pp. 300-304 et passim. Apple quotes from Science ... A Process Approach, Module One. (Lexington, Ginn and Co., 1974).

36. Bowers, op. cit., p. 326.

CHAPTER VII

A CRITIQUE OF TECHNOCRATIC IDEOLOGY:
UNVEILING ITS ALIENATING EFFECTS

...(The) application of systems theory to the
teaching process ... is likely to transform
teaching and learning into a mechanical,
positivistically oriented process... (Its)
language is not concerned with the truth
claims of statements, the adequacy of values
people live by, or the discrepancy between the
energy demands of our culture and the carrying
capacity of the ecosystems. In effect, it
creates an encapsulated technological universe where only technological and management
problems are real. [1]   C.A. Bowers

R.L. Why aren't you doing your work, Alphonso?

A. I thought we were going to read today.

R.L. That's what we did--you just had reading
group.

A. But, I thought we would read today.

R.L. We did, Alphonso. That's what we just
did. We looked for 's' sounds in your book,
did two 's' pages in your workbook and here is
the worksheet you should be doing right now to
find some more 's' words.

A. But, I thought we would read today, you
know READ read ! [2]
                    Rita Roth (Journal Entry)

We have presented a picture of influences of
technocratic ideology on American schools in the
1970s. Schools are gripped by it because it represents the taken-for-granted values and mode of thought
of the managerial leaders of society. Alice Rivlin
reflected the sense of its inevitability in her
comments describing PPBS (Planning, Programming,
Budgeting System) as simply the "common sense approach
to decision making" and said that "hardly anyone
favors a return to muddling through." [3] She acknow-
ledges the imperfections of its cost/benefit
methodologies, but is confident that progress depends
primarily on developing more effective performance

133

measures as incentive for "accountability" and higher productivity. Progress essentially is a matter of doing more of the same, but with greater sophistication. Eventually education can be treated as a production function in cost/benefit terms. If this is, indeed, the course of common sense and technical efficiency why not simply get on with it?

The blunt answer is that it has to be opposed because it is destructive of the best of our traditions - the concept of a liberalizing education for free persons. That tradition is rooted in an image of human beings as capable of transforming the world to support growth of human potential. This assumes an emancipatory function for education. Liberal learning teaches us to read, discuss and study to attain critical insight into traditions and social conditions that enable us to understand our human condition. It empowers us to make intentional choices to transform our social and individual lives. In Bowers terms, "The idea of critical consciousness is tied to the traditional liberal view of individual dignity and a reconstituted view of the rational process.... It is also grounded in an ideology, but one that does not subordinate the individual to the technique or status of an output." [4]

In this chapter we shall attempt to clarify how technocratic ideology in education is destructive of that ideal.

A. The Philosophical Critique

We start with the conviction that the nature and danger of technocratic ideology must be understood more fully. An ideology is an interlocking set of beliefs and assumptions by which members of a society make sense of their daily experience. It provides the basic assumptions for conceptualizing reality; these assumptions and beliefs often make it possible for certain groups or classes to benefit more from the system than others.

In this case we are talking about a technocratic ideology which is becoming the taken-for-granted way for symbolizing reality by the managerial leaders in the institutions of this society. In education, it shows up as the rational efficiency model, which is borrowed from techniques of scientific management from industry. As noted earlier, it has structured the mind set of managerial leadership to think of the work process in terms such as mechanisticity, reproductibility, measurability, componentiality, self-anonymization of the worker etc.

In the last chapter, we noted our hunch that there is something debilitating about that model which divorces it from human reality. In this chapter we want to show first, that the technocratic ideology is flawed at its philosophical core because it is out of touch with what is distinctive about us as human beings, and secondly, that observational studies of competency oriented education point to its trivializing effects on learning.

Eventually we shall attempt to explain why we agree with Bowers that technocratic ideology transforms teaching and learning into a mechanical positivistically oriented process, "where only technological and managerial problems are real."

The roots of the technocratic view of reality lie deep in the history of western culture. We have neither the space nor the competence to explore the sources in depth. The attempt to understand the ideology, however, must include an effort to understand examples of the philosophical issues at stake. These include the kinds of answers given to the classical questions about the nature of human life and the good society. Our thesis is that the new ideology is at odds with the answers given to those questions in the Western tradition of education as the liberalizing of experience.

Technocratic ideology, in its behavioristic aspects, reduces humans to organisms whose behaviors are to be shaped by benevolent behavioral engineers, thus subtracting from the human condition the possibility of considered free choice. It substitutes the expertly controlled society for the free society, capable of transforming itself through critical reflection and intentional action.

One way of seeing what is at issue is to compare the positive science image of human nature and its concept of truth seeking, with two powerful twentieth century humanist critiques of positivism: that of the phenomologists (e.g. Edmund Husserl and Paul Ricoeur) and the critical theorists of the Frankfurt school of Marxist humanism (e.g. Jürgen Habermas, Herbert Marcuse, Erich Fromm et al.). Our goal is a modest one of selecting aspects which bear on our purposes. There are extensive writings by the spokesmen of each position and a large interpretive literature. In addition, there are papers by James Palermo and C. A. Bowers which provide insightful analyses of concepts which bear on educational issues.

The phenomenologists (related to the existentialists) and the critical theorists have been European philosophers who have taken their stand against Anglo-American empiricist-positivist traditions. While there are points of differences between them, they agree in differing sharply with positivist science's way of viewing human existence. Their critique of positivism is based, in part, on a return to an image of human nature, upon which the liberalizing concept of education of the West was based.

Positivist science and educational techniques derived from it are seen as a source of human alienation - alienation being a condition in which the person has part of his human-ness taken away. This happens in any process which involves the "thingification" of humans - which reduces them to the role of passive objects in the world. Marx saw an example of this in the social relations of capitalism, under which relations with others are transformed into the thing-like relationships of commodity exchange. Laborers are transformed into labor commodities whose "value" fluctuates according to the natural law of supply and demand. The human being is thus "...depressed spiritually and physically to the condition of a machine and from being a man becomes an <u>abstract activity</u> and a stomach."[5]

A fundamental way in which positivist science contributes to the "thingification" of man is by its operating assumption that man is to be studied and understood as nothing but another object in nature. We shall return to an elaboration of this point.

For the moment, however, we note that the critics - who for shorthand purposes, we may label the humanist critics - point to the fact that the positivist interpretation of what man is, is a radical departure from the liberal traditions of a free person in a free society. <u>Human</u> reality, from the Greeks onward, was seen as different in kind from the physical order.

Sophocles expressed the Greek sense that there is something unique and worthy about man in the scheme of things when he had his chorus say,

There are so many strange wonders, but nothing more wonderful than man.

As the classical scholar C. M. Bowra phrased it:

(For the Greeks,) Man serves a purpose in the scheme of things and realizes his full nature in it. This is to develop his <u>areté</u>, or inborn capacities as far as he can...In the fifth century... areté was found in the full development of the individual within the social frame.[6]

The function of the good society was to organize itself to help humans reach the limit of their gifts. From the perspective of the Greek tradition, humans are different from the physical order by virtue of the human capacities of language, reason, and consciousness, which enable them to have self-awareness of their own existence and condition. Through discourse and reasoned inquiry they may gain insights which enable them to transcend their animal organism aspect.

From this view, it does violence to people to study them only in terms of their behaviors. From the humanist perspective, being in the world as a human being is being here with nothing less than an ethical task - to support the project of becoming more fully human. This carries with it the obligation to oppose conditions which cause part of our human-ness to be taken away.

In the language of the phenomenologists, "the human life world" includes not only the realm of present behavior, but the historical community of our past, as well as the possibilities of our future. The human task, as for the Greeks, is social-self formative activity. It is to take action, guided by rational insight, to serve the end of human areté or excellence.

Rational insight, which can grow out of critical dialogue, can enable the unveiling of what is repressive or alienating. From this perspective, there is no value free, neutral role for humans, or for investigators of human existence. Unveiling the effects of technocratic ideology (and its companion positivist science) involves creating an understanding of how it distorts human reality and diverts us from our ethical project.[7] At a basic level, it substitutes the language and thought processes of positivist science for critical reason. Put in other terms, it substitutes the control techniques of monologue for the liberating processes of dialogue.

According to the phenomenologist Edmund Husserl, the origin of the positivist distortion derives from Galileo's mathematization of nature. From Galileo's time forward, empirical positivist science approached the world as a reality which was to be quantified, controlled and manipulated. The methods of the physical sciences, based on a materialist, mechanistic view of reality, provided us with impressive, lawful, quantifiable explanations of the physical world. Because of the undeniable power of the methods, the assumption grew that these modes of truth seeking were the only legitimate ways.

Gradually, critics have countered by revealing distortions that result when the positivist, mathematicized universe is identified with the human life world. Human reality, treated as part of a positivist-conceived nature, becomes another object to be mastered. Positivism's primary interests in prediction and control are transferred to the human life world itself. As positivist science merges with the human life world, both become constructs within a mathematical logic.

Human reality is diminished when placed under the aegis of the positivist model. That model is neglectful of the reflexive power of human understanding and reason. As Paul Ricoeur pointed out, understanding is more than a form of knowledge in the usual sense of a subject-knowing, object-known relationship. [8] Understanding is rooted in the power of reflective self-understanding - in the capacity for appropriating the meaning of events for the purpose of directing the formation of our own selves and society; in the capacity for gaining insight into how cultural history (including the appearance of positivist science) affects the quality of our lives; in the capacity for projecting alternative futures and making choices to guide action.

A positivist science, constructed within a mathematical logic, lacks insight into its own historical origins in the physical science model. It lacks awareness of the wholeness of human existence, and lacks awareness of moral/political interests and consequences. In the absence of such understanding it takes its validity as self-evident. Eventually it becomes hurtful to children and their teachers. We need to acknowledge that. A more adequate "science" would recognize the limitations of its positivist dimension and honor the importance of the truths of the larger human life world for an adequate education.

Those who have unveiled the presuppositions of positivism have shown its underlying interest in control which, when institutionalized, becomes social control. Husserl saw the historical origins of this in Galileo's new science, with its grounding in geometry, the art of measuring. With this as the ground, the overriding goal of positivist science becomes experimental prediction and control. "The ability of the experimenter to predict within a prescribed environment of the physical world is correlative to his ability to control the environ-

ment."[9] When the positivist view of nature is made
one with the human life world, the central interest
becomes identifying the natural lawfulness of human
behavior which can lead to prediction and control.
(We may recall Alice Rivlin's statement regarding
planned experimental variation: "Information necessary
to improve the effectiveness of social services is
impossible to obtain any other way.")[10] The positivist scientific method gradually becomes identified
with the human life world itself - "hidden and unrecognized, the positivist method is used to translate
the life world into a mathematical form."[11]
       Such efforts to reduce the human being to
another object within nature purport to be objectively
neutral - a disinterested study of human life by
physical science methods. But as Habermas pointed
out, the "truth" which derives from positivist science
is not the neutral picturing of objective fact, "It is
instead the filtered residue of a life world reality
that has been reduced to mathematical terms." This,
Habermas maintains, enables the positivist to preserve
his transcendent interest of control. By choosing to
work within this broad control orientation, and
preserving his grip on a method with which he is
comfortable, the positivist conceals from himself the
way in which his operations have distorted understanding of human existence. "Quite simply the
experimenter accepts the second order mathematically
idealized life world as his most primitive data. This
mystification of lived experience is embedded in both
the methods and logic of positive science itself."[12]
       Having limited his view of reality to what his
methods can handle, the positivist limits his description of "reality" to <u>language</u> permitted by goals of
physical observation and control. Such observational
language appears to be scientific, "theory free",
neutral and objective. Yet to insist on limiting
descriptions of human existence to language of the
physical order is a "violation of neutrality" in the
violence it does to our human nature. As the language
and logic of positivist method become incorporated
into the scientific management rationale of our
institutional leaders, it begins to be seen as the
standard way. To improve productivity of a technical
system requires technical tools; the language and
techniques of positivist science provide the means for
systems analysis and control. The language and mode
of thought of technocratic ideology become the "recipe
knowledge," the way of thinking and speaking in
systems saturated with its style. The grammar and

139

technical terminology used in work place speech reflect the assimilation into consciousness of the technocratic world view. More and more, daily talk describes reality in terms such as input, output, system components, performance objectives, sequencing instruction, instructional packages, etc. As all of this becomes the taken-for-granted way of thinking about the work of teaching and learning, it becomes difficult "to distance" oneself from it in order to become aware of its consequences.

In short, critics who argue the need for aware-ness of the alienating effects argue that it manifests itself in two related ways which tend to be concealed: First, in a false impression of political neutrality by claiming to be concerned only with a simple goal of increased efficiency and second, by the imposition of a restricted language of "efficient production" which captures the way our minds work and detracts our energies from concerns with liberalizing experience. It tends to restrict interactions to a controlling form of monologue through which the subject manipu-lates the object. This may give the appearance of communication in that words are exchanged. In fact, the exchange is monologue, with a reduction in the mutual exploration of meaning through dialogue in which each is "really present" to the other. In Martin Buber's terms I-It monologue takes the place of I-Thou communication.

Positivist method (and its offspring, techno-cratic ideology) appears to be value free to its practitioners: "We aim only to improve efficiency." But this bland concern obscures the political, parti-san nature of its orientation. The technocratic ideology dictates that activities be organized accord-ing to the principles of rational efficiency, assessed according to measurable outcomes and legitimated by the production oriented language of industrial ma-chines. The insistence that the only real concern is with productivity and its pay-offs has the effect, as Habermas put it, of "repressing ethics as a category of discussion." [13] The single-minded passion for measurable production rules out reflective criticism of the technocratic ideology itself.

Technocratic ideology asserts itself most obvi-ously in many ways through the language of teaching and learning of the positivist behavioral scientist, B. F. Skinner. His orientation undergirds much rationalistic school reform. Skinner's "science of human behavior" analyzes human learning in terms of environmentally conditioned events. His operationalist methods of employing schedules of positive reinforcement enable the experimenter or practitioner to control the environment to shape desired patterns of behavior.

As Skinner adapts the operationalist model to teaching, the teacher must learn to control the learning environment so that the student elicits the proper behavioral responses. The teacher's task is to arrange reinforcing environmental contingencies so as to lead the student to emit "correct" behaviors - or answers. As Skinner puts it, special techniques based on the science of human behavior "provide a much more effective control of behavior."[14] Control, effected by numerous verbal responses to the child, enable the teacher to replicate learning conditions, so she can predict what will happen and which she can technically reproduce repeatedly. Skinner's behaviorism reduces teaching to "...a subject/object relation wherein the subject is controlling the object and its...behavior."[15]

Educational practice is transformed from the subject/subject relationship of dialogue of the liberal tradition, into the subject/object relationship of behaviorist technique. Because all of this is done under the imprimateur of "scientific pedagogy", the domination of the experimenter or teacher over the human "object" is obscured. Behavioral engineering is simply assumed to be the scientific way, i.e. the most efficient way to secure a larger number of correct responses.

From the time of Edward L. Thorndike, John Watson, and the social efficiency philosophers of the early twentieth century, control-oriented pedagogy has been a major force in American educational theory and practice. Currently, it insinuates itself through a language filled with terms like "behavioral objectives," "behavioral modification," "competency- based criteria" etc. When talk about teaching is captured within the empirical-positivist language frame, the lived experience of teachers gets reduced to "schedules of scientific facts and procedures." All of this is fundamentally alienating, as students become organisms whose behavior is to be "shaped", and knowledge is reduced to units of correct responses to be mastered.

Learners seem to be acting when, in fact, they are controlled. Their actions are simply reflections of the commands of others. Behavioral designed learning simply recapitulates the environmental conditions engineered by the teacher or curriculum programmer. When a learning activity is defined as "a

correct elicited response," the liberal ideal of
reaching forward into the world for meaning and self
understanding disappears, for teachers as well as
students. When the behaviorist rationale comes to
define teaching, teachers as well as students must be
socialized to its ideology. Teachers must internalize
into consciousness the assumptions, definitions and
categories required to create classroom reality in
terms of behaviors, atomized units of instruction,
reinforcers etc. In doing so, teachers become encapsulated from their human life world - with its rich
complexity of intending, interpreting, valuing, and
the feelings of uncertainty, fear, affection, humor,
frustration etc. Teachers are under pressure to
become the carriers of the alienation of technocratic
ideology.

Teachers begin to perceive themselves as behaviors or responses which will facilitate control of the
learning environment. The teacher becomes the boss -
the student the obedient (and consumer-rewarded)
worker. Each has become "thingified" as have also the
inert "elicited responses" passed off as "knowledge."
Can we feel the pathos of it in Alphonso's experience
with "the reading period?"

    R.L. Why aren't you doing your work, Alphonso?
    A. I thought we were going to read today.
    R.L. That's what we did--you just had reading
        group.
    A. But, I thought we would read today.
    R.L. We did, Alphonso. That's what we just
        did. We looked for 's' sounds in your
        book, did two 's· pages in your workbook
        and here is the worksheet you should be
        doing right now to find some more 's'
        words.
    A. But, I thought we would read today -- you
        know, READ read

                      Rita Roth (Journal Entry)
And if that isn't enough, we may listen in to another
"lesson in reading:"

    Mrs. R. What is that?
    Cassandra It's my book, In a People House
    Mrs. R. Put that away and do your reading,
           Cassandra. You have lots to do in
           your folder and two pages in your
           workbook.
    Cassandra looks puzzled. She says nothing.
    Mrs. R. repeats what she said.
    Mrs. R. Put that book away and do your
           reading. You have lots to do in

your folder and two pages in your workbook.

Cassandra puts her book away, opens her worksheet folder and begins to write. A small group of children come to the reading table with Mrs. R. They are working on vowel sounds, short and long.

Mrs. R. (immediately after the group is seated). Name the vowels, Zia. (She does) Say the short sounds for the vowels, Charlie. (He says them) Bill, what's the opposite of stand? (He doesn't answer) Read the short vowel words, Joyce.

Her tone is direct, crisp, quick. They are working with the following vocabulary: fit, sit, pit, lit, hit, etc. Zia reads:

Zia: Can a kit hit a lot?
Mrs. R. Billy?
Billy: No
Mrs. R. Why can't a kit hit a lot? Zia?
Zia: (She looks puzzled) I don't know what that means. Does it mean he is waiting for his turn?
Mrs. R. No. Read it to find out. Does anyone know? "A kit can't hit." Why?
Anna.   A kit just can't hit.
Mrs. R. Yes Zia, can you hit?
Zia: Yes, I hit a lot!
Charlie: I hit a home run!
Mrs. R. (Ignoring Charlie's comment) Read the next page silently and I'll ask you about it. (To a child waiting) Questions, please![16]

(Rita Roth, Journal entry)

B. Observational Critique

Our glimpse at the doubts of the philosophical critics of the rationalist efficency model of education ended with brief excerpts of teacher procedures consistent with the model. We continue now to explore at greater length observational reports of life within schools committed to "mastery of the basics." Educational and popular journals have been replete with theoretical arguments for or against competency oriented education, but there has been little observational data on the day-to-day operations of such schools. Fortunately, a colleague of mine, Professor

143

Marilyn Cohn, has made available observational records and conclusions of her research in a district heavily committed to a "back to basics" orientation.[17] One cannot claim that one study yields "the truth" about the new efficiency reform movement. But the research was conducted with disciplined participant observation research procedures in a middle class suburb of the American Midwest.

Professor Cohn's two and a half month research study was sponsored by the Center for Evaluation at Western Michigan University. The original contract was for a study of the impact on fifth and sixth grade children, of a new instructional television series entitled "Think About." It became broadened, however, to all subject areas and to many kinds of school interactions as it became clear that the larger opportunity was to study a school thoroughly committed to "back to basics" education. In addition to in-depth participant observation techniques in one fifth grade classroom, the teaching-learning process was studied by extensive interviews of students, teachers and administrators, and by participation in parent relations activities.

Because of limitations of space we shall limit ourselves to presenting brief descriptive materials followed by major conclusions of the investigator.

(1) "Back To Basics" at Forest Hills (all names are fictional)
(Research of Marilyn Cohn, Washington University, St. Louis). [18]

The essence of the Forest Hills approach is contained in the title of the "mandated retention-promotion policy" passed by the Board of Education. One elementary principal expressed the abruptness of its appearance as follows:

We came back to school in August and we found that we had a retention promotion policy thrown at us. The Board wrote it, unbeknownst to us all, and the Elementary Division ended up writing the administrative guidelines....

The features of the policy relate to the national trends we noted earlier, in which lay policy makers prescribe specifics of professional practice. The policy, passed by the Board, dictated the need for a clearly delineated set of "fundamental skills" and a corresponding set of tests. Since neither existed, committees of administrators, teachers and subject area consultants produced both. They brought forth a

List of Skills to be mastered at each grade level in (1) communication (reading, writing, composition, spelling, speaking), (2) mathematics, (3) science, and (4) social studies, and a set of measurement items for each skill area.

While teachers experienced stress concerning test score results, both teachers and administrators seemed generally supportive of the idea. In fact, one school person said, "Everyone wants to take credit for the idea."

The principal of the Roberts School, Dr. Madison, agreed completely with the community's charge to concentrate on the "basics." He had no trouble implementing the plan in a way that fit his idea of creating a school that is a pleasant and predictable work place - with well established routines and orderly conduct.

He told the investigator how he turned the retention-promotion policy, announced by the Board, into a highly profitable experience for all affected:

I made a little flip-chart with pictures and I went into every room...I told them we have this new rule and what is your responsibility?...We would have a little rap session with them and flip through it and so on... The monkey is on the kids' backs for responsibility. Not all of them have accepted it and they pay the price, but very few kids have we retained that it hasn't been profitable for.

We may note in passing that no one seems to have thought it significant that teachers were not consulted prior to implementation procedures. Dr. Madison is, however, a strong believer that "to keep achievement up", he must create a "positive environment." So he frequently gives "positive reinforcement" to students for good performance, and gives "strokes" to teachers by sending them "happy grams." He keeps parents supportive and happy by monthly meetings about school accomplishments, and by requiring his teachers to send home every Friday a folder filled with each child's work for the week.

Professor Cohn spent considerable time observing the plan in action at the level of the fifth grade class of Ms. Church. Professor Cohn prefaces her field notes of this class with the observation that the procedures recorded were characteristic of Ms. Church's teaching style and classroom organization. She noted also that, in spite of a daily blackboard activity schedule, which included reference to social

145

studies and science, each day tends to break down into the same three large segments - spelling and language, reading, and math. Ms. Church explains this as her way of coping with the test pressures, "covering myself in certain areas (reading, math and language arts) so that they don't realize what is not being done in others (science, social studies or health)." For example, during the first quarter there were math, reading, and spelling groups every day, but no lessons from social studies or health texts. However, the week before the quarterly grade cards, the children were assigned a map skill worksheet and a "weekly reader" for a social studies grade, as well as a drawing of the human eye for a health grade. Where reading is concerned, the experience of the children in Ms. Church's class was almost identical to what Alfonso and Zia experienced. Since those incidents of "reading" seem sufficiently vivid, we shall turn to Professor Cohn's account of a lesson in Ms. Church's class of one of the other major areas - mathematics.

10/30 12:15 <u>Math</u>

Ms. Church announces: "I want to see the Bionic Brains, the Page 11 people. Three children arrive at the back table. Ms. Church tells them to "exchange papers" and then writes 30 answers to subtraction problems on the chalkboard. After papers are returned and checked by the owner, students are asked to read scores aloud so that she can record them. Two of the three who scored high (100% and 97%) -- are told "to go on to page 12." To John, who scored 77%, she says, "That's better than yesterday, but you can do better. Correct your paper before you go on to page 12."

12:25

"Okay, the rest of the Bionic Brains." Six come to the round table. She again says "exchange papers" and then puts answers to page 12 (35 in all) on the chalkboard. After grading and returning papers, children read aloud their scores, "Rita, 8 wrong, that's not good--you'll have to do something else. Carla, Stanley, Susie, and Ken, go and do the test on page 28. Rita, correct your mistakes first. Stanley, erase the board. Dan, good, all right, do page 12 and then go on to the test. Rita, (her head is now on the table and she looks dejected) you can leave now."

12:45

Ms. Church looks up and says, "Who's supposed to get T.V.?" (Two kids go out). As she begins to analyze Ken's mistakes, Rita comes back with her corrections. She works about two minutes with Ken, asking questions, like "what is 6 from 9?" and then she sends

146

him back. "Just do two rows and put down the time you stop so we can see how long it takes you." She works a minute or two with Rita: "You still have this wrong. How can you take this from this? Rita, you are forgetting your basic facts. Bring me your textbook. Okay, turn to page 28. There are 20 problems, check these and see if you can pick up your mistakes." (She stops math for "ThinkAbout.")

Ms. Church (1:25 p.m.) "I want to see the last group-- the Mathematical Menaces" (high group). Three arrive. She begins by reading aloud a group of answers from yesterday's assignment and then she asks the students to put their answers to another group of problems, dealing with the function rule, on the chalkboard. Only one gets his problem right. She helps others see their mistakes by asking them questions, and collects papers--saying "Aren't you lucky I'm not taking grades today? Now turn to pages 40-41." Ms. Church reads the introductory sentences and then talks through the examples. Students are asked to work out problems 1 and 2 on page 40 and number 4 on page 41. They do them correctly. Then she asks if using nine, three, and six, can they make a mathematical statement? Three can and one cannot. She asks the three to leave and she works with Terry until he says, "I get it." It is 1:55 and she tells everyone that they can go to the the restroom and eat their snacks. While they are gone, she gets flash cards for Ken and asks the two girls who sit at his island to help him to learn his facts.

We limit ourselves to presenting this one selection from the field notes but we remind the reader that Professor Cohn saw this excerpt of the teaching style as characteristic. Elsewhere she described it as "a total reliance on the teacher's guide and text; a mastery approach." We present next Professor Cohn's summary and reflections on the meaning of her total experience in the Forest Hills schools.

Perhaps the first and most obvious feature of this learning environment for students is its passive quality. As shown above, students spend the bulk of their time sitting and working independently at their desks or in small math and reading groups following directives or instructions; doing, checking, or grading practice exercises and tests.

A second but related aspect of this environment is that the work itself comes through to students as a potpourri of discrete skills and isolated concepts which seem to bear little connection to each other, to underlying principles, or to the rest of their life experiences.

In both reading and math, skills are invariably taught through worksheets with little or no opportunity for practice or application in life-like situations. Just as students do not look at a book with a table of contents to learn how to use one, they do not go beyond worksheets to "distinguish between fact and opinion" or beyond rows of already set-up problems in the text to develop the ability to use subtraction to solve problems. Thus while there is surely an underlying structure and an overarching purpose to the daily curricular diet in Ms. Church's mind, the chopped and diced quality of each of the main courses oftentimes keeps the student from knowing why the menu was planned in the first place.

A third characteristic of the learning environment that emerges from the transcript is the preponderance of activities which call for low levels of thinking and brief narrow responses from students. The above excerpts from reading, for example, reveal a program with a heavy emphasis on mechanics wherein individual skills are taught through a "molecular" and "mastery" approach. For each skill there is an invariable sequence of pre-test, skill lesson, workbook practice, post-test, review exercise, and mastery test. And for each question within the sequence there is one narrow correct answer. In fact so much time is spent on drill and recall questions related to mechanics, relatively little time is left for the reading and discussion of stories. Over the 2½ month observation period, the students read only four stories, although "reading" groups met daily. And, as can be noted above, when students do finally read a story, the "discussion" involves a mechanically read set of questions from the guide which asks for one-word answers of fact or detail. In like manner, math work generally consists of practice in computation which requires only knowledge and recall of basic math facts.

A fourth aspect of student life that surfaces in the excerpts is the emphasis on grades and getting the right answer. Large segments of class time are devoted to testing, checking and recording of grades. Moreover, as can be seen above, students are warned to read carefully so as not to get "wrong answers" and are told to consider themselves "lucky" when their teacher doesn't record grades from lessons where there was a general lack of understanding.

A fifth and final quality that is suggested by

the transcripts is that the learning environment is strongly controlled by Ms. Church. Berlak and Berlak (1981)[19] delineate three particular control dilemmas facing elementary teachers which help describe the authority structure that students experience in Ms. Church's classroom. They speak of the teacher vs. child "time" dilemma which asks who controls the beginning point and duration of activities; the teacher vs. child "operations" dilemma which asks who controls what students are to do in the various curricular areas; the teacher vs. child "standards" dilemma which asks who sets and monitors the standards for evaluation. In Ms. Church's case, the answers are clear and consistent. Ms. Church totally controls "operations" and "standards" and controls to a high degree "time."

Because she asks most of the questions, holds all of the answers, and determines the nature, sequence, and time of activities, students exercise almost no control over their learning environment.

Thus the picture that begins to unfold is that of a work place where the main order of business is the learning of facts and narrow skills in an isolated, molecular, and passive fashion. The paper-pencil exercises which provide opportunities for learning and practice of the "basics," the "discussions" that are essentially recitations, and the mastery tests require only the lowest levels of thinking. Students are rarely told or shown the rationale behind what they do nor are they given much choice as to when and how to do it; nevertheless, they are expected to comply in an unquestioning manner.

Now if one believes, as John Dewey did, that students learn what they experience one might legitimately speculate that students in such an environment might tend to (1) search for "the right answer" more often than for understanding; (2) have difficulty in applying facts and skills learned in the classroom to actual problem solving situations; (3) see themselves as unable to act or control their own learning or decision making; (4) conclude that school work has little connection with the rest of their lives.

There is more than enough data stemming from interviews and observations of Ms. Church's students to move somewhat beyond the speculation stage. A first case in point involves the area of mathematics. After weeks of watching all math groups practice doing subtraction "problems" from their text, I observed the slowest reading group puzzled by a subtraction problem of relatively simple nature. The children were

149

"discussing" a story about the first woman cosmonaut and the dialogue went this way:

    Ms. C. (reading from the guide): How old was _____ when she entered the Soviet training program for cosmonauts? It doesn't tell you in the story but there is enough information for you to figure it out.

    Students: No answer

    Ms. C.: O.K. Look on Page ___ it tells you the year she was born. Now look on page ___ it tells the year she entered the training program. Now what do you have to do with those years to find out her age.

    John: Add

    Ms. C.: No

    Steven: Subtract

    Ms. C.: That's right - now Steven go ahead and find the answer for us.

Steven turns over a worksheet, does some quick figuring and shouts out an obviously incorrect answer. Ms. Church asks to see his work and then shows the rest of the class how he erred by putting the year of her birth on top and the year of her entry on the bottom. Steven then comes to the board, reverses numbers and gets the correct answer.

This incident, I think, illustrates quite clearly that at least some of the children (perhaps only the slowest) were simply rotely performing the operation of subtraction during math time rather than learning how to use subtraction to solve actual problems. Throughout the observation period, there were similar example of rote and therefore meaningless learning.

A brief encounter with a single student provides a second illustration. In this instance, the behavioral evidence involves a student's interest in getting the right answer at the expense of understanding, and the data was recorded as follows:

    In today's reading group the students are checking work sheets on "distinguishing fact from opinion". Students were to read a number of paragraphs and put "F" for fact and "O" for opinion in the blank in front of each. Ms. Church reads the correct answers and has students check their own work and read aloud their scores while she records them. Those who have mistakes are told to correct them. Kathy, who got all of them wrong, leaves Reading group and returns within one minute to have her "corrections" checked. Surprised to see her back so quickly, I

ask her how she reread all those paragraphs so
quickly. She replies: Oh, Dr. Cohn, don't you
know about kids? We like to do things fast. I
got them all wrong and so I just erased them and
put in the opposite. Kathy then marches up to
Ms. Church who glances approvingly at the
"corrected" version and puts a smile face on the
paper.
Many times throughout the observation period students
"corrected" their work by using Kathy's method or
"copying" from a friend. As a result, everyone's
Friday folder was filled with papers with smile faces.
    Ms. Church was, of course, not totally unaware
of some of the problematic aspects of the "basics"
thrust in her building and district. On several
occasions she expressed a number of concerns - all of
which revolved around accountability in terms of
grades and test scores. She spoke of personal pressure, for instance in this way:
    I felt the pressure very strongly. Now this
    is the first year we didn't have a printed
    list of class scores listed separately but I
    do feel that our principal bases a lot of his
    evaluation on a teacher's test scores. I
    don't think he takes into account where the
    kids were or what type of child you have, or
    if the class tends to be a higher average
    class or lower average class.
A related concern was that the highly valued test
scores might in fact be of little value:
    ...And the ironic thing is that if you give a
    skill test after you've studied it, then most
    of them can get an 80% on it. You wait a
    couple of weeks, and then you give it to them
    and they'll say, 'Well, why didn't you give
    this to us before? We've forgotten it.' So
    do these tests really show that they've
    mastered? If they can't master it two weeks
    later, or even a month later, have they really
    mastered it or have we really just been
    teaching it so we can make a little chart of
    however we want it to look?
A final concern was that the current "basics" curriculum was less interesting for students:
    I find I don't have as much time to devote to
    some of the more creative aspects of teaching
    or to some of the projects we once did. It's
    more of a mundane routine type of teaching
    that's done. We do that because there's no
    getting around it. Every quarter you have to

151

come up with those grades and you have to have
something to base it on. So you tend to do
things you can grade easily. Discussion and
inquiry projects -- you just don't have time
for. Holt's a great inquiry curriculum, but
you can't grade the activities -- it's all
teacher evaluation and it's only what you
think a child is putting into it.

Nonetheless Ms. Church clearly endorsed her district's
current emphasis on the "basics" and never explicitly
or implicitly indicated any discomfort with her
students' preoccupation with "the right answer," view
of learning, inability to apply facts and and skills,
lack of self-esteem, and control over their own learning and decision making. The precise purpose behind
the "Back to Basics" movement in American education is
probably no easier to reach consensus on than is a
definition of the "basics" or an evaluation of the
effort. For some, the intent may be a focus on the 3
R's; for others it may be the establishment of minimum
competencies; for still others it may be a respect for
order and authority. For many, it may be all of the
above; for a few, it may be none of the above. It is
difficult to imagine, however, that for anyone the aim
was ever rote learning of narrow skills, low levels of
thinking, passivity, lack of confidence and self
esteem, and pressure on students to achieve high
scores at almost any cost. These, however, all appear
to be possible outcomes with Ms. Church's interpretation of the "basics."

Summary Reflections

Professor Cohn's observations and commentaries
carry their own potent message. Since, however, we
began this chapter with the contention that teaching
as management of instruction is inimical to the
emancipatory values of liberal education, we add some
personal comments which bear on the point. I concede
that Professor Cohn's research does not provide the
final word about "back to basics." I assume, however,
that her account is far from being atypical of teaching students in such programs, I admit further that
the goal of helping children become proficient in
basic skills is necessary and defensible. I believe,
however, that Professor Cohn's research helps us see
the management instruction model for what it essentially is: a dull control system, with a monologue
style of communication and interpersonal relations.
It is a _training_ approach to learning, with a re-

stricted speech code which tends to force talk and thinking about education into what can be accommodated by a "management of instruction" frame of reference.

The life of students and teachers is limited to the behavioral activities that "count." They "cover" discrete measurable units of information. They rarely expend energy in talking with sentences which come from their personal life world. They emit "right" or "wrong" responses. They master bits of information and try to win on tests. The system is alienating in the literal sense of "alien" - without significant ties. Persons are alien to themselves, to each other, and to the informational content they are "mastering."

We may recall the experiences of Alfonso and Zia with "reading" in the management system mode. The pressures seem to limit reading to a decoding of words into their constituent parts as approved by the manuals. This is the reading that "counts." Decoding is, of course, a significant aspect of learning to read. But to the extent that fixation with it dominates, Alfonso's yearning to "<u>Read</u> read" gets little attention. We can sense the attenuation of reading as a liberalizing experience. Alfonso's call to "<u>Read</u> read" reflects the human need to listen and reflect on passages that were personally meaningful. It contains a call for the need to explore with others meanings which might be missed by one alone; a call to raise questions about the goodness or badness of human action. When students are not equipped to conceptualize, or communicate social experience, silence and distortion result. (We witnessed Alfonso and Zia retreat into silence when their efforts to reach out were overruled.) To honor the need to explore experience, on the other hand, moves the elementary child in the direction of what C.A. Bowers calls a liberating "cultural literacy"20 - a type of reading to which the management model pays scant attention.

Seen from this perspective, the issue is whether children will be passively socialized to the ways and values of the technocratic culture, or whether elementary children, will get initial experience with features of learning which may help them to become insightful about their personal lives, and to become critically aware of what is nurturing or destructive in social life.

To put it another way, the issue is whether we shall define teachers as "managers of instruction" or carriers of liberal culture. To shift the emphasis in teaching to the liberalizing of experience changes our expectations of the work of schools. We would be asking schools to be places of work and learning, committed to the liberal tradition of the Greeks - to help learners to develop their unique areté, or "inborn capacities, so far as they possibly can" and, in Bowra's terms, to ask if the institutional or societal arrangements enables

A man to throw his full personality into what he does, which sustains him in powerful exertions and impels him to unusual efforts, which sets his intelligence fully and actively to work, and gives him that unity of being, that harmony of his whole nature, which is the spring of creative endeavor.[21]

To work in that way requires that teachers and students be present to each other with the wholeness of their persons. It means a willingness to recognize the uniqueness of each and an insistence on expecting a committed effort from each. The good school becomes one, in Dewey's words, where "a social return is demanded from all and opportunity for development of distinctive capacity is provided for all."

If we ask teachers to submit to the technocratic image of teachers as "managers of instruction" we ask them to deafen themselves to the claims and obligations of that liberal tradition; we ask them to forego engaging in the exploratory dialogue so dear to the Greeks; we ask them to restrict their talk to the speech code of management ideology which yields responses which can be objectively marked right or wrong.

The kind of learning experienced by students and teachers in such "right answer" schools diminishes them as persons. It would also appear to be dysfunctional. It ill-equips them for a world of turbulent change, and for a future world which may demand of them flexible, self-initiated learning, mutual problem solving, and a capacity to take group responsibility for the quality of shared work.

Even worse, a system like that can appear to be immovable to the people within it. They begin to experience themselves as passive, powerless, and even lacking any right to question it. Unfortunately, they may even learn to find security in it. If the system is perceived as "just the way the world is," and if it seems to belong to "them", with "myself" lacking any sense of ownership in it, life within it can drift into a matter of "acceptance," spiced with efforts to beat the system on the fringes. Witness Ms. Church's decision to cover herself by giving the appearance of teaching social studies, science and health, while actually ignoring them in order to concentrate on testable areas which count. Witness Kathy submitting a whole list of undigested "corrections" to replace "the wrongs" and getting a "smiling face" mark of approval.

The passion for efficiency can turn a school into an aggregate of isolated individuals spurred by self-centered desire to win high test scores. Such a school loses the quality of being a polis unified by an ethical commitment to nurture the collective human excellence in the school community. Just where this tendency can lead was illustrated by developments in a district near Forest Hills in the spring and summer of 1981.

There is a state requirement that a Basic Essential Skills Test (BEST) be given yearly to eighth grade students. It measures performance in reading, mathematics, and government/economics. A teacher (an eleven year veteran and former nun) was fired for "knowingly passing test answers to students." Other teacher monitors were given reprimands for "coaching students by suggesting that they were 'doing o.k.' or that they should 'go over the test again' or similar expressions." [22]

The State Teachers Association, in defending the accused teacher, charged that the district's top administrators had put pressure on teachers to bring up scores by unorthodox means, including winking at lax security during the test. [23]

The source of fear is an annual spring chart which lists in rank order how children in each district scored on the Basic Essential Skills Tests. The Teachers Association said the chart has become an obsession with some school administrators who feel compelled to bring these scores up "at any cost." On the other hand the Superintendent of the district in question replied that "nobody is pressured," and explained the jump in district scores from 49.7 percent in one year to 77.1 percent the next by the fact that "a lot of teachers worked very hard preparing these kids."

Whatever the facts, the case brought out some interesting information. Other administrators complained that tax payers tended to judge general education programs simply by BEST test scores. Educators feel under heavy pressure to modify curriculum and procedures to increase scores. One district's scores went up in one year from 58 percent to 80.2 percent. When eighth graders in another district were required to retake the test after a suspicious number of tests turned up with perfect scores, only 20 percent passed compared to 68.6 percent in the previous year. School administrators in a major city were reprimanded after teachers were told to use the previous year's test to coach the students by giving them practice on items from a former test.

Multiple explanations are given for all of these events. We don't need to know who is "right" or "wrong" to see the consequences. There is something pathetic about communities reducing their ideas about children's learning to the scores they win on tests, then pitting teachers, principals, schools, and school systems against each other to see who will "win" in competition over test scores. It is a mean view of education and it yields mean results. From the perspective of the Deweyan tradition, what you see emerging here is the breakdown in schools of a sense of community, or of shared social living.

Dewey was skeptical of a view of schooling which had students working in competitive isolation from each other, and which then attempted to give them moral training by exhortations or "lessons in morals." He argued, on the contrary, that the moral traits of a person who is a worthy member of society, such as discipline, natural development, responsibility and social efficiency come from daily participation in the social life of a school as a community of learners. These traits come from the serious effort to become educated, by joining with others in the pursuit of meaning and understanding - "the reconstruction of experience." For a school to have a vital social spirit it must "be a community life in all which that implies", (work and play, communication, cooperation, shared activity, aesthetic expression):

> the measure of the worth of the administration, curriculum, and methods of instruction of the school is the extent to which they are animated by a social spirit. And the great danger which threatens school work is the absence of conditions which make possible a permeating social spirit; this is the great enemy of effective moral training. [24]

While we have been critical, nothing useful is accomplished by being too glib about Back to Basics and related phenomena in American education. There is no doubt that the movement is a response to deep yearning among large numbers of Americans. It is no single thing. Without pretending to understand it completely we offer conjectures which seem plausible.

156

We have been through two decades of traumatic change and repeated frustration with the malfunctioning of many of our institutions. The fall-off in College Board scores seems to parallel weaknesses in industrial productivity. Divorce rates soar, and sexual mores veer from traditional norms. There has been massive erosion of respect for legitimacy of authority across institutions. Educators are among those endlessly demanding more money, while inflation puts relentless strain on pocketbooks and nervous systems. The temptation to seek simplistic answers when, in fact, there are none, can be strong.

"If they can't get kids to read, write, figure and 'learn the basics' what can they do?" Why not insist that teachers be accountable in terms of measurable results - like people in business? Insistence on results in numerical terms seems a no-nonsense way of eliminating the fuzziness of more intangible goals. If learning is reduced to mastery of dull fragments, "Well, that at least will teach them the values of the work ethic which they'll need for survival in a rough world anyway." As we saw in Forest Hills, the idea can win strong support among teachers and administrators who are under the gun to get results.

Our doubt has been with whether the way to significant learning is to treat education as a "technical production function" which can be improved by the engineering and control techniques of scientific management. With all of its "rational" appeal, the critical dimension which scientific management fails to engender in its linear push for efficiency, is human commitment and morale.

This is increasingly recognized in industry and in other institutions besides schools. Edward M. Luttwak of the Georgetown Center for Strategic and International Studies identified the consequences of a narrow systems management style for the American military establishment: "Management techniques and systems analysis have created U.S. armed forces that may be efficient but not very effective."[25]

In comparing the Israeli and American defense establishments, Luttwak sees the American effort much more heavily endowed with engineers and systems analysts. The problem, he says, is "a deformity, a real deformity at the very center of our defense establishment." Serious study of warfare, he maintains, has been suppressed by the brutal imposition of analytical techniques which measure wonderfully what they measure but which ignore the really significant

157

aspects of war:

> The tactical, the leadership, the morale, the
> skill are so much more important than the
> material things. Yet the different techniques
> we use, the systems analyses, the programming,
> all capture only the material aspects. For
> example: Every person who has seriously
> studied war knows that it is critically
> important to allow the combat unit to develop
> kinship and solidarity. Men under fire don't
> fight for their country; they fight for their
> buddies. Everyone knows this and every
> serious army makes it a point to have very
> stable structures, regiments and the like.
> But that is not efficient. For simple effi-
> ciency you want to have all the manpower in a
> big pool and send the correctly trained person
> where he is needed most. But when you move
> the guy, you are disrupting two organizations;
> and there is no way you can put the morale -
> the terribly important but completely unmea-
> surable development of solidarity - into those
> computers."[26]

The result, Luttwak thinks, is that it is hard
to think of a major successful American military
operation since the Inchon landing in the Korean war.
Military organizations are much more technical than
schools. Luttwak's reminder is that even in the
military, a one-sided technical push for efficiency
can reduce actual effectiveness. Human institutions
become poor and ungainly when the persons they are
composed of lose a sense of identity with the work at
hand - when they are alienated from the work and each
other. We could sense that, as an unlovely factor in
the schools where "coaching" and "cheating" were going
on to beat the system - "their system."

Robert Pirsig, in a memorable book of the 70's,
Zen and the Art of Motorcycle Maintenance, helped us
see what was going on with his description of alienation as "technological ugliness" - a condition where
subjects are separated from objects.

Pirsig takes his readers on a lengthy "chautau-
qua" in which he pursues the source of technological
ugliness in our time, by trying to discern the
difference between good and bad motorcycle maintenance. In an early comment Pirsig says "in that
strange separation of what man is from what man does
we may have some clues as to what the hell has gone
wrong in this twentieth century."[27]

A bit later in commenting on the tensions

between aesthetic experience and scientific explanation he says, "What you've got here, really, are <u>two</u> realities, one of immediate artistic experience and one of underlying scientific explanation and they don't match and they don't really have much of anything to do with each other... You might say there's a little problem there."[28] At the intellectual level, Pirsig is conveying a feeling of the split between the rich immediate, personal, subjective experience of the human life-world which the phenomenologists insist we honor, and the mathematically rational way of structuring knowledge of the world of the positivist science tradition. In applying this to the problem of the nature and sources of technological ugliness Pirsig says "What's wrong with technology is that it's not connected in any real way with matters of the spirit and heart. And so it does blind, ugly things, quite by accident and gets hated for that."[29] He conveys one image of the ugliness in a scene familiar to all of us.

You go though a heavy industrial area of a large city and there it all is, the technology. In front of it are the high barbedwire fences, locked gates, signs saying NO TRESPASSING, and beyond, through sooty air, you see ugly strange shapes of metal and brick whose purpose you will never see. What it's for you don't know, and why it's there, there's no one to tell, and so all you can feel is alienated, strange as if you didn't belong there. Who runs and understands this doesn't want you around. All this technology has somehow made you a stranger in your own land."[30]

Pirsig captures the sense of technological ugliness in another way with his image of the bad motorcycle mechanic. He reports an incident where mechanics butcher the repair of his engine. As he seeks to understand why, he starts noting the features of life in the bad work place: (1)"The radio was playing loudly." He notes it is difficult to think hard about what you are doing while snapping fingers to the music. "Maybe they didn't see their job as having anything to do with hard thought, just wrench twiddling." (2) "Speed was another clue." They were slopping things around in a hurry - figuring they could get money that way, and (3) The big clue seemed to be in their expressions - good-natured, friendly, easy-going - and uninvolved. "They were like spectators...There was no identification with the job." - or

159

the machines. They were on the job, "they had something to do with it, but their own selves were outside
of it, detached, removed. They were involved in it
but not in such a way as to "care."[31]

They had never <u>appropriated</u> for themselves a
personal understanding of the functioning of the
machine - in terms of the interconnections of its
parts so that they could improvise creatively when the
manual or the tool kit did not yield a ready answer.

The bad mechanics were manual-bound, "right
answer" mechanics with a non involved "spectator" way
of being at work. Pirsig saw parallels between their
styles and the style of the technical manuals he had
written for a living.

> These were spectator manuals. It was built
> into the format of them. Implicit in every
> line is the idea that 'Here is the machine,
> isolated in time and in space from everything
> else in the universe. It has no relationship
> to you, you have no relationship to it, other
> than to turn certain switches, maintain
> voltage levels, check for error conditions...[32]

We are capable of technological ugliness and
bad maintenance. But Pirsig reminds us that we are
also capable of technological beauty.

He was haunted by a vision he had glimpsed one
morning while a soldier on an army transport ship in
Asia - a vision of a Korean wall "shining, radiantly,
like a gate of heaven, across a misty harbor." Since
the vision returned to him repeatedly he came to see
it as symbolizing something very important - an act of
technological beauty:

> It was beautiful, not because of any masterful
> intellectual planning or any scientific
> supervision of the job, or any added
> expenditures to 'stylize' it. It was beauti-
> ful because the people who worked on it had a
> way of looking at things that made them do it
> right unselfconsciously. They didn't separate
> themselves from the work in such a way as to
> do it wrong...Their way to solve the conflict
> between human values and technological needs
> is not to run away from technology. That's
> impossible. The way to resolve the conflict
> is to break down the barriers of dualistic
> thought that prevent a real understanding of
> what technology is - not an exploitation of
> nature, but a fusion of nature and the human
> spirit into a new kind of creation that
> transcends both. [33]

Pirsig's metaphors help us see that the one-sided truths of positivist science and technical management can lead to technological ugliness in educational practice - and to bad maintenance of "the motorcycles we call ourselves."

But we are destined to continue along that destructive road only if we ignore conditions which open the the possibility of "technological beauty." The Buddha, the Godhead, resides quite as comfortably in the circuits of a digital computer or the gears of a cycle transmission as he does at the top of a mountain or in the petals of a flower.[34]

NOTES

1. C.A. Bowers, "Emergent Ideological Characteristics of Educational Policy," Teachers College Record, (Vol. 79, No. 1, September, 1977), p. 50.

2. Rita Roth, Literacy acquisition, schooling and knowledge control. (unpublished Ph.D dissertation, Washington University, St. Louis, MO, 1982).

3. Alice M. Rivlin, Systematic Thinking for Social Action. (Washington, D.C.: The Brookings Institution, 1971), p. 3.

4. Bowers, op. cit., p. 53. (I am obligated to Bowers for helping me see the connections between technocratic ideology and positivist science.)

5. Karl Marx, Economic and Philosophical Manuscripts. (London: Lawrence and Wishart, Ltd., 1959 (tr.)), p. 25.

6. C.M. Bowra, The Greek Experience. (Cleveland: The World Publishing Co., 1957), pp. 198-199.

7. I have been influenced significantly by the work of James Palermo on phenomenology and critical theory. He, of course, is not responsible for my interpretations of his work. See James Palermo, "The Stagnation of Positivist Educational Theory: A Hermaneutical Critique," n.d. (1980?) (unpublished ms., State University College of New York at Buffalo). Also useful for an introductory summary: Richard J Bernstein, The Restructuring of Social and Political Theory. (Philadelphia: University of Pennsylvania Press, 1976), Part III "The Phenomenological Alternatives".

8. See Paul Ricoeur, "Ethics and Culture," and "The

Hermeneutical Function of Distantiation," <u>Philosophy Today</u>, (Vol. 18, Summer, 1973).

9.   Palermo op. cit., p. 21. (See also Brian Fay, <u>Social Theory and Practice</u>. (London: George Allen and Unwin, 1975).

10.   In Ernest R. House, "Evaluation as Scientific Management in U.S. School Reform," <u>Comparative Education Review</u>, (Vol. 22, No. 3, October, 1978), p. 396.

11.   Palermo, op. cit., p. 23.

12.   Trent Schroyer, "Marx and Habermas," <u>Continuum 8</u>, (Nos. 1 and 2, Spring-Summer 1970), p. 55.

13.   Ibid., p. 38.

14.   B.F. Skinner, <u>The Technology of Teaching</u>. (New York: Appleton-Century-Crofts, 1968), p. 9.

15.   Palermo, op. cit., p. 32.

16.   Rita Roth, op. cit., 1982.

17.   Marilyn Cohn, "Back to Basics: A Case Study of Student Learning" Unpublished, 1980. Washington University, St. Louis, MO.

18.   Ibid. In the account which follows I quote frequently Professor Cohn's research report.

19.   Ann Berlak and Harold Berlak, <u>Dilemmas of Schooling</u>. (New York: Methuen, 1981).

20.   C.A. Bowers, "Cultural literacy in developed countries," <u>Prospects</u>, (Vol. VIII, No. 3, 1977), pp. 323-335.

21.   Bowra, op. cit., p. 197.

22.   <u>St. Louis Post Dispatch</u>, July 27, 1981, p. 1.

23.   <u>St. Louis Post Dispatch</u>, August 2, 1981, Section 1-BB.

24.   John Dewey, <u>Democracy and Education</u>. (New York: MacMillan, 1916), pp. 415-416.

25.   John Dewey, "A Critical View of the U.S. Military establishment, <u>Forbes</u>, (May 26, 1980), p. 37.

26.   Ibid., p. 28.

27. Robert M. Pirsig, <u>Zen and the Art of Motorcycle</u>
<u>Maintenance</u>. (New York: Bantam Books, 1974), p. 27.

28. Ibid., p. 54.

29. Ibid., p. 162.

30. Ibid., p. 16.

31. Ibid., pp. 25-26.

32. Ibid., pp. 26-27.

33. Ibid., p. 284.

34. Ibid., p. 18.

CHAPTER VIII

TO UNDERSTAND IS TO INVENT:
SOCIO-TECHNICAL THEORY AND LEARNING
AT WORK AND IN SCHOOL

The basic principle of active methods will
have to draw its inspiration from the history
of science and may be expressed as follows:
to understand is to discover, or reconstruct
by rediscovery, and such conditions must be
complied with if in the future individuals are
to be formed who are capable of production and
creativity and not simply repetition.[1]
Jean Piaget

In this chapter we are going to explore how
challenges to the mainline efficiency tradition, by
democratic redesign of work theory, might be reflected
in changed ideas about learning - learning at work and
in school. More specifically we shall follow the
contention of work theorists such as Philip Herbst
that democratic socio-technical work changes will
require corresponding changes in the theory and
practice of school learning. Beyond that, in Chapter
IX, we shall examine Herbst's argument that the new
work redesign can become a "leading edge" for wider
social reform - reform toward a more conserving, human
"well-faring", post-industrial society.

Before entertaining such a seemingly far-
fetched idea, we might first confront a skeptical
perspective about the possibilities of such reform
within a capitalist economy. A tough-minded example
is Marxist criticism.

A. Reflections on the Marxist Perspective
Regarding School/Work Relations

The Marxist argument, in brief, is that schools
in capitalist societies reproduce in their structure
and functioning the social relations of capitalist
production. Marxist theory places the production
system of capitalism and class conflict at the center
of an explanation of school/work connections. It
holds that capitalist enterprises exact a surplus from
the labor power of workers in relation to their wages,
in order to expand capital. To be efficient and
maintain command, capitalists introduce a minute
division of labor combined with hierarchical-technical
control of the production process. The consequence is

that workers are deskilled and lose control of both the processes and products of their own work activity. They become alienated human beings.

In order to obtain worker acquiescence to the domination of the social relations of capitalist control, the schools have an important role to play. They reproduce the ideological beliefs and class differences which characterize capitalist production. They reproduce the division of labor in the minutely monitored and measured units of instruction; they teach the behaviors and attitudes of compliance, e.g., work hard to win approval of authorities, acquiesce to bureaucratic rules, depersonalized roles, etc. By differentiated certificates and curriculum statuses, the educational system sorts out potential workers and managers according to the class divisions of the society. In other words, Marxist analysis presents an image of a dominant capitalist class molding schools to reproduce exploitable labor for capitalist expansion, and to produce attitudes in the work force which will dampen tendencies towards working class discontents.

Henry Levin in an article "Education and Work" [2] (1983) points out, however, that the standard Marxist thesis about a complete correspondence between schools and work is an exaggeration which does not fit the complexities of American life. In asking why there is less correspondence between school and work than Marxist theory projects, he suggests another analysis. There is a tension between two social forces in U.S. democratic, capitalist society which helps explain the mixture of correspondence and lack of correspondence between work and school life. The state is seen as an arena for struggle between the needs of capital and of people who labor for capital.

The legitimacy of the state, which is subject to periodic democratic elections, is dependent on providing popular reforms, e.g., a fairer distribution of social services such as health care and social security for the elderly, unemployment compensation, etc. At the same time it creates policies to support the needs for private capital accumulation. An ongoing political struggle ensues between factions of both capital and labor to establish the outcome in the policies and actions of the state.

The schools, situated within the state, reflect the same contradictions: the need to meet demands for popular and egalitarian reforms, and the pressures of capital accumulation. The schools then "are in opposition to themselves in being organized to satisfy

166

the needs of two masters with conflicting goals."
They respond with "policies which represent an attempt
to meet the needs of both the democratic and egalitarian aspects of schooling and the authoritarianism
and hierarchical ones that are needed for reproducing
labor for capitalist firms." The result is the
creation of an autonomous dynamic for schools which
places them under the control of neither capital nor
labor. This order of complexity explains how the
schools in part correspond to the ideology and practices of capitalist work places, while they also are
"far more equal and provide more opportunities for
upward mobility than the work place."[3]

But another factor is at work which presses for
a new type of school/work correspondence. American
ideology holds that democratization of opportunity is
provided by access to public schooling which opens
possibilities of upward mobility: high educational
attainment can lead to higher income and social
status. The twentieth century, in fact, has seen an
impressive expansion of the school system aimed to
accommodate all aspirants. This accomplishment,
however, brings other consequences. It produces a
larger number of educated persons than the economy
provides jobs for and, as we saw earlier, a more
highly educated work force tends to be more resistant
to the authoritarian, fragmented social relations of
Taylorized work. The discontent of "overeducated
workers" poses potential disruption for productivity
and capital accumulation. Concern about the disruptive potential is leading to awareness of the need to
address disaffection in the work place. One response
is the move to increase worker participation by
various forms of work place democracy.[4]

In Levin's view, moves toward greater worker
participation and collective decision making could
have profound implications for schools. If the
emerging system of production requires more collaborative, problem-solving human interactions it, in turn,
could require school experiments with more liberalizing forms of learning for students and teachers.
The conditions begin to arise that call for a new
stage of work/school "correspondence."

B. New Work and Learning: The Case of High Technology

One test of whether there is evidence to
support the possibility sketched by Levin is to see if
it gets any confirmation from events on the frontiers

of new work, i.e. high technology production. There
are instances where such production supports the kind
of collaborative, problem-solving interactions Levin
speaks of. At the same time we need to guard against
self-delusion. The value contradictions of the
culture operate here as elsewhere and will be in
contention for the forseeable future.

We get a vivid sense of this in Larry
Hirschhorn's analysis of the situation in the high
technology nuclear power industry, with events at
Three Mile Island as an illustration.[5] There is a
growing awareness, Hirschhorn says, that cybernetic
technology cannot replace human work but leads to
workers, technicians and supervisors actually taking
on more complex roles. A basic reason is that inevitable failures of cybernetic processes built into
production require a higher order of coping responses.

In his analysis of events at the Three Mile
Island accident, Hirschhorn identifies a lesson we are
beginning to learn: "The more complex the machinery,
the more complex are the possible varieties of machine
failure. There are moments when only human intelligence can diagnose and correct unforeseen breakdowns.
To prevent catastrophes, machinery must be designed to
permit human intervention, and workers must be trained
as problem solvers, not merely machine tenders."[6]

At Three Mile Island there was a lack of
flexible response to the complicated set of events
which unfolded. Multiple failures included poor
maintenance, bad design of the console and the control
room, error of judgment and inappropriate training.
These "errors," says Hirschhorn, did not derive from
failures to operate a machine correctly, but reflected
a failure by the engineers and managers to design a
system that integrated effectively worker intelligence
and technical processes. Analysis of the situation
reveals basic contradictions resulting from a conflict
between old industrial mind-sets and the actual
demands of the new post-industrial production systems.

On the one hand, the philosophy and training of
engineers leads them to create designs based on the
ideal of the regularity and lawfulness of the solar
clock. In technical systems, "feedback" controls are
designed to cope with predictable errors and failures.
Workers are treated as extensions of the mechanical
system. The aspiration is to control their actions
through training programs and system design so that
their responses will be specific and predictable. On
the other hand, cybernation is a product of fallible
humans. It cannot eliminate errors and, in fact,

raises failures to new levels of complexity. Hirschhorn's analysis of the failures at Three Mile Island and on the abortive helicopter mission to Teheran, leads him to conclude that "workers in cybernated systems cannot function as passive machine tenders, looking to instruction manuals for the appropriate response. This suggests an entirely new definition of work in a post-industrial setting. Skills can no longer be defined in terms of a particular set of actions, but as general ability to understand how a system functions and to think flexibly in solving problems."[7]

In spite of this, Hirschhorn finds that the traditional mind set of engineers and managers makes them reluctant to help workers gain insight into system designs, or to train them to think conceptually beyond lists of responses to a series of anticipated problems. He found that training at nuclear plants is typically conducted by utility officials or vendors who sell training packages to companies. These trainers are technically competent but their courses are usually geared to the Nuclear Regulatory Commission's qualification examinations. The aim is to test competence on routine tasks and familiarity with specific emergency procedures. The aim is not to deepen workers' understanding of the physical, chemical and system features of the reactor process. The result is a kind of training which ignores requirements for the kind of expanded learning that would equip workers to cope with the unexpected.

Even while these mismatches between concepts of training and the new technology continue to happen, there is growing experimentation with alternatives. The general trend in cybernated industries is to locate workers in control rooms where they manage the manufacturing process from a distance. In the chemical industry, for example, continuous "batch processes" are controlled by micro-processor operations. While not subject to nuclear catastrophe possibilities, failures in the system can become a major cost of production. Workers must not only be prepared to respond to emergencies but be prepared to adjust when new machinery or new products are introduced. Hirschhorn points out that some manufacturers are recognizing the need to create designs that permit fruitful interactions between technology and human intelligence. Thus a Canadian plant, which manufactures the alcohol which has to be "customized" for use in a variety of things such as soaps, carpets, containers, etc., designed a computer process not simply

to automate production, but which supplied workers
with technical and economic data so they could solve
problems of customizing, and could test their own
production decisions. Workers who develop a facility
for experimental decision making become more knowledgeable and contribute to a constant upgrading of
the manufacturing process.[8]

Moves in these directions involve a fundamentally different conception of the interactions of
workers and machines. Hirschhorn points out that the
emerging logic of post-industrial work places tends to
leave both management and unions in a paradoxical
position.

Management, to operate and protect the new
machinery, needs highly trained workers, trained to
think independently; but its traditional interest in
control mandates a work force with limited skills and
aspirations. There is an uneasiness among some
utility owners, that moves toward autonomous work
teams with highly trained problem solving skills could
become threats to the basic prerogatives of management.

Other problems are posed for trade unionists.
Traditionally union solidarity has been secured by
emphasizing a class division between management and
workers. But this tradition is in conflict with the
professional character of work transformed by cybernated processes. In fact unions, to protect workers,
need to seek upgrading of competencies and broader
worker involvement in plant operation. They need to
assure workers' rights to understand the technology
which they use. Such moves, which recognize the
paraprofessional status of better-educated workers,
may further blur the increasingly unclear line between
workers and managers. There is fear among union
officials that this could lead to erosion of union
security. It could also lead, however, to new and
different opportunities. There is growing dissatis-
faction among engineers, middle managers and other
professionals who chafe at being under-utilized or in
being victimized by bureaucratic size and politics.
Imaginative unions might become a counterpoint to
represent all employees, workers and managers who are
seeking new perspectives and goals for work life.
They might assume leadership of an "oppositional
culture" aiming at a new integration of company goals
with protection of professional competence and needs
for professional growth.

Hirschhorn concludes:
The logic of the post-industrial workplace may

force a radically different conception of production work upon both managers and trade unions. Managers may be forced to share real power with their workforce, not for the conventional purpose of improving morale or smoothing industrial relations, but because technological exigencies and market pressures simply demand more knowledgeable, autonomous workers. The old-fashioned class politics of industrial society is giving way to a new post-industrial politics, in which representation of worker interests by trade unions will turn on a very different set of issues, such as education and access to information.[9]

We may note briefly that Hirschhorn's position receives confirmation by Louis Davis's studies of computerized continuous processing methods in the chemical industry. There is a growing recognition that success with the new cybernetic methods depends on planning with designs which include, jointly, the technical and the social systems.

Davis notes that when innovative technology replaces older methods, two significant changes take place: (1) changes in work roles, and (2) changes in the means of securing successful economic operation.

The new work roles call for skills in performing abstract activities and require self-initiated responses to stochastic, or randomly occurring, events. Such responses are usually non-programmed, non-scheduled ones that are drawn from a substantial repertoire of responses built up through experience and foresight....Successful continuous-process operation places a high premium on individual commitment to act when needed....Anticipating and responding to stochastic events and minimizing their effects leads to roles for workers as diagnosers, adjusters, and controllers of variances under stochastic conditions --in effect, as systems supervisors, a role that requires individual commitment and the ability to act when and how needed. In view of this high dependence on worker commitment a socio-technical system must include a design that will build such commitment.[10]

The growing concern is how to design interlocking technical and social structures that will support the learning needed for adapting to rapid and unexpected demands from the environment. Equally important to adaptability is the need for commitment. High

171

technology work processes cannot function with workers who are alienated or detached from the work. Socio-technical and related theory holds that commitment is dependent on the degree of autonomy and control given to people at work: "increased autonomy contributes to a worker's job satisfaction, sense of personal freedom and initiative, and self-esteem -- and this kind of self-investment tends to build a commitment to the job ..."[11] This way of viewing the task of work design is a far cry from the utopian vision of many engineers-that higher levels of technology would permit engineers to build "people-proof" systems that would free organizations from dealing with the imponderable complexities of human employees.

Operating from these assumptions, Davis says, new designers are beginning to believe that the worst approach is to try to impose bureaucratic, discrete, programmed ways of working. The alternative is to design social systems which give considerable scope of authority and freedom of action to those involved in the work. The key need is to maximize learning through the design of technology, and through the structuring of work units so that workers can learn to exert greater control over unpredictable variables. Instead of employees having fixed jobs, work teams are created in which employees have flexible work assignments to facilitate acquiring a wider range of knowledge and skills. Technology is designed to give team members feedback information needed to regulate the system, and computer programs provide information to operators so that they can "operate at any time in the context of evolutionary operations."[12] Reward systems are designed to pay people for acquiring knowledge and skill, related to the functioning of the whole system, rather than for performing specific assigned tasks.

We may remind ourselves that there are strong value orientations in the culture to resist the sharing of intelligence and control. The mechanistic, atomistic rationale of the natural sciences, upon which the training of engineers is based, inclines them to prefer the controls of "perfect clock" designs. Management ideology, which assumes the unchallenged rights of ownership and management to control the production system, is made uneasy by alternative conceptions. We should have no illusions that the mind set of the Taylorist tradition has disappeared. Work orientations related to it are still dominant and attempts can be made to design high technology work to de-skill even highly educated employees in order to exert technocratic control over

172

them. One study contends, for example, that computerized electronic switching (ESS) at A.T. and T. is being designed to de-skill and depersonalize work. Its potential for decentralizing work, so workers could use it to diagnose and solve problems, is undeveloped.[13]

We may recall Hackman and Oldham's appraisal in Work Redesign that high technology can be designed to follow either of two scenarios: "fitting humans to jobs," or "fitting jobs to humans." And Mike Cooley, author of Architect or Bee (1981) warns that computerization can be "Taylor's latest disguise." We shall return to the contradictory possibilities in the next chapter. We turn first, however, to how emerging democratic socio-technical theory relates to concepts of learning.

C. Socio-technical Theory and Concepts of Learning: Norwegian Theory and Practice as Pioneer Cases

In the previous section we reviewed qualities of human work required in emerging high technology organizations. We noted that they may turn to socio-technical theory as appropriate for the challenges they confront. While the work world in the immediate future will be split between scientific management and socio-technical modes, the latter theory clearly deserves serious attention by educators. In addition to offering features required by high technology it may also offer clues for securing "good work" in schools themselves.

If one seeks a literature on the implications of socio-technical theory for education, one finds very little. Energies so far have been focused on work itself. Since, however, "new work" places must support the learning of their members, the questions of what kind of learning, and eventually what kinds of schools for preparation, cannot be ignored.

While the literature is scarce, I shall pursue two lines of investigation. First I shall review the writings of Philip G. Herbst, associated with the Norwegian Work Research Institutes, who was a pioneer in "new work" theory. Then we shall explore ways in which Norwegian work sites themselves have become learning communities and how the work itself relates to the learning theory developed by Herbst. We shall note the effects on approaches to learning in the Norwegian schools with which these work places have associated. Finally we shall turn to some parallel developments in the U.S.A.

173

1. Philip B. Herbst on two models of school learning, the "production" model vs. the "research project" model

Philip Herbst was a charismatic leader in work redesign projects initiated by the Norwegian Work Research Institutes in the late sixties and early seventies. In his seminal Socio-technical Design: Strategies in Multidisciplinary Research, he devotes a chapter to the implications of new work structures for educational organizations.

Herbst assumes that constant technological and social innovation is the dominant reality with which institutions must cope. The need grows to create educational organizations which can equip persons to adapt to indeterminate change. Educational institutions themselves must respond to rapid growth in knowledge and shifts in expectations of their clienteles.

Herbst's premise is that the possibility for creating educational organizations appropriate for any era depends on the model used for structuring educational tasks. He makes a socio-didactic analysis of the basic assumptions that have been built into twentieth century schools and finds that educational tasks have been structured on a simple "production-process model" paralleling the Taylorist tradition in industry. In many ways schools have taken on the organizational features of the traditional factories. They have not yet responded to the learning characteristics of the emerging new work world.

To clarify his thesis, Herbst differentiates two fundamentally different types of work tasks: determinate tasks involving "production type learning" modes, and indeterminate tasks requiring "research type" learning modes.[14] Determinate tasks are those where every element is specifiable and the outcome is predictable. (The manufacture of Model T Fords would be an example.) Herbst creates a formula to identify this production-type task: $\mathcal{T}(S_1) \longrightarrow S_0$, where "a specific operation or method" ($\mathcal{T}$) is applied to an "initial situation" (S_1), to produce a "specified predictable outcome" (S_0). For example, to assemble auto parts (S_1) a controlled production line ($\mathcal{T}$) was used to produce the standard Model T Ford (S_0).

Indeterminate tasks are divided by Herbst into three varieties:
(a) One variety is indicated by the formula $?(S_1) \longrightarrow S_0$. There may be a given initial situation and a required outcome and the problem or unknown factor is

174

the means to use to get from the initial state to the outcome. For example, when the engine room of a ship (S_1') may need to be cleaned (S_0) the method (m) may be left undetermined ? if the crew is permitted to create its own task force which will take initiative in reaching the goal. In this case it becomes a research-type task. On the other hand, if the methods are prescribed in detail and executed under bureaucratic scrutiny, the work has remained as a production-type task.

(b) We may have a task where new material (S_1) is given and the problem becomes how can we use it? $?(S_1)$ $\longrightarrow$? For example, if a school gets a micro-computer, the staff might be brought into the thinking about what ends to use it for and how to use it.

(c) Finally there is the fully indeterminate task where no element can be specified at the outset ? (?) $\longrightarrow$? This is the type of task which increasingly emerges with advanced technology. For example, in the case of the Norwegian merchant marine, traditional ship organization was based on the production type model $(S_1) \longrightarrow S_0$. The standard ship was operated by top down control from the captain through the ship's officers to crew members each of whom had a specific rating which qualified for a specific task. But as changing computer-oriented technology transformed the nature of the ships, the old production type model increasingly became dysfunctional. New training programs could not be implemented before technological changes upset the planned design. The new type of ship required flexible, multiple-skill trained personnel who could identify the problems and form themselves into flexible autonomous matrix groups to help the ship perform its mission. Workers who participate in this kind of indeterminate work task are actively engaged in a learning process. In Herbst's words,

> Those who are involved in a process of change are required to be able to identify relevant characteristics of the existing situation and to discover potential directions of change towards the objective. The exploratory implementation of one or more alternative first steps of a change process is then evaluated to define new alternative options which only now become visible. It is in the process of change that the objective aimed at becomes more clearly structured and definable and the characteristics of what was the initial situation become more clearly defined.[15]

We can understand why the socio-technical work

theorists repeatedly refer to Jean Piaget's To Understand is To Invent. Those who are at work in fully indeterminate type tasks (?(?) ⟶ (?)) cannot be people who know only the discrete steps of a manual or work book. They have to understand the whole system by recreating it. Then they may know it in terms of its holistic interrelations. To facilitate change they have to be able to generate and convey ideas, and hear the ideas of others, and identify working plans to meet problems.

2. Socio-technical influences on educational practice

As Norwegians on the ship Balao began to work more and more in the "indeterminate research learning" style rather than the traditional "production task" mode, they discovered they had to turn attention to the schools which were training personnel for the merchant marine. They found that the schools and teachers who were not in touch with the new developments were becoming isolated from maritime reality. The younger personnel were losing respect for out-of-date teachers and programs. A decision was made to bring teachers aboard the ships. Teachers were integrated into the work process itself which gave them a sense of being on the frontiers of learning and enabled them to communicate as equals with ship's personnel who were working in the autonomous, matrix, task force mode. Teachers, however, also taught classes in their specialized skill areas which were valued as components of an integrated training program. When teachers returned to their schools on shore they began to introduce problem-oriented projects consistent with the emerging learning style they had seen on ships.

Later I was able to visit a secondary school in Stavanger which was pointed out to me by the merchant marine researchers as a place exemplifying moves in the new direction. The Jonas Øegland plant produces bicycles and industrial robots among other products. It has moved in the direction of shop floor democracy with autonomous work group teams. After management and the union made a commitment to the idea of worker involvement, planning groups were initiated in collaboration with people from the Oslo Work Research Institute. As Einar Thorsrud, a consultant, put it, Øegland is one of the initial companies "developing their work organization in the way so many will have to do in the future. Their great advantage is that they have no fixed concept of what they want. This

176

enables them to operate in free waters. The workers evolve their own systems and share the problem-solving in a step-by-step development."[16]

I saw one assembly line area where the workers, with managers acting as guides and counselors, developed plans to break up the traditional line. We do not need the details here but the team-work modes of producing the bicycles and controlling quality turned this lagging department into one of the most efficient in the plant.

I then visited the Gand Viderengaende Skole in Stavanger, a secondary school which has established experimental working relations with the Øegland Plant. I observed classes in electronics where students were working on project problems which had been identified in consultation with factory work groups. For example, several students were working on a problem from the industrial robot division. There was a problem in measuring the range of movements of the robot. When the solution was taken back to the plant, it didn't work. The teacher said he and the students then became aware that in talking with the production team the first time, they had not had a precise understanding of the problem. So they got back into the situation and were making another try at it.

The teacher expressed both satisfaction and anxiety about the new style of teaching. He was impressed by the creativity and involvement of the students. But he felt considerable pressure to invest time in study "to keep up". He was uneasy about the time required for project study methods which made students innovative, but which did not seem to leave time for systematic instruction in micro-processor theory and similar knowledge he believed necessary. It is important to recognize that risks are taken in making changes and that reflection on the problems of change is a form of learning that must accompany the change process. The Director of the school explained, however, that the general idea was receiving support in that it was being incorporated in an extended form in plans for a new school. The basic socio-technical model was being built into aspects of the third year program as follows:

A school steering group is being composed of elected pupils and teachers and representatives of work groups from industry. The steering committee will allocate study projects into several courses of study:

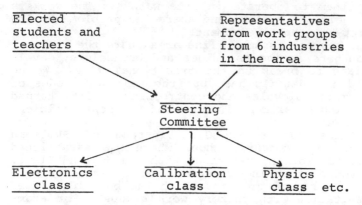

Beyond this, the Director explained that Norwegian Education officials and representatives of collaborating industries are developing a plan for a post-graduate thesis program which can be completed by people who have entered industry. A practical or theoretical industrial problem will be identified by a candidate. His plan for thesis research will be placed under the supervision of the head of the appropriate department, for example, a department of professional engineers; and there will be consultation with appropriate personnel in the University. If the thesis is well executed, the candidate will be assisted in entering advanced training in a University.

The Director saw these developments as giving continued encouragement to students who learn to like problem-solving, research-type learning. They will be able to continue on-going, research-oriented projects when they enter industry after secondary education. He said industry begins to take on more of the quality of a learning experience for both workers and managers and moves a step in the ideal direction advocated by Philip Herbst where "everyone ought to be a researcher".

A basic point in Herbst's socio-didactic analysis is that the way school tasks are structured affects all aspects of the dynamics of school life. The basic distinction is between production-type tasks and research project-type tasks. He quotes the findings of a Dutch researcher, J. Roggema (1969) who showed that students spot with high consistency the difference between "schoolish" and "non-schoolish" teachers. In describing this research, Herbst says,

> The schoolish teacher splits his subject into small isolated bits, which have to be worked

on and learnt one at a time. Students are
required to follow rigid instructions. The
performance of students, both in terms of
following instructions and in terms of the
results obtained, is judged simply as right or
wrong. The teacher claims complete autonomy
for himself as an expert, while allowing
little or no autonomy to his pupils. Subjects
that especially lend themselves to being
taught in this manner are mathematics and
foreign languages. A machine teaching pro-
gramme is an extreme example of this type of
teaching technique.
Non-schoolish teachers give their students
autonomy to investigate, discuss, and find out
for themselves. The teacher defines his role
as a resource person for the activities of his
students. The teaching is problem-oriented.
Where drill is needed, the purpose and meaning
are explained. Judgement of performance is
not simply in terms of right or wrong, but in
terms of the development of increased ability,
competence, and independence. [17]

An important finding in Roggema's study was
that any subject can be taught either way. The way
that educational tasks are structured has significant
effects on both the type of relations between students
and teachers, and the appropriate criteria for performance evaluation.

On the basis of his analyses, Herbst sees
growing discrepancies between the type of task definitions in schools, and the task definitions in industries under turbulent change. Secondary schools
typically are organized around separate subjects. The
research problem-oriented tasks of higher technology
industry do not split up the field of knowledge in the
same way as the school subjects, and they require a
type of organization based on cooperation rather than
on competition. "Many types of problems encountered
on the shop floor, in a hospital, or in a family
require an understanding of social-psychological,
economic, technological, and political aspects and
their inter-relationships." [18]

The "schoolish" teacher aims to have his
students follow instructions and to perform precisely
a predetermined program. Original ideas of students
are seen as non-compliant behavior, so curious students are often forced to choose between being passive
or being seen as rebellious. This type of school
organization fulfilled its function to produce persons

179

who were attached to traditional production processes and who were to subordinate themselves to the control of managerial authority. It also often produced alienation from school tasks. Resort to external rewards or punishments and competitive arrangements are major means of keeping the system functioning. Industries themselves now have to become capable of "learning" to meet change. In order for students to be adequately prepared for entrance to such places the young should learn in schools which also are capable of "learning as institutions". Ironically, many schools whose programs are rigidly prescribed by centralized authority have less capacity for "learning" than some of the newer work places. Teachers and administrators are worn out by keeping the system running, by being made subordinate to prescriptions of external authorities, and by having to keep tab on reluctant charges.

Herbst calls then for more autonomy for individual schools with meaningful roles for some representative committees like the Steering Committee of the Viderengaende Skole in Stavanger. Centralized boards of education would still have system-wide responsibilities but their consultative, facilitative roles would rise sharply in importance and their prescriptive, control functions would diminish. Pride would be taken in fostering schools skilled in getting students and teachers involved in personal learnings which relate to the changing social reality.

In Herbst's view this does not mean that all "schoolish" type teaching is bad. There are needs for systematic specialized learning experiences. One of the avenues to be explored seriously in the eighties will be to see how many of these can be programmed into computer-assisted instruction. That "technical" dimension is a necessary complement to the "research-project, non-schoolish methods" which now need to be expanded. For example, at the university level, Herbst sees retention of academic specialties as well as interdisciplinary research projects which might be expanded also into post-university polytechnical centers. [19]

One of Herbst's colleagues, Dr. Max Elden, Director of the Institute for Social Research at Norwegian Technical University, at Trondheim, Norway has described how researchers' own concept of the nature of research was affected by democratic work philosophy. In an article, "Sharing the Research Work"[20] Elden points out that when socio-technical research began in the 1960s, the researchers were

heavily involved in making diagnoses of problems, and
actively engaged in suggesting ideas for changes in
work. By the 1970s, theorists like Herbst and
Thorsrud became aware that they could be building
contradictions into well-intentioned efforts. The
goal was to help employees acquire self-sustaining
learning so they could initiate change. The process
could be impeded by heavy initiatives taken by "socio-
technical experts - in-charge - of change."
     Elden describes what happened to researchers
like himself when they asked, "How can we support the
kind of learning people need in order to take charge
of their own work places?" He describes with candor,
anxieties he experienced in shifting from his academic
research training to techniques of shared participative research. He describes how he helped workers in
a Norwegian bank learn to define their own problems,
decide on research strategies, and decide how they
wanted to make use of his expertise. He notes his
uneasiness about losing his authority as administrator
of research as the bank employees formed autonomous
work groups which took their own active initiatives.
He learned that people at work could, indeed, conduct
investigations that led to effective results. He
learned also that they welcomed his assistance when he
was willing to make contributions meaningful to them
in their own terms. They insisted, for example, that
problems and conclusions be stated in words they
understood. The result was that the research report,
which was received by the work force with avid interest, was written jointly by two bank employees and Dr.
Elden. The research process itself became an experience in new learning.

3. Communities of learners to free intelligence for good work

     Herbst's analysis suggests that both work and
schools which are being transformed by knowledge
and/or technology have to become "institutions capable
of learning". The socio-technical critics challenge
the orthodox management assumption that that can be
accomplished through more controls by technical
experts over a pliable work force. From the socio-
technical perspective, workers at the site have to be
learners and participants. It is relevant to consider
what is required to make this possible. More is
needed than personnel who have been injected with
useful information. They have to come to perceive
themselves as thinkers and doers - which can best

181

happen when they are learners - in a community in which the habits of growing in conceptual insight, and in habits of collaborative problem solving become a way of living.

Herbst's analysis points in that direction, but I believe significant dimensions can be added by recalling aspects of Dewey's thinking. There are parallels, of course, between Herbst's view of effective learning for our time and Dewey's analysis of the reflective, problem-oriented modes of scientific inquiry, as models for "the freeing of intelligence". We may recall that Dewey in following the model of science was led to design his school as a "community of learners" for teachers as well as students. This derived from his idea that to secure reflective thinking (i.e., "research project-type" learning) several conditions needed to be created to nurture the process: (1) a quality of community respectful of individuality which is the source of creative, aberrant ideas and (2) dialogue as the critical mode of communication. In Dewey's words, "The final actuality is accomplished in face-to-face relationships by means of direct give and take. Logic," he said, "in its fulfillment recurs to the primitive sense of the word: <u>dialogue</u> in which ideas are communicated, shared, and reborn in expression." 21

As I had the opportunity over several years to observe and conduct interviews in situations where work and learning were being redesigned in "the socio-technical" direction, I became aware that differences beyond specific techniques were involved. The gestalts were different.

I am suggesting that the goal of getting "good work" in industry or school requires more than a technical restructuring of behavior - even more than assigning "problems" instead of "production tasks". It requires, I believe, going beyond the habit of seeing people in terms of their "behaviors". It requires helping people get in touch with the full range of their powers as whole persons: the power to see what is there, to project ideas, to risk confrontation, to express trust and anger and fear, to gain insight into personal and institutional histories and their effects, to act to make reasoned change. To move this way requires building "communities of learners" marked by respect for individuality and dialogue.

There are instances from both my experiences in Norway and the U.S.A. which lead me to be confident about that assertion. For example, on the ship Balao, researchers report that after several years of moving toward organizing work around autonomous, matrix groups and defining tasks through ship-wide planning, "the entire ship's community is strongly characterized by learning."[22] They are now seeing this as a result of a complex shift in dynamics from an older work structure which fostered isolation to the creation of a ship's community with rich interactions.

The ship's captain, for example, expressed relief at being released from a state of isolation from the crew which formerly was considered necessary to maintain crew discipline. As the whole ship became more technical and the crew was mastering new conceptual and skill competencies, the captain, in the new pattern of dining with the crew, had a chance to be part of the talk about technical changes and problems. Also, he expressed satisfaction in getting to know the crew as persons, learning about a crewman's problems with a new wife, learning about pop music culture, etc. He himself learned to play the hand organ and could become part of ship recreational life. Instead of having to concentrate mainly on control and discipline, he said, "I now see that I need these people." At the same time his leadership was needed. Could he gain acceptance of his authority and maintain effectiveness by leading in a new way?

Once it was recognized that the ship's organization had to support the learning of everyone, the total ship's life gradually was transformed. Physical quarters on new ships acquired equality of provisions, with each cabin having its own air conditioning, desk and shelf space and access to the library and conference room. Study groups were formed not only for technical matters but for social-cultural topics. The new ship structure made it possible for people to do things together in ways that cut across old barriers such as the separation of engine and deck crews. A ship's committee was formed to consider ways of improving recreational-cultural life. Passive activities like watching movies gave way to activities where people constructed or worked on things together.

The researchers were told by trade union officials that in union conferences, seafarers from ships like the Balao stood up more frequently to say something, and argued points more effectively. The researchers also found evidence of less tension in family life and more involvement in community activities on shore.

It would be a disservice to portray ships like the Balao as problem-free utopias. The range of human

183

stresses and weaknesses still have to be dealt with. As noted previously, however, the basic commitment is to the new ways. The reality test is that the Norwegian merchant marine is more than holding its own in international competition.

Beyond that, there is the suggestion in the Norwegian experience that once you help people get in touch with their powers to learn, spill-over effects begin to happen. There seems to be less willingness to let learning be confined to the limits of pre-scribed programs. Something happens when an "ordinary person" gets the experience that" I have words to say about the world," and "I will be attended to." The exchange of ideas, and the experience of helping to create solutions to daily problems are experienced as satisfying. When they feel so empowered, their learning capacities express themselves in multidimen-sional, unpredictable ways. It is not too far-fetched to say that they begin to sense an ethical right to have access to such experiences and even the right to have the aesthetic experience of bringing unclear events to satisfying, consummatory resolutions (Dewey's way of portraying the essence of the aesthe-tic dimension of experience.)

In any case, the decision to bring everyone into learning seemed to transform the nature of the ship community, and that is worthy of serious reflec-tion. It contributed to produce the autonomy and commitment required in the emerging world of work.

An interesting phenomenon for educational policy makers to note is that work places which survive by moves toward socio-technical design begin to take on features of the liberalizing ideal. They introduce features of communities designed to help people experience a wider range of their powers and to put those powers to work - and this often from those who had only been silent and disregarded. It would be ludicrous to push the idea too far. It seems clear, however, that the newer work places do not suggest that schools define themselves merely as "production functions" which process students through narrowly functional instructional programs.

Work places that "work" (including schools) may, more and more, have to nurture learning in the Deweyan sense of "freeing intelligence". We have to start creating continuity of experiences in schools and work communities which support that kind of learning.

The Norway example illustrates that: (1) when people start down the democratic socio-technical road, questions about the nature of learning and schooling tend to be raised. (2) If "new work" requires the empowering of people to learn reflectively and to act based on that learning (features of the liberalizing ideal), then continuities are needed between "new work" and schooling. The notion arises that the kind of learning that needs to be supported in both institutions is the liberal "freeing of intelligence" type learning. (3) The strange hypothesis emerges that if we seek ideas about how to make schools centers of liberalizing learning, we might turn to these new work places for useful clues. The question of what conditions support the freeing of intelligence (or what thwarts it) can be pursued productively both within schools as work places and within work places themselves.

D. The Socio-technical Idea and Learning in the United States

Is there anything in the American experience which adds to Norwegian thinking about work/education relations? I have had the opportunity to visit situations where socio-technical type work redesign is in practice in this country. In the United States, questions about linkages between "new work" and education have scarcely been raised. But if we follow the hypothesis that one can gain insights about conditions for freeing intelligence by looking at work place democracy, then I believe we can advance our understanding. I offer several examples as instructive.

In brief contact with the Harman International Industries plant, in Bolivar, Tennessee, and its researchers I noted that changes in work and changes in attitudes about learning went hand in hand. In this auto-mirror manufacturing plant in southern Tennessee the work force was not highly educated - many had not finished high school. But there were indications that people were gaining a sense that they could learn what they wanted to learn and they were enjoying it. It radiated from the work sites to the larger life of the plant. It made a difference in morale and quality of work accomplished.

For illustration I cite the worker-managed Harman Mirror referred to earlier in Chapter III.[23] The June 1979 issue describes an employee counseling program for alcohol and drug dependency problems:

Several months ago a group of people got together because of a mutual concern for the

well-being of people in this plant. They
wanted to find out what they could do to help
those who were having difficuly helping
themselves....The members of the task force
committed themselves to studying similar
programs which other industries had put
together. We wanted to come up with something
which would be uniquely ours...rather than
just copying what someone else had done. A
group of the task force even took a trip to
Tarrytown, New York to examine a similar
program first-hand.

The _Mirror_ then submitted the policy statement
(stressing confidentiality) which came out of months
of planning, and described a training program for
worker-counselors that had been set up for 40 supervisory people and 32 shop stewards which was to be
expanded for other people in the plant.

Another article was headed "Things You Always
Wanted to Learn But Didn't Have the Opportunity":

At Harman International in Bolivar that
opportunity is a way of life. We have a
school here that is based on the idea that
what an employee wants to know is of sufficient importance that he/she should be given
the opportunity to learn it. Classes are
constructed for employees and are taught by
other employees who have some expertise in the
subject area. Sometimes employees agree to
teach a class that they don't know anything
about. But they are willing to learn about
the material in such a way that they can
become facilitators in the education process.

The article then mentions Mike Bass, a material
handler at the assembly plant who teaches a class
after work, in drawing. Students range in age from 10
to 50 and typically say, "I didn't think I could draw
a straight line. Look at my picture." Mike, they
say, teaches people to be excited about their lives
and to be interested in new challenges. Other vi-
gnettes include a picture of a black worker, driving
his tow motor, who had just completed a course on how
to repair the truck he had merely been the driver of
before. A shop steward is shown teaching others to
play the mountain dulcimer which he had built.

These events suggest that when a person starts
being treated as a person instead of as a hired hand
an important shift occurs: a shift from being a
passive instrument to being an active learner. At
Harman this was accompanied by the emergence of a

community that supported desires to learn. When these conditions are created, beginnings can be made toward realizing a part of E.F. Schumacher's description of the function of "good work", i.e., to give a person a chance "to utilize and develop his faculties; to enable him to overcome his ego-centeredness by joining with others in a common task."[24] People formerly treated as "nobodies" with "nothing to say" began perceiving themselves as learners, even within the severe restraints of factory production.

The Harman experience, while taking place in a non-high technology setting, replicates in part the Balao experience. When people are given an opportunity to think and participate in a climate of trust and shared responsibility - unanticipated capacities for individual and group learning emerge. Both the work and the persons benefit.

The key qualities of democratic communities, respect for individuality and dialogue, assist the liberating of intelligence. They are related to another dimension of the liberal ideal, i.e., that free persons have the ability to act, to enhance well-being. This, in turn, requires the capacity to gain insight about past history that was destructive and the will to generate alternatives.

I saw evidence of such learning in talking with U.A.W. members and their management counterparts who were engaging in "employee participation groups" (EPG's) in giant auto plants in Flint and Detroit - a development related to Quality of Work Life (QWL) efforts.[25] Motivated by a sense of crisis over the possibility of plant closings, these were people engaged in the scary process of frank union/management talk about the relations of quality of production and quality of work life. There was a combination of healthy skepticism and a heady sense of discovery in their venturings.

I want to make clear that I am reporting on interviews with union and management participants who are not starry-eyed, true-believer zealots. They are people who are feeling their way into a new style of work, which seems like a better bet. I heard comments from managers like, "We are leery of Quality of Work Life (QWL) lingo." A union man added, "We want to create our own terms." A management person said, "QWL sometimes seems murky. We don't know how to do it. We want to know where we can learn." But I heard also comments like, "It's the best thing that ever happened around here."

Repeatedly I was given accounts of "how it used

187

to be" and "why we moved to QWL." I was told about
the deep suspicions at the beginning stages - suspicions that are still strong among many workers and
managers. Union people in Flint pointed out to me a
huge 250 pound man who had told the management representatives at the first QWL workshop, "I don't trust
you, and I don't trust these union guys who are
jumping into bed with you. But I am willing to try
this workshop because you are paying me for time off
to be here. I'll pay attention. But if I catch you
s.o.b.'s lying or conning me, I'm walking out." He
stayed, they said, and hasn't missed an EPG meeting
since. "He seemed to have a hunger for something that
was happening in his group."

At this plant in Flint I had a meeting with the
production manager, union and management representatives, and EPG "facilitators" from the U.A.W. and
management. The production manager said, "You have to
understand the history we come from. Foremen in the
auto industry were part of a tradition to exert
authority forcefully. Once we "wore a tie", we became
managment. We had to show we were the boss. We had
to know the answers - know how to yell at them. We
had authority and our job was to exercise it."

On hearing this, I mentioned comments I used to
hear in the neighborhood I grew up in. When a man
became foreman he would say with pride, "I got six men
under me," and if it went well, "Now I got twenty men
under me." One manager commented, "Ok, that says it
all. That is our history as managers in the auto
industry."

Union and management representatives at a
second plant confirmed this tradition of management/
union relations. Here I talked at length with two men
(one "union", the other "management") who now jointly
conduct QWL workshops from which Employee Participation Groups get started if workers request them. This
time the union man did most of the talking. His
language reflected the violence of assembly line work.
Tim (union) and Bob (management) agreed that they
could not have been seen walking through the plant
together three years before. Tim said, "This plant
was going down the tubes and we all knew it. Absenteeism was high, we had one of the worst quality
records. At one time we had a backlog of 7000 grievance procedures. Three to four hundred people would
be working 'under penalty' at any one time. Flash
strikes were frequent. It was hell. Each side was
out to screw the other."

After production of a major unit was shifted to

a plant in another state, management came to the union and said, "The hand-writing is on the wall. We're done unless we can turn it around." As part of a last-ditch effort they asked for union volunteers to visit the Tarrytown plant. At Tarrytown the volunteers sensed immediately a different climate. The hate and the violence were missing. They learned about the QWL idea and some union volunteers reluctantly agreed to go to a week-long seminar to get checked out on the idea as well as communications skills, conflict resolution skills, etc.

Tim said, "Frankly, I thought it was b.s. but I would go for the ride since they were paying me. My union President said, 'Give me a report on whether or not we should go along with these guys.' I was skeptical of all these personnel people, but as it went on I saw they were talking to me as a person - not as an arm or a leg, and I began to realize we had some of the same fears."

After the seminar, the Union President asked, "Well, are they out to screw us again?" Tim said, "I knew I was out on a limb - a lot of guys were ready to say that I had jumped in bed with management. But I told him, 'This is what we need.'"

Both Tim and Bob recalled their great fear when they were ready to start their first QWL workshop. After a rough beginning, with some hard names tossed at Tim, it went well. Now Tim and Bob are in their second year of running workshops. They have seven EPG's* in action and QWL style has begun to operate. "We have the best QWL Workshops anywhere," Tim said. Bob's comment was, "And that is from the guy who four years ago we saw as one of the meanest union s.o.b.'s in the plant. We hoped he would get hit crossing the street to work."

When I asked what kinds of changes were happening Bob said, "We tell the guys on the line in effect, 'You are the experts on this. We will listen to you.

---

* They told me eventually they could see as many as 50 EPG groups. They were, however, resisting management's urging to expand more quickly. "We need to understand what we are doing and learn as we go along," they said, "and we want to adhere strictly to the principle that no EPG group gets started unless a request comes from the shop floor. Guys are beginning to trust the idea when they see it as something they can use for what is important to them. If we lose that by expanding too soon, we lose the ball game. It will be junked as one more gimmick."

189

We want input from you.'" The plant is functioning
again. The trend is to "try to get decision making
made as low as possible." In newer plants the goal is
to design production to give the people at the work
site immediate computer feedback on the quality of
their product. If someone "screws up," the new
attitude is, "Let's see if we can figure it out and
get it together better next time. If a whole section
does well, we might have a steak dinner. We still may
fire people and use grievance procedures but the whole
atmosphere is different - and we do good work."

This fragment is a pale reflection of the range
of feelings and talk I experienced with a variety of
people in the QWL settings. To me, though, it illustrates growth in the value choice dimension of learning. When conditions are created which free people
from isolation and atomization and enable them to
confront what is problematic in their lives, they may
gain insight through talk, study and reflection on
what is happening to them. They may generate ideas
for alternative actions and weigh the results. They
become acting agents instead of passive objects.

I have tried to make clear the skepticism about
the QWL idea that exists alongside the endorsement of
it by some who see it as a better way to work and
live. Among those drawn to its support, there is a
note of pathos in their recognition that "it could
become another gimmick if the big shots try to make
their reputations off of it." One point is clear, the
new moves never could have happened if the historical
management model of one-way, top-down talk and control
had prevailed.

While in Flint, I also had a look at U.A.W.
participation in a project that provided a glimpse of
how QWL thinking might affect education.

In the fall of 1981 I visited a newly instituted secondary school program in Flint, Michigan - a
Pre-Employment Center where secondary school students
are given a variety of orientations to work experiences. Flint is dominated by the auto industry, so
orientation to present reality and future trends are
included. Instruction is given by people who have
experienced industry changes - the shifts from manual
work to more automated processes with computer-
assisted quality control, the emergence of work units
requiring people working together, etc.

The United Auto Workers Union provides instructors for part of the program which includes the
history of unions and the quality of work life idea.[26]
In order to orient students to the newer work styles,

union instructors developed exercises in which teams of students were given tasks such as disassembling the steering mechanism, or the front end of a car and then figuring out as a group how to re-assemble it. They had to plan strategies for both disassembly and assembly. They were given practice in quality evaluation and compared their efforts with those of other student teams. Students were then taken to the plants to see the relation of the section they had assembled to the total process of producing the car.

In this rudimentary example we may see the tendency of the socio-technical rationale to pull concepts of learning toward the "research project-type" model.

E. Good work at school

We have seen how democratic work place reform supports a style of learning that is alternative to the "production process" model. We end this chapter by looking at examples of how socio-technical work theory might relate to work in schools. It is appropriate to put such an exploration in juxtaposition to examples of the technocratic approach to teaching described in Chapters VI and VII.

In looking for examples of what meaning the democratic work place ideal might have for work at school, I had no difficulty finding ideas that are congruent because just as some American teachers are drawn to the efficiency control values, others feel the need to resist them. I shall describe two examples of such resistance: first an example about one teacher's ideas about classroom work for children; and another about the school as a work place for teachers.

1. Learning to read.

In the last chapter we saw examples of the teaching of the 3 R's that reflected the influence of the rational efficiency ideology. In this chapter I present ideas of a black teacher about teaching "the basics" to black students - ideas which grew out of her resistance to the efficiency control approach.

She had read Herbst and others about democratic work. In her search for a pedagogical equivalent she turned to the ideas of Paulo Freire for the teaching of reading or literacy. She saw Herbst and Freire sharing a common desire to create more liberating practices of "work" as alternative to paternalistic, hierarchical control models.

Before looking at her ideas for classroom work, we turn first to some features of Freire's ideas which provided the background for the teaching strategies she adopted. Freire deals with pedagogical questions more specifically than Herbst and in more philosophical depth. It is worthwhile to examine Freire's position at some length even though he writes about a dissimilar Brazilian culture and speaks about teaching reading to illiterate peasants rather than to children. Freire helps us see how contrasting approaches to teaching relate to our prospects as human beings: teaching can provide an "education for the practice of freedom", or it can "anaesthetize" - at its worst, reduce persons to the passive condition of "the culture of silence".

Paulo Freire was coordinator of the National Literacy Program of the Ministry of Education in Brazil during the administration of President Goulart until the military coup of 1964.

Our quest is to seek insights from Freire's efforts to identify educational practices which liberate the learning of peasants instead of causing them to passively retreat into "the culture of silence" which immobilizes them. We hope to find clues in his ideas for teaching literacy which will help us identify features of classrooms marked by good work.

It will be useful to compare Freire's ideas with the "back to basics" approach of Forest Hills teachers which we examined in the last chapter. Their approach was the "production process" variety described by Herbst as "determinate work tasks" where every element is specifiable and the outcome is predictable. In Freire's work we shall find this described variously as verbalist, monologic, "false" education, as contrasted with problem-posing, dialogical, "education for the practice of freedom".

Freire's conception of good education is rooted in his basic image of what it means to be a human being - "a human being face to face with the world... <u>in</u> it, <u>with</u> it as a being who works, acts and transforms the world." [27] Humans are marked off from animals by their distinctive capacity to employ language to understand, act on, and transform the world. Therefore the way one learns to read - learns literacy - has fundamental consequences for what s/he can become in the world. Learning to read is a social event - it must be learned from and with others. There is a basic issue for either children or illiterate peasants learning to read. Either they will experience the process of learning literacy in a way

192

which puts them in touch with their power to be makers and agents of action; or they will experience learning to read as a matter of giving a correct performance for the teacher-expert. They become "domesticated" right response givers.

Whatever Freire writes on, including the teaching of literacy, his core frame of reference in defining choices is whether a policy supports or thwarts the primary vocation of "becoming more fully human". Further clarity about his ideas of what it is to be human is essential to understanding his work.

To be human first of all is to be in interaction with the world of nature - and with other humans. It is to experience that world as an objective reality capable of being known - while animals, cut off from that possibility, can only make contact with it. Man's active, knowing relationship with the world frees him from being limited to a single reaction pattern. Through communication/language, humans organize themselves, choose and test responses, and change the world and themselves. Through language, humans relate to the world with critical awareness which makes choice possible - instead of the reflex actions of animals. Through critical perception, they are aware not only of nature but of the accumulated learnings of culture and of their histories - "they reach back to yesterday, recognize today, and come upon tomorrow."

The quality of the way humans relate to the emerging context is vitally signficant for life possibilities open to them. "To be more fully human" means to have a relation of integration as opposed to adaptation. Integration results from the capacity to adapt oneself to reality plus the critical capacity to make choices and to transform that reality.[28] When we lose our ability to make choices and are subjected to the choices of others; when decisions are no longer our own because they are imposed by external prescriptions, we are no longer integrated. We have "adjusted" or "adapted". We have become objects instead of integrated active, human subjects.

Humans as integrated subjects respond to the challenges of the environment and humanize it. They, in collaboration with their fellows, add something to it of their own making. They can develop awareness of the critical themes and issues of their times and project solutions to problems which enable them to live as integrated subjects. As such they constantly alter reality by the way they are at work in it. Without such active critical awareness and participa-

193

tion, they can become mere onlookers manipulated by events or by those who impose solutions for purposes of domination and control. As disempowered "objects", they may feel "crushed, diminished, converted into spectators, maneuvered by myths which powerful forces have created....Tragically frightened, men fear authentic relationships and even doubt the possibility of their existence."[29]

Freire applied his analysis to the kind of teaching he saw illiterate Brazilian peasants receiving from the agricultural experts. Having been habituated by their historical experience under paternalistic feudalism to perceiving themselves as objects, he saw them failing to respond to teaching by experts about scientifically enlightened agriculture.

In reflecting on these failures in both teaching about agriculture and in the teaching of reading, he distinguished between the teaching methods of monologue and dialogue - dialogue secured good work in farm and school - monologue failed.

Freire's message about how to get good work in schools centers on his distinction between the two methods of teaching. When Freire confronts the questions of when education can become a liberating experience to help humans get on with their primary vocation, he speaks of it as "education for the practice of freedom" and contrasts it with education as "a form of technical aid or assistance".

"Education for the practice of freedom" must be a form of teaching/learning which is freeing for the teacher as well as the student. In teaching as technical aid, the assumption is made that knowledge is something that the teacher has acquired like an object that can be given out, handed over - as something to be received by the recipient as completed, finished. This is the one-way process of transmission by monologue or "verbalizing". The student, treated as a depository, is transformed into a "thing".[30] Education that liberates, by contrast, involves an on-going relation between teacher and student both of whom are subjects and in which the educator "permanently reconstructs the act of knowing".[31]

In seeking to clarify the differences, Freire distinguishes between knowing as an element in a process of "depositing", and the act of knowing in which teacher and students are active partners in the creating of knowledge.

> Knowing, whatever its level, is not the act by which an object docilely and passively accepts the contents others give or impose on him or

her. Knowledge, on the contrary, necessitates the curious presence of subjects confronted with the world. It requires their transforming action on reality. It demands a constant searching. It implies invention and re-invention....In the learning process the only person who really <u>learns</u> is s/he who appropriates what is learned, who apprehends and thereby re-invents that learning; s/he who is able to apply the appropriate learning to concrete existential situations. On the other hand, the person who is filled by another with 'contents' whose meaning s/he is not aware of, which contradict his or her way of being in the world, cannot learn because s/he is not challenged. [32]

A learning situation where teachers and students are jointly engaged in a problem-posing situation is one where "how" and "why" questions take precedence over "who" and "what". In problem-posing or problematizing, the teachers seek to raise the level of critical awareness of meanings and issues in the life-world which both they and the students share.

Problematizing, in which questions are raised about matters in the real lives of students and teachers, "is so much a dialectic process that it would be impossible for anyone to begin it without becoming involved in it. No one can present something to someone else as a problem and at the same time remain a mere spectator of the process. S/he will be problematized even if methodologically speaking, s/he prefers to remain silent after posing the problem, while the educators capture, analyze, and comprehend it." [33]

Teachers who are not mere technicians never allow themselves "to be bureaucratized by high-sounding repetitious, mechanical explanations." In the problematizing process, when students ask a question, engaged teachers in their explanations "remake the whole previous effort of cognition". This re-making is more, however, than a repetition of answers teachers already know. "It means making a new effort, in a new situation, in which new aspects which were not clear before are clearly presented...." [34]

Teachers who engage in this kind of action "re-enter" problem-situations and in so doing find new roads opened for themselves as well as for their students. This is how and why teachers continue to learn. They experience the growth of person-hood that emerges from the dialogue of communication.

Education is something quite different for teachers who do not make this effort. It becomes a form of "technical aid" in which "knowledge" is transferred or "extended" to passive students who are denied the active participatory experience of really knowing - the kind of knowing in which knowledge is personally appropriated or won through the active meaning-seeking process of dialogue.

The classroom as a good work place thus "is not a class in the traditional sense, but a meeting place where knowledge is sought" and not merely trans-mitted.[35]

We are ready then to note the approach to teaching of an American black teacher, Ms. Ordia Harrison,[36] who resisted the "production-process" model of teaching. She saw parallels between what happened to de-skilled workers in Taylorist-type work settings, Freire's descriptions of peasants who retreated into the culture of silence, and the many black students from the ghetto who came to define themselves as non-learners. She turned to Freire for ideas to make her classroom a good work place for her children and herself.

On reading Freire Ms. Harrison wrote:
Freire strongly opposes an educational setting in which the teacher is assumed to always be the one who knows everything (expert), while students are assumed to know nothing of significance -- 'absolutizing ignorance'. Forcing students to remain in such a learning environment dulls the critical spirit and capacities of the students. An even more debilitating result which stems from such an environment is that students come to believe that they are, indeed ignorant -- they have no words to say in the learning situation -- and, therefore, their ignorance justifies the presence of the teacher. Feeling helpless, they abdicate to the teacher by passively listening and saying little or nothing at all, becoming part of what Freire calls 'the culture of silence'. In this sense, students are depersonalized and come to behave as mechanical robots. They become domesticated.

She worked out both a set of recommendations and a description of personal practices consistent with her values of a more liberalizing/liberating education for black children. I take the liberty of using her own words at length just as I previously presented the observations of "back to basics" teaching by Dr. Marilyn Cohn.

Ms. Harrison's approach to teaching literacy:

Working off of Freire's suggestion that teachers fit their actions into the framework of the cultural conditions of the learners, I have come to believe that teachers should allow children to bring their knowledge and experience to bear on the reading process. What could create more interest in learning to read than to have minority students develop their first reading books from their own experiences?

Photographs may be taken of the children at school, in their homes, or public housing units, in hospitals or clinics, etc. -- all located in their own community. In addition, photographs may be taken of the children in settings which depict their normal play sites -- vacant lots, alleys, abandoned buildings, streets, etc. With the children as characters in the visual images (photographs) presented by the teacher, they can be guided in critically analyzing the existential situations shown in the photographs.

Analyzing their existential situations, the children, with guidance from the teacher, can discuss the problem of housing, education, health care, etc., in a <u>slum</u>, as well as discussing the problem of finding adequate play or recreation sites in their neighborhood and the dangers or hazards involved in using their present play areas. Thus, the students can come to perceive the <u>slum</u> as a problem situation. These children (including Kindergarteners and first graders) learn to read reality without knowing how to read and write linguistic symbols. Concepts like slum, poverty, hunger, etc., filter down to become the stuff of daily life for Black children living in the poor areas of the inner city, who have never read, written, nor heard the abstract terms.

At this point, one can develop an appreciation for the use of the language experience approach in the teaching of reading. Through use of the language experience approach, the teacher may tune into the language of the children and gain insight into the generative words (those words most weighted in existential meaning and greatest emotional content as well as typical sayings and expressions linked to the experience of the students) that should aid the students in developing awareness of their humanity. This task may be accomplished by having the children dictate and/or write stories to accompany the photographs.

The teacher may subsequently type the children's stories in large print to accompany the pictures. These sheets (containing pictures accompanied by children's stories) may be laminated and given to children to become pages in their "own reading books." Together, the photographs and the children's stories tell "the story" with a clarity and an absolute truth that traditional primers cannot.

Key words (linked to the existential experiences of the children) which are consistently found in their stories, may be utilized in the initial development of the students' sight vocabulary and word meaning skills. Rather than beginning the children's initial reading experiences with pressure from the teacher to learn isolated letter sounds or a list of isolated words (as currently practiced in many school settings), the children learn to recognize many words to which they can attach their own existential meanings. These words can, indeed, serve as a frame of reference for subsequent learning of phonetic skills.

When teachers attempt to fit their actions into the framework of the cultural conditions of minority students, and to assist both the students and their parents to emerge from the "culture of silence," they are not resistant to inviting students and their parents to bring their knowledge and experience to bear on the learning process. In this type of learning environment, older students may combine reading with history by tape recording interviews with their parents or grandparents (who have lived for a long time in the local community) to produce books. There is much to be gained in an educational setting when the creative power of these oppressed people is emphasized.

By becoming "involved" in such an activity with my own students in an urban ghetto, we learned that an older member of the community had trained three world heavy-weight boxing champions, one of whom he had taken off the local street corner and who had encountered problems with the law. He informed us of how training of black boxers was taken over by "organized" groups, thus taking it out of the hands of local people like himself. Both local trainers and young black boxers were "forced" to abdicate under pressure from "organized" groups. This led us to a critical analysis of the boxing arena from an economical, social and political perspective.

Through participation in the learning activities described above, students may come to "perceive the normal situation of man as a being in the world and with the world, as a creative and re-creative being who, through work, constantly alters reality

198

(Freire, 1973:63)." By means of simple questions, such as "Who made the bicycle? Who produced the reading books? Who trained the three world heavy-weight boxers? Why did they do it? How did they do it? When?," students are encouraged to get in touch with their "own capacities." They discover the value of their "person" and their people -- to know that they are "cultured." For example, by discovering himself to be a maker of the world of culture -- having a creative and re-creative impulse -- the minority child also discovers that culture is just as much a "first reading book" produced by himself and his peers as it is the work of the Ph.D. who writes books -- that culture is all human creation (Freire, 1973:47).

In the learning environment described above, the language of minority children is viewed as an asset in the learning process rather than as a defi-cit. This is not to state, however, that these individuals should not be made aware of and taught to speak standard English -- "given the nature of American society." However, teachers should not devalue the language of minority children by referring to it as "dialect" while referring to standard English as "language": "The superiority and richness of the latter is placed over against the poverty and inferi-ority of the former" (Freire, 1975: 126).

It is incumbent upon teachers to provide opportunities for dialogue with minority children through which they critically analyze the "problem of language" in contemporary American society. Minori-ties must respect and preserve their language -- their language is a part of their culture. To deny their language is to deny their culture which, in turn, is a denial of their own being.

Black urban minorities did not "choose" to be born in nor live in urban ghettos, but they are there; therefore, they must learn to deal effectively with their surroundings and to give their own meanings to their existence. Brought up in a society that begins early to preach to them the "myth" of the "American Dream" (equality and equal opportunity for all, meritocracy, etc.), through what Freire terms "inten-tional" education, minority students may discover contradictions in the myths as well as contradictions involving the oppressive situation in which they find themselves. They may compare daily life with T.V. screen "reality".

In "education for the practice of freedom", teachers and students must take a political stance,

199

questioning the meaning and nature of knowledge itself and peeling away hidden structures of reality -- viewing knowledge as problematic. The import of teachers taking a political stance through which they emphasize the relationship between knowledge and ideology, is eloquently addressed by Freire (1975):

> Education as an act of knowing confronts us with a number of theoretical-practical questions: What to know? How to know? Why to know? In benefit of what and of whom to know? Against what and whom to know?.... Thus, in concerning myself with what should be known, I am also necessarily involved with why it needs to be known, how, in benefit of what and in whose interest, as well as against what and whom (p. 100).
>
> ...The definition of what to know -- without which it is not possible to organize the programmatic content of educational activity -- is also intimately related to the overall plan for society, to the priorities this plan requires, and to the concrete conditions for its realization....Defining what needs to be known in order to organize the content of educational activities demands political clarity of everyone involved in any part of the planning (p. 101).
>
> ...The organization of programmatic content of education...is an eminently political act, just as politics is an attitude which we assume in the choice of the techniques and methods for the concrete accomplishment of the task....The knowledge of how to define what needs to be known, cannot be separated from the "why" of knowing or from the other implications of this act to which I have referred. For this reason, there are no neutral specialists, no owners of neutral techniques in the field of curriculum organization -- or in any other field, for that matter. There are no neutral "methodologists" who can teach how to teach history, geography, language or mathematics neutrally (p. 102).

Through the type of "problem-posing" education described above, students develop their power to perceive critically the way they exist in the world with which and in which they find themselves. They come to view the world not as a static reality, but as a reality in process, in transformation. Hence, minority students (through their own development of critical and conscious awareness) may come to realize the factors that oppress them and also realize that their oppressive situation is not a "determinism". Instead, it is one that they can transform.

There is no need to claim that Freire's rationale for teaching, which Ms. Harrison turned to, is the one right way consistent with "good work in school". I am saying that one teacher who cared deeply about "liberating the intelligence" of her "ghetto culture" children, and who wanted good work for herself and her students in Herbst's sense, found Freire's model appropriate. Freire sought a mode of teaching that would combine productively the technical knowledge of the experts with the human experience and wisdom of the peasants.

Ms. Harrison wanted her children to become literate in the liberating sense. To do that she had to honor the technical dimension of her craft - she had to help her children learn the methods and techniques of "decoding" and word recognition. But she felt compelled to go beyond that - to help them to use language - written and oral, which enabled them to see significant features in their daily social reality, and enabled them to draw on the experience of their personal life worlds. While engaging with them in genuine talk about their shared reality, she became a learner also. (In the mutual exploration of ideas, anyone can teach and anyone can learn.) The subject matter skills, personal experience, and awareness of social reality were brought into fruitful interaction.

It is not inappropriate to contrast Ms. Harrison's experience with a counter approach to teaching reading described by Bruno Bettelheim in "Why Children Don't Like to Read":

Word Recognition -- "decoding"...deteriorates into empty rote learning when it does not lead directly to the reading of meaningful content. The longer it takes the child to advance from decoding to meaningful pleasure in books, the more likely it becomes that his pleasure in books will evaporate ...The child must become convinced that skills are only means to achieve a goal, and the only goal of importance is that he become literate -- that is, come to enjoy literature and benefit from what it has to offer.[37]

201

2. Autonomy and sense of mission: key to good work at school.

> Adherence to norm-referenced standardized test scores as the standard for judging student, teacher, and school performance has led quite naturally to a stultifying approach to accountability. There is nothing wrong with the idea of being accountable -- that is, being required to give account. The problems and injustices in contemporary approaches to educational accountability stem from the fact that all the richness, shortcomings, interpersonal relations, successes and failures are reduced to a few figures, much as one records profits and losses in a ledger book... Relatively few (superintendents) have internalized, let alone articulated, the view that the prime measure of their success is the quality of life in the schools under their jurisdiction."[38]
>
> John Goodlad

As we have seen, the teaching profession, like the larger American society, is split between attraction toward values of the business efficiency orientation and the democratic-humanist tradition. There are sizable numbers of educators and parents who feel that education is perverted by the current emphasis on rationalist efficiency. We have just looked at a teacher from an impoverished urban area who reached for an alternative to what Herbst called the production-process model. In closing, we turn to another educator from a very different background - one of the most prominent students of American education, John Goodlad: Dean of the Graduate School of Education, University of California, Los Angeles; director of research for I/D/E/A, education arm of the Kettering Foundation; and director of the long-term study of Schooling in America supported by eight major foundations. Goodlad also resists the technocratic ideology and offers a counter argument, unrelated to Freire, but congruent in important respects with the values of the socio-technical model of good work.

John Goodlad has expressed his misgivings about post-1970 trends in a number of writings. We refer primarily to one of these, "Can Our Schools Get Better?", Phi Delta Kappan, January, 1979.

Goodlad argues that our schools cannot offer better education as long as we cling to the current emphases. Like the socio-technical theorists, he holds that efforts to secure improvement by rationalist-technical means are futile because they are out of touch with the reality of learning and living in schools. The norm used to judge schools - norm-referenced standardized test scores, "the linear reductionist model that squares nicely with the manufacture of paper cups and safety pins and the basics of bookkeeping" - is entirely inadequate and, in fact, corrupts the educative process. It has led, he says, to the practice of letting the first six letters of the alphabet and two numbers representing scores or percentile ratings as the sole evidence for judging the adequacy of an individual's or a school's performance. This tunnel vision reductionism leads to an avoidance of asking genuinely important questions about a liberalizing education: whether the curricula of students are well-balanced, whether their interests and curiosities are aroused, their talents unleashed, their creativity stimulated, and their sentiments and tastes refined. It leads to a failure to be seriously concerned with how students spend precious growing-up time in schools, and how they feel about what goes on there. When the fixation is on test score results, "large numbers of parents apparently suffer no pangs of conscience in withholding support or love or inflicting pain and humiliation purely on the basis of these letters and grades. Others bestow gifts and lavish praise on their achieving children with little thought as to whether their marks were obtained with little effort, through cheating, or at the expense of peers, some of them friends and neighbors." [39]

This adulteration of the quality of life in schools goes on in spite of the fact that there is no convincing evidence that schools have become more "efficient". Criteria which would give a saner perspective on the health of students and teachers at school are ignored. Criteria such as: How many registered students in major American cities are absent and walking the streets? Why? How many suicides occurred as a direct consequence of grades or test scores? What schools have trouble keeping children home even when ill because they are so anxious to be at school? How much attention has been given to the effect of legislators' prescriptions on principals' paperwork, and on teachers' freedom to be creative in designing learning experiences suited to the diverse needs of their students? How much opportunity has been provided for local faculties to bring their ideas to bear on improving the quality of life in their work places?

"Accounting questions" like these, says Goodlad show the breadth of responsibility which ought to be acknowledged to try to improve schools. They reveal, also, "the folly of concentrating the bulk of our time, energy, and resources on those ubiquitous test scores."

Besides being concerned about the narrowing effects of test-oriented accountability, Goodlad in his 1979 article also ventured hunches about negative side effects. In addition to anticipating increased alienation and drop-out rates, he guessed that back to basics might yield improvement here and there on test scores, but "those more complex intellectual processes not easily measured will decline at an equal or greater rate." [40] Evidence which came in several years later proved him to be an accurate forecaster.

In the fall of 1981, the National Assessment of Educational Progress found that over 100,000 students tested demonstrated "very few skills for examining the nature of the ideas that they take away from reading." They are less adept than students a decade ago in analyzing literature, and are less knowledgeable about classics such as Tom Sawyer and Robin Hood. The report pointed out that most students showed a capacity to answer multiple choice questions requiring literal or inferential skills and demonstrated mechanical and grammatical writing skills, but the majority lacked problem solving strategies and critical thinking skills, enabling them to go beyond simple reactions to literary passages. The report commented that the skills lacking were the ones most needed to prepare students for a society marked more and more by information overload - where the need is to sort important information from the trivial. It concluded, "A society in which habits of disciplined reading, analysis, interpretation and discourse are not sufficiently cultivated, has much to fear." [41]

The situation is similar in mathematics. Organizations such as the National Council of Teachers of Mathematics, the National Council of Supervisors of Mathematics and the National Science Foundation sounded warnings about consequences of a limited back to basics focus. They point, for example, to a survey by the National Assessment of Educational Progress which showed that in spite of the back to basics emphasis the computational ability among 9 and 13 year olds remained virtually unchanged from 1973-1978, and among 17 year olds it dropped sharply. Students were generally able to add, subtract and multiply as well, but there was an appreciable drop in their problem solving ability.

The National Congress of Parents and Teachers joined the criticism, pointing to the pressures on teachers to drill students on skills that will produce good showings on the tests. They concluded that "overemphasis on basics has a tendency to teach children only those things for which they will be tested, a tendency that leads to mediocrity."[42]

In sum, a variety of critics accept the necessity of drill in computation but deplore the current stress on recipe learning, which is failing to teach children the flexibility and suppleness of mind needed to attack new and unfamiliar problems. Slavish devotion to computational skills is analogous, they say, to teaching children to spell and punctuate flawlessly, but not to write an intelligible sentence. Students are not learning the language of mathematics.

Seeing these trends developing suggested to Goodlad that it is time to seriously consider the possibility that attempts to make the system better by applying more of the current principles actually makes education worse. "Some responsible legislators are becoming aware of the fact that their good intentions, expressed in bill after bill -- many of them under-financed and most of them hopelessly tangled in regulations and procedures of accountability -- are compounding the work of school personnel."[43] Initiatives of local schools atrophy as their energies and resources are consumed by mounting bureaucratic demands to meet uniform legislative prescriptions. School systems begin to drag along like dinosaurs which may collapse because of sheer weight and lack of mobility.

To do better, Goodlad says, we would first have to accept the proposition that ideas for educational change that are based on the model of factories and assembly lines simply are out of touch with realities of work in schools. They are based on assumptions which are not true to the facts: the assumption that improvement follows easily from applying a theory of rationality that calls for precisely delineated, measured goals; the assumption that educators are passively impotent - incapable of improving schools; and the assumtion that there is more intelligence outside the schools than in them. We now need to turn from the reductionist processes in schooling and "turn toward learnings rich in opportunities to derive varied meanings, and devise creative, individual approaches to understanding and problem solving."[44]

Goodlad says we can identify schools in the

past and present which achieved "marked success in whatever they set out to accomplish." When identified, they reveal a picture quite different from the reductionist model: schools such as Evanston Township High School or New Trier High School of an earlier era; or, the handful of black high schools that produced 21% of our black Ph.D.'s during one period of our history - schools such as McDonough 35 High School in New Orleans, Dunbar High School in Washington, D.C., and Booker T. Washington High School in Atlanta.

None of these were improved by single, outside interventions, however well-funded. Each of these dynamic schools had a great deal of autonomy, "a sense of mission, unity, identity, and wholeness that pervades every aspect of its functioning....The people connected with it have a sense of ownership, of belonging to a special institution. 'I teach at' or 'I attend Union High' is spoken with a sense of pride."

Studies of these schools show that the values, dedication and strength of the principal is a key factor in creating a sense of mission. Such a principal is a person with a strong sense of potency, "one who takes a position on issues and is not regarded as a pawn of the superintendent or of strong individuals or groups within the community."

Where central administration is concerned:
the superintendent recognizes the school as the key unit for change and improvement, encourages principals to be captains of their ships, works directly with them as often as possible rather than building a wall of central office administrators between them and himself, and supports them even while disagreeing with them. A significant part of the budget -- the discretionary part -- is built from the bottom up, with each school principal bringing forward plans projected several years into the future, plans developed collaboratively at the site level...a school that is well along toward becoming a good place to work and study is the school that can take on virtually any project with reasonable prospect of success.[45]

Practices like these do not occur by happy accident. They occur when educators and community leaders have the values which support them and the will to sustain them.

Where the instructional program is concerned, effective school leaders reject panaceas and simple

206

solutions. They recognize that good schools need, as
Daniel Tanner pointed out, comprehensive programs
which include a dynamic tensional balance between
respect for intellectual rigor of the subjects,
sensitivity to the interests and differences of
students, and a concern for relating study to social
history and issues. [46] By knowing that trouble develops when any one of these is neglected, they are less
vulnerable to sloganeering either for "back to basics"
or for "freeing the children".

In a summary statement, Goodlad says:
I have implied throughout that schools will be
better if legislators, school board members,
parents, and superintendents see themselves as
responsible and accountable for enhancing the
effectiveness, unity, and sense of mission of
the single school. This may mean passing less
rather than more reform legislation, reducing
rather than increasing district-wide programs
and demands, giving more rather than less
autonomy to principals and teachers, and using
contextual as well as outcome criteria as
measures of successful performance." [47]

It is obvious that Goodlad's rationale for good
work at school supports pluralism and autonomy at the
school level. One of our success stories has been the
magnet schools development, which brings together
teachers, students and parents with shared interests.
Goodlad's ideas parallel closely the recommendations
of the socio-technical theorist Philip Herbst of
Norway. Herbst called for more autonomy for individual schools, with an increase in the consultative,
facilitative roles for central school administration
and a corresponding diminution of their prescriptive,
control functions.

While Goodlad has confidence that we can
identify the qualities of effective schools, he is
less confident that we have the determination or
desire to implement them. He says he is not at all
sure that the American people are ready to put the
criteria for good schools "ahead of the marks and
scores we worship mindlessly in much the same way our
supposedly more primitive ancestors worshiped the gods
of thunder and fire."

Goodlad points to sharp divisions within the
teaching profession. Many superintendents are enamored of the efficiency model. They see power as finite
and decentralizing - as undermining their authority.
"Relatively few have internalized, let alone articulated, the view that the prime measure of their

207

success is the quality of life in the schools under their jurisdiction." Many superintendents are more interested in crisis management, public relations and budgetary specifics than assuring "that resources and support get to the school ships at sea."

Principals themselves find a certain protection in seeing themselves boxed in by the demands of the district office and the ever-growing routines of management. When these elements are combined with the status elements of the job, principals tend to play their cards close to their vest, "making their lonely job even lonelier." This puts some of them in conflict with counter yearnings for collegial relations through which they could explore solutions for the problems for which they were not prepared."

Teachers themselves may find security in concentrating on improving student scores on the tests that count. It becomes convenient to avoid coming together with administrators and colleagues from the wider school to examine the total educational programs for children and youth. By fixating on test score results, teachers themselves can obtain a penumbra of status by being rated as "persons concerned with standards".

If one asks if this does not make for isolation or alienation, there may be spoken or unspoken replies: "So that's the way it is with everyone. The kids might as well learn the way it really is. Keep your nose clean, get your points, punch out on time, and try to get your cut. That's what made us what we are today."

There is no guarantee that we want anything other than that - either in our schools or in our work places. There are, however, the other possibilities that we have created in both institutions. We know how to build in both directions.

NOTES

1. Jean Piaget, To Understand is to Invent: The Future of Education. (New York: Grossman Publishers, 1973).

2. Henry M. Levin, Education and Work. (Program Report No. 82-B8, Stanford: Institute for Research on Educational Finance and Governance, December 1982). The report was prepared for the International Encyclopedia of Education: Research and Studies (1983). For an elaboration see Martin Carnoy and H.M. Levin, The Dialectic of Education and Work. (Stanford: Stanford University Press, forthcoming). I am indebted to Levin for his

insight about the discrepancy between Marxist "reproduction" theory and the realities of American life. I am responsible for the ideas developed in this section.

3.   Ibid., pp. 19-20.

4.   Ibid., p. 25.

5.   Larry Hirschhorn, "The Soul of a New Worker," Working Papers Magazine (Vol. IX, No. 1, January/February 1982).

6.   Ibid., p. 44.

7.   Ibid., p. 45.

8.   Ibid., p. 46.

9.   Ibid., p. 47.

10.   Louis E. Davis, "Optimizing Organization-Plant Design: A Complementary Structure for Technical and Social Systems," Organizational Dynamics, (Autumn 1977), p. 6.

11.   Ibid., p. 5.

12.   Ibid., p. 10.

13.   David Newman, "Work and Technology in Telephone," Dissent (Winter, 1982), pp. 58-59.

14.   Philip Herbst, Socio-technical Design. (London: Tavistock Publications, 1974), p. 181.

15.   Ibid., p. 183.

16.   Einar Thorsrud, "Listening to the Workers Produces Results," International Management, (February, 1980), p. 41.

17.   Herbst, op. cit., p. 185.

18.   Ibid., p. 186.

19.   Ibid., pp. 194-195.

20.   Max Elden, "Sharing the Research Work: One Way of Initiating a Process of Employee Management Change," Trondheim: Norwegian Technical University, 1977.

21.   John Dewey, The Public and Its Problems. (New York: Henry Holt and Co., 1927), p. 218.

22. Ragnar Johansen, "Democratizing work and social life on ships: a report from the experiment on board M.S. Balao," Report of Ship Research Group, Work Research Institutes, Oslo, Norway, 1979. Supplemented by interviews with Mr. Johansen at Work Research Institute, Oslo, May 14, 1980.

23. The Harman Mirror, Bolivar, Tennessee, June, 1979, pp. 2-4.

24. E.F. Schumacher, Small is Beautiful: Economics As If People Mattered. (New York: Harper and Row (Torch Books), 1973), p. 51.

25. Interviews in Flint and Detroit, October 14-16, 1981.

26. Tri Center Pre-Employment Center, Flint, Michigan, October 14, 1981.

27. Paulo Freire, Education for Critical Consciousness. (New York: The Seabury Press (A Continuum Book), 1974), p. 154.

28. Ibid., p. 4.

29. Ibid., p. 63.

30. Ibid., p. 88.

31. Ibid., pp. 152-153.

32. Ibid., p. 88.

33. Ibid., p. 154.

34. Ibid., p. 151.

35. Ibid., pp. 150-153 et passim.

36. Ordia Harrison, "Education as practice for freedom and socio-technical theory," Unpublished paper, Washington University, St. Louis, MO, 1981.

37. Bruno Bettelheim, "Why Children Don't Like to Read," Atlantic Monthly, (Vol. 248, No 1., November, 1981), p. 25. (For more on the point see Bruno Bettelheim and Karan Zelan, On Learning to Read: The Child's Fascination with Meaning. (New York: Alfred Knopf, 1981)

38. John I. Goodlad, "Can Our Schools Get Better?," Phi Delta Kappan, (Vol. 60, No. 5, January, 1979), pp. 342, 347.

39. Ibid., p. 343.

40. Ibid., pp. 343-344.

41. St. Louis Post Dispatch, November 12, 1981, p. 1.

42. St. Louis Post Dispatch, November 17, 1981, p. 1.

43. Goodlad, op. cit., p. 345.

44. Ibid., p. 344.

45. Ibid., p. 346.

46. Daniel Tanner and L.N. Tanner, Curriculum Development: Theory Into Practice. (New York: MacMillan, 1980).

47. Goodlad, op. cit., p. 346.

48. Ibid.

CHAPTER IX

BEYOND "GOOD WORK": SOCIAL RENEWAL

Enterprises in both government and private
sectors must create new modes of operating
efficiently,....It is no longer correct to
label some procedure efficient if it exacts
intolerable social costs, proves grossly
wasteful of resources, or imposes its
mechanistic rhythms on the operator.[1]
                                    Dennis Goulet

We have failed to lay the groundwork for real
democracy: we have omitted the thorough-going
and continuing critical education of the whole
population, upon which alone responsible
representative government can be based![2]
                                    Ernest Becker

     In ending, we return to themes initiated in the
opening chapter. Before making some concluding
comments about education, I want to consider another
significant dimension about "new work" projected by
the theorist Philip Herbst, in Socio-Technical Design.
His argument is that something more fundamental is
involved than how to improve productivity for economic
survival. In Herbst's view, democratic socio-
technical theory could become a "leading edge" for
wider social change.After a description of Herbst's
contention, I will give examples of how re-thinking,
begun in places of work has, in fact, broadened to
larger social issues. Then I will end with summary
reflections about education which relate to the new
work possibility.

A. "Good Work" as "leading edge" for social change

     One of the high points in my investigations was
to meet the thinking of the pioneering socio-technical
theorist Philip Herbst, through his writings and
through personal conversations in Trondheim, Norway.
In the preceding chapter I turned to Herbst to explore
connections between socio-technical theory and work in
our schools. I want to refer to him once again in
exploring the idea that this work theory has significant implications for societal transformation at the
broadest level.
     Philip Herbst, in "The Evolution of World

Models" in Socio-technical Design, allies himself with the perspective of Fred Emery and Eric Trist in Toward A Social Ecology, in seeing us in transition between a late-industrial stage and a potentially less destructive post-industrial era. Socio-technical work design is seen as a "leading edge" toward the forming of a social order, based on the principle that productive development depends on human conservation or "well-faring" of all.

As Herbst sees it, in the late industrial (or "modernist") model, the significant challenges seen as problematic for survival are located in the properties of the environment. Life is seen as man fighting against his environment. The locus of change and power lies in the physical environment, which man can understand scientifically in order to subdue it. The fundamental characteristic of the environment is that it is a cluster or aggregate of elements. This is the model, in terms of which classical science built its theories of universal determinist laws. In this world, man's predominant relationship is not to himself, but to the world of external objects. Armed with the tools of science to conquer the environment, man stands apart from and against it. This results in a basic contradiction in his condition.

In the active mode, standing god-like outside the world, man controls, masters, and subjugates the environment. In the passive mode it is the environment that shapes, governs and determines his behavior.[3]

The orientation of a science that is atomistic, mechanistic and deterministic, which permitted mastery of the environment, also provided the conceptual base for the creation of bureaucratic organizations based on the principle of "redundancy of parts." The classical organizational design to secure productivity assumes a system of uniform replaceable parts. When "fixing" is needed, one turns to the engineering expert who provides the thinking required "to restore efficiency." The pathologies of this engineer's model emerge, Herbst wryly observes, "when man begins to treat man as part of the physical environment. In the active mode, he perceives and masters others as objects. In the passive mode, he experiences himself as object, as a cog in the machinery."[4]

In the late industrial stage, the solidity of the "modernist" model is called into question: the source of challenge comes from a fundamental change in the relationship of man to his environment. The environment, once confidently being brought under scientific control, is marked now by new orders of turbulence. The organizational patterns designed to increase control, are themselves increasingly marked by unruly complexity, size, and dysfunctional change which become increasingly repugnant and unacceptable to humans.

The symptoms of breakdown appear in both the work world of the adults and in the school world of youth and their teachers. Those who cling to assumptions of technocratic ideology assume that the only way to "fix" the turbulence is to step up the control and supervision of the parts. The possibility that the "expertise" itself may be the source of escalating the turbulence, seems beyond comprehension.

Herbst suggests that the predominant issue in a post-industrial era which may be emerging, centers on "the dense interdependent ecology of life on this globe ... There is no outside to man's world. The existential loneliness of humanity is not overcome by space flights. Man takes his environment along wherever he goes. The system has taken the environment into itself. Each part has the rest of the system as its environment and each part is the environment for others". [5]

What has receded, Herbst says, is the independent physicalist type environment, "which could be conceptualized as an aggregate or cluster of elements and which provided the basis for the immutable laws of classical science." These laws have not ceased to operate in so far as they are valid, but they no longer provide the conceptual base for understanding the problems of the present unsettled environment. "This is because the behavior of man, the relationship of man to man, and the social ecologies that have come into being do not conform to the universal and immutable principles of classical science." [6] The capacity to deal successfully with this order of change depends now on building a learning, value-choosing capacity into the system itself.

The traditional hierarchical style, based on the separation of doing, planning, and deciding becomes increasingly inappropriate, and is replaced by work groups in which these functions are integrated. "The members of these groups will to an increasing degree be able to participate in policy decisions, and be capable of using specialists as consultants." [7] The shift then is from a feeling of alienation to a feeling of autonomy.

Herbst's image of a possible post-industrial world model sees the emergence of such organizational

qualities foreshadowing and supporting more general
social changes. In shifts to a post-industrial world
model, decisions to move toward freeing the intelligence of people at work to cope with rapid change
introduces an essentially new factor - the potential
for technological choice within the organization.
Herbst's experience in the Norwegian industrial
democracy projects led him to believe that people at
work can design technologies and social relations to
meet technological change and to create a more satisfying quality of democratic social living.

The critical condition for gaining control
over social change in industry and society as
a whole becomes, then, that we utilize the
option of technological choice. To the extent
that the choice of future technologies is
directively correlated with social and educational changes over the same period, stability
and directionality of societal development can
be achieved. This is a necessary but not
sufficient condition. Man has become able to
create his future society, not as he has done
so far, blindly and unknowingly, but within
limits, consciously. What he is faced with is
the problem of deciding what kind of future he
wants. [8]

If a world model more conducive to well-being
is to emerge, the key problem lies in what goals to
achieve. Values and ethics become the central concern. And the means must be congruent with the ends.

From this perspective, socio-technical theory
may be seen as an alternative mode of thinking to
replace the "atomistic, aggregate" orientation of an
ailing late industrialism. It moves away from a
concept of science and technology with mechanistic
assumptions about nature and production toward a more
ecological view of the world. It moves toward a model
of integral efficiency which assumes we have to learn
to produce efficiently while optimizing human values.
It moves toward concepts of production which would
capitalize on distinctive human capacities to see the
relation of parts to the whole, to communicate effectively in generating hypotheses to cope with problems,
and to tap personal, subjective dimensions of learning
instead of only the abstract/rational.

As we have seen, a forerunner of work of this
type may be seen in some high technology work processes, where a relatively small number of well educated
workers need to respond to random, unpredictable
developments. Intellectual involvement, learning,

communication and commitment increasingly get located in primary groups where thinking and acting are integrated. People who are "left out" or who are "out of it" become a threat to the well-being of the activity. Therefore the question of how to sustain involvement of the whole range of human capacities of everyone in the system becomes essential.

This "world model" requires a kind of science of human behavior that is not ethically neutral, but which has a responsibility to determine the choice of technologies which support the learning of all persons in the system. According to Herbst, the shift to the new world model requires the capacity and opportunity to participate in "research style", inquiry type learning. This requires the values which Dewey said are essential to engage in scientific inquiry - values of individuality and community.

So far we have focused on characteristics of a new world model within organizations which see that effective functioning requires attention to questions of ethics and values.

It is, however, increasingly apparent that post-industrial development is a global matter and the situation at the world level has become a social ecology. Restoring sanity in work, by helping people become persons again, can make an important contribution to raising awareness about the quality of life. While this is important in itself, it obviously does not speak directly to a whole array of economic problems: world-wide depression, unemployment, inflation, world-trade imbalances, and economic power concentrations in multi-national corporations. There is a huge gap between the ethical concept of work place democracy and the prevalent situation in society at large.

Late industrial development has spawned enormous casualties of people who are "not in" the system at all. In developed countries, large numbers of unemployed are concentrated among racial and ethnic minorities, the old, the young, and single women heads of families. In developing countries, the masses are relegated to a mean existence of bare survival by the power elites committed to preserving privilege. We need to note, too, that socio-technical trends to extend participation to highly-skilled workers may actually exacerbate the dualism between the "haves" and "have nots." In "Silicon Valley" in California, for example, engineers and other highly trained personnel in computer industries may work in inter-disciplinary, collaborative project task forces, while minority women who produce the silicon chips may be working under mind-killing, monotonous, unhealthy labor situations.[9]

Herbst himself argues that high technology itself is not a guarantee of humanistic reform. Computer technology, for example, may be designed to bring closer the goal of complete, rational machine control which requires no human participation or intervention. "It is possible that god-like mysterious power will be projected upon computer programs, to which effective decision-making authority will be transferred and which may for a time permit the survival of centralized hierarchical organizations."[10]

Herbst and colleagues simply point to the waste that results when human capacities are unutilized; and that technical and social health can be restored when people are "brought in" as whole human beings - as demonstrated with low-skilled workers in assembly plants, as well as people in high technology industries. These may be seen as "leading edge" examples of a well-faring world model where ethical choices about uses of technology and social relations are made for sane social and personal development. No one knows if they are aberrants or forerunners. They do exist embyronically in the master institution. They may function as laboratories where growing numbers of people begin to raise questions about the quality of life under technology. The observations of end-of-the twentieth century observers like Victor Laszlo and Denis Goulet, who were mentioned at the beginning, convey a sense of a new order of urgency about needed economic-social change. Ervin Laszlo, looking at the world from the perspective of a United Nations researcher in the closing decades of the century, described the needed change in ways which underscores the ecological ethic which complements the democratic perspective: "In this world the one who survives is the one who is the most symbiotic with his fellow men and his environment, not the one who is out for immediate materialist gain to the detriment of nature and other persons."[11]

If our time calls for such major shifts in values, are we justified in holding that the redesign of work we have described as socio-technical can be considered a significant contributor? It is obvious that the shifts Laszlo, and Goulet call for will require very broad efforts - from philosophical re-conceptualizing to institutional/societal restructuring. There is no single right place to begin. It is possible, however, that the small changes made in

the daily work life of thousands, eventually hundreds
of thousands, can contribute as much or more to the
evolution of salutary change than broader political/
philosophical debates. A fundamental question is, how
do we change mind-sets of people who have been immersed in the ideology of "modernism?" We are bogged
down in the consumerist ethic and passive privatism
spawned by it. Questions about quality - what has
been happening to the quality of our daily lives - and
to the quality of life on the planet have been crowded
out of consciousness.

Stewart Ewen, in Captains of Consciousness,[12]
pointed out that from the 1920's onward, mass advertising equated consumerist quantity with life quality.
Boredom and resentments in corporate work places were
contained and muted by promises of individual attainment and consumer rewards. The focus on consumer
goods pay-off satisfied aspirations for "higher
standards of living", and it tended to isolate individuals and channeled their energies into meeting "time
payments" on the latest purchase. In twentieth
century American work, the kind of goals included in
Michael Maccoby's concept of "social productivity",
such as concern for individuation and democracy were
notable by their absence. The legitimate goal of work
was assumed to be increasing the size of the pie by
well-engineered techniques combined with efficient
control of labor by management. In school, working
for grades as pay-off, in an atmosphere of firm
control, provided the parallel preparatory function.

If the culture has been immersed in passive
consumerism, what is the case for work place democracy
as a significant development for change? To be blunt,
it helps to return to people the sense of their
capacity to be learners - to be engaged actors in ways
where they can see the results of their actions. The
critical shift is not the re-shuffle of work assignments - a new "program." When people in their daily
work lives begin to experience themselves as active
questioners, communicators, learners and collaborative
problem-solvers the groundwork for change in which we
can have confidence may be laid. That was Thorsrud's
hunch in Norway: that individual activation and
learning at the job were necessary conditions for
involvement in larger social issues, hence, the
decision to stimulate the democraticization process at
the bottom of organizations.

In short, I work from the idea that without the
experience with democracy as social living in daily
life, ideological political/economic shifts at the

219

macro level can easily degenerate into more of the same old techno/bureaucratic manipulations. We have had enough twentieth century experiences with shifts from private to state ownership to know that this can be the dismal case.

I think there is some evidence that the evolution of "going through the institutions" is a possibility. I want to reflect on experiences I have noted in work change situations in this country and abroad that give support for that type of evolution. In pointing to examples that involve different levels of transformation, I by no means intend to imply that some "inevitable line of march" is indicated. I do suggest, that when people are brought into liberalizing learning at work, it can lead to their wanting more of it, and it may move in democratic humanist directions.

Our brief foray into the field of work redesign in the direction of work place democracy, suggests that when a shift is made from "control in a closed system" to the "support of learning and participation in open systems," opportunities emerge for plural and unpredictable developments. Howard Carlson caught the style in saying that the "quality of work life" idea should be viewed as an ongoing process wherein people and organizations are always at transitional stages of development. The root idea is the view of individuals as unique human beings: "needing the freedom to grow, to develop, and to make use of their education, experience and talents." Organizations as well as individuals are also seen as parts of open-ended transition - moving, for example, "from external to self-regulation to interdependent sources of control." Later the process aims at bridging "to new and extra-organizational combinations of people, new ways of involving people in problem-solving and other organizational processes, and new mechanisms for transforming the potential of individuals and the organism into operating reality." Finally, even an American Quality of Work Life theorist like Carlson - much more politically cautious than European "industrial or economic democracy" theorists, sees that the values implicit in his model have the implications of a "social movement" beyond the work place, which relates to "societal development as a state of transition in itself."[13]

Real world change, if it happens, will reflect the value contradictions in the culture. Results will, therefore, be complex and confusing, especially since a key issue is whether there will be significant

220

shifts in location of power and control.

It is a fact that much work place change is introduced unilaterally by management simply to improve "bottom-line performance." With that tradition at work it is a safe bet that if socio-technical terminology becomes popular, it will, in many cases, be perverted or manipulated to keep management's control intact. A tool to combat such tendencies is to judge practice against the principles of work place democratization described in Chapter I.* On a continuum of real world change we will find examples of pseudo work place democracy at one end of the scale, as well as examples of genuine democratic change at the other end. Awareness grows that there is a crucial choice between paternalistic "humanizing" of work, seemingly preferred by most American management, and a genuine exploration of the meaning of democratizing of work.

Since our goal has been to clarify the possibilities of change when democratization principles are adhered to, we now note examples which point to the range of wider institutional changes which may emerge when those principles are honored.

By growing gradually from changes in daily experience, people at work may gain self confidence about their capacities to create conditions which expand their freedom to act in life satisfying ways.

In talking with people in the auto industry who have been involved in the initiation of Employee Participation Groups of 12 or 15 people, it seems to be clear that first moves involve cautious steps to make very concrete changes - like improvement in ventilation or lighting at the work site. There is initial skepticism that requests will be heard or acted on. A request for a simple tangible change becomes a trial to see if trust is possible. If the reply is positive, the way is open for taking another look and trying another idea.

The Scandinavian experience indicates how broader types of questions may evolve. In Sweden, for example, production teams as they have moved toward becoming autonomous matrix groups, have expanded significantly their way of seeing and organizing the

_____
* (1) Workers must influence decisions during the planning and change process, (2) Changes must lead to increased worker autonomy, (3) Workers must share in economic benefits, (4) Workers must be free to withdraw if they no longer evaluate the changes positively (See Chapter I, p.4).

221

work place. At a SAAB plant, the team not only builds
auto bodies, it has taken over many of the functions
heretofore reserved for skilled craftsmen and white
collar employees. It does most of the maintenance of
its machinery, most quality control, and manages a
$100,000 to $150,000 budget for equipment. Work
groups are taking over the training of new members.
Production teams also have introduced new concepts of
management. A team is composed of seven workers. Six
work in pairs while the seventh serves as coordinator,
seeing that materials arrive and stepping in when
there is an absence. The coordinator functions as a
foreman, with one difference: the position is rotated
among members of the group on a weekly basis. [14]
     In the Øegland plant in Stavanger, Norway,
production teams not only assumed the responsibility
of hiring new workers, but raised questions which
involved relating the values of redesigned work to
community problems. They decided that since new ways
of working in production teams had been good for their
mental well-being, maybe they could make a contribution to the community through their experience.
Planning committee representatives from several
departments met with officials from the juvenile
correctional bureau to discuss hiring a few young
people who had committed crimes, were in trouble with
narcotics, etc. The general hypothesis was that young
people might gain a sense of self-respect and purpose,
if they could become successful members of collaborative production groups - that this might be more
effective than sending them to juvenile detention
centers. During a trial and training period of eight
weeks the municipal authorities pay the wages. If the
young people succeed in the probationary period they
are put on the company's payroll. In one department
which I visited, nine such young people had been
brought in during the past year. Three had quit or
were not accepted. The other six were making it. [15]
     In the process of this move, the teams also
raised questions about the desirability of having a
wider range of ages in the work groups; and they
developed a policy of hiring women half-time, who
split a full shift. They found many women were
looking for half-time employment, and the mix of full
and part time workers gave the factory more flexibility. In Stavanger, where there is a serious labor
shortage, women on both a full-time and part-time
basis were entering the whole range of work. Some of
the older men had trouble accepting the fact that many
women learned faster and worked more carefully in

222

roles such as welders and machinists, that traditionally had been considered the prerogative of men. Some
were moving into leadership roles such as the woman
who was the safety officer in the bicycle assembly
plant.

The significant point about these Scandinavian
incidents is not that they led to specific developments such as assisting young people in trouble. The
point is that they were open systems which encouraged
people at work to reflect on their experience and to
consider new ideas supporting "integral efficiency."
Both the rationale and the structure of work enabled
persons to experience themselves as subjects who could
generate ideas for more satisfying living.

B.   Beyond the Work Place: Economic Democracy

At another level, in the 1960s, working people
in a number of northern European countries began to
ask for involvement beyond the work place in management decision making. Industrial democracy becomes
broadened, then, to economic democracy.

After World War II, a number of major European
countries passed legislation for creating work councils in all large plants. These work councils are
groups of workers in units of a plant, that represent
the workers in various decisions relating to the work.
In 1972, legislation in West Germany specified that
work councils have a right to financial information,
and to initiate discussion about new methods and
standards in work. The councils have a voice in
determining work schedules, welfare, hiring, expansion
or cutback of production, introduction of new technology, mergers and plant closings. They may raise
issues about the physical work place, the bonus
system, and fringe benefits. In Sweden, the law
required workers' concurrence on all important decisions, including the sale of the company and the modes
of production. Where negotiations break down, the
areas of dispute are taken to national panels or
ultimately to a labor court. Similar developments
with work councils have taken place in Norway,
Denmark, France, Belgium, and Holland.

A number of European countries, with West
Germany in the lead, have moved beyond work council
procedures to co-determination, wherein workers
participate with management in decision-making on
company policy at the level of the Board of Directors.
In 1976 Germany passed the first economy-wide co-
determination law. As a result, German workers make

223

up between one-third and one-half of the Boards of Directors in hundreds of German companies, including banks, hotel and restaurant chains and firms involved in public transportation and services. Decision making becomes more complicated because more interests have to be taken into account, but evaluations by the economic Ministry noted the advantages as outweighing the disadvantages: there has been an increase in "social peace" with a very low incidence of strikes compared with the U. S. A.; job reductions and retraining have been accomplished without major conflicts; and Germany's economic performance has been one of the strongest in the world.[16]

Steps in this direction have emerged as European trade unions have recognized that workers are affected by how power and control are exercised beyond the work place. In commenting on these developments, we shall note the difference between European and American unions on the issue of challenging the unilateral rights of management to control decisions regarding the production process.

A number of West European trade unions, recognizing that power and decision making are exercised at different levels within the industrial system, have developed a "package" strategy for seeking a share of power.

The first formulation of such a package-oriented policy was adopted by the Swedish Labor Organization Congress in 1971. It included: (1) labor representation on boards of directors, for purposes of observation and feed-back of information to work councils; (2) an increase in the powers of work councils so they can deal autonomously with planning, staffing, and training questions at work; (3) democratic involvement in work design to increase the autonomy of workers; (4) strengthening of collective bargaining to deal with wages and working conditions; and (5) involvement in federal legislation to limit managerial prerogatives. For example, legislation in Sweden and Norway has been passed guaranteeing union influence over the planning of work when new technology is introduced, and for the protection of achieved autonomy at the work group level. Beyond action at the local and national levels, the Swedish Labor Organization has shown a growing awareness of the need to create international worker organizations to counter the power of multi-national corporations.[17]

These experiences are still in their infancy, and tensions over arrangements for capital/labor sharing of power are aspects of a long range, on-going debate. The European trend is toward a recognition that in a democratic society "management's unilateral right to manage" is more and more an empty slogan. There is a growing awareness that the right to manage is really dependent on the consent of a democratic society and, in particular, on the consent of those managed. Acceptance of decisions by management is dependent on whether such decisions are perceived as legitimate by workers and the public.

In the United States the history of labor-management relations has been very different. Social class cleavages have been less sharp, and labor unions have rejected affiliation with democratic socialist philosophy. American unions in general have given very little support to ideas for nationalization, worker-ownership, or worker-share in management. The general tradition has been to seek strong unions which would concede to management the responsibility of managerial decisions, i.e., to determine the nature of the products, the location of plants, the methods and processes of manufacturing, and administrative decisions such as governing financial, marketing and pricing matters - while the unions would seek to wrest concessions from management in return. American unions have deliberately chosen a narrow role of organizing workers, and then representing them in collective bargaining for tangible benefits and certain limited rights. This has led them to see their power as dependent on a sharp distinction between labor and management. Consequently there has been little enthusiasm for union representation on boards of directors, even though this brings access to company records, because putting union members on boards will blur the sharp distinction between employees and employers - a distinction which gives unions and their leaders their identities.

This carries over to attitudes toward worker-owned enterprises. Thus a left-liberal union leader like William Winpisinger commented: "Ownership? I view that as a catastrophe." His reason was that ownership may put workers and unions in the same bind as serving on a board. They'll lose their identity. "Pretty soon you'll get workers managing the workers, and you'll have management managing the workers all over again." [18]

Beyond that, where the great corporations are concerned, American union leaders have tended to dismiss the idea of worker control as so unrealistic that it is scarcely worth comment. As Jerry Wurf, president of the American Federation of State, County and Municipal Employees put it, "The concept of workers' control is an exciting one for soapbox oratory and rap sessions in the faculty lounge. It's just not realistic to talk about under the social, political and economic system in this country."[19]

With that kind of history, it is not hard to understand the existence of a good deal of ambivalence toward work place democracy by union leaders. This is due partly to lack of clarity as to what the term includes. Unions rightly have perceived that management inspired job enrichment and "human relations" projects have sometimes been used to forestall or weaken unionization.

At the same time, other union leaders like Irving Bluestone, have urged unions to take leadership in democratic work place reform when there are adequate safeguards for unions. Growing numbers of unions, under the lash of foreign competition, are joining in collaborative quality of work life projects. They don't advocate worker ownership or plant management, or even representation on the board. They do advocate work place arrangements which encourage rank and file workers to analyze their own jobs, to identify issues affecting their life at work, and to help design changes on matters not ordinarily covered by the basic contract.

In view of this background, Carnoy and Shearer in Economic Democracy are undoubtedly correct in holding that in the United States, moves to explore extension of democratic values to economic life will have to take root in forms and methods indigenous to our cultural history. They will not come from foreign ideologies or the European socialist tradition. They will stem from "the American radical tradition of populism, whose primary value always was democracy."[20] In line with this labor union tradition, workers, so far, have preferred participation in their immediate task environment rather than on broader issues of the corporation.

Nevertheless, the economic crisis of the early 80's has been acting as a stimulus to change traditional union-management relations. American unions have begun to question whether management should have the sole power of decision to move production geographically to cheaper labor sites. Unions are asking for more detailed corporate financial information when workers are asked to take cut-backs in benefits. Unions also have been joining with management in exploring alternatives to old-time adversarial traditions. Workers and management have even begun to

226

explore life-time job guarantees of the Japanese variety, with the profound implications for relationships which go with that.

In short, American workers are rapidly being drawn into new levels and degrees of involvement as they confront disturbing changes centering around corporate survival. Events are pushing workers and management in the direction of seeing that the health of a corporate organization depends on the quality of inter-dependencies of all people at work. The Taylorist control system, with which the century opened, which left labor uninformed, unconsulted and uncommitted, is under challenge. New kinds and levels of learning are required by all concerned as there is a growing sense of the symbiotic nature of the system. Management and labor are having to learn the attitudes and skills to function within a more open, evolving system. Management has to learn to listen, consult, provide information and feedback, and share the process of evaluation and re-planning. Labor is confronted with puzzling questions about how such developments relate to traditional adversarial labor-management relations.

Historic changes are under way in corporate life; primarily these have been structural changes within organizations. We find few signs, however, of the emergence of the social-ecological perspective Herbst spoke of: a perspective with a vision of a post-industrial "world model" in which there is conscious <u>ethical</u> selection of <u>technological choices</u> to effect changes that will serve the "well-faring" not only of people at work, but also of the surrounding society. Collective bargaining within the market economy has been primarily a contention between the power of management and of organized labor about how to share the fruits of free enterprise. What is lacking is a system of ethical accountability. There is little evidence of serious efforts to create what Willard Wirtz called a needed "new economics": an economics taking human potential as its starting point and which would "measure all major enterprises in terms of their comparative drain on dwindling natural resources and the comparative use of...human resources." This would lead us to start evaluating our economic activity in terms of its contribution to Net National Strength (NNS) rather than to Gross National Product (GNP).[21]

There has, in fact, been little sustained effort to embrace the more limited goal proposed by Michael Maccoby: to replace the free market, quanti-

227

tative measure of productivity with a broader concept of "social productivity" designed to meet ethical criteria such as:

(1) not endangering the safety of workers or the health of the community through pollution, or endangering consumer welfare through harmful products,

(2) not damaging the mental health of workers by conditions denying them dignity, democratic rights and opportunities for learning and personal development,

(3) not unduly increasing social inequity by increasing the personal power of a few, or by discriminating on the basis of race, sex, age, beliefs,

(4) not leading to loss of employment. (Without job security, economic productivity is socially unproductive.)

Maccoby expressed the hope that progressive unions might take the lead in developing such a new definition of "social productivity" and the policies it implies (1979).[22]

If American unions did not take bold steps in this direction, the same cannot be said of the Shop Stewards Committee of Lucas Aerospace Industries in England. The Lucas story deserves extended commentary, because it points to controversial new questions about power and values which may enter debate in the years ahead.

C. A New Order of Questions: The Case of the Lucas Aerospace Industries

The Lucas Shop Stewards Committee has raised a radically new set of issues. Its members claim the right to produce socially useful products; the right to produce in ways which conserve a healthy relation between people and the environment; the right to propose alternative work to combat lay-offs; the right to invent technology and anti-hierarchical relations which support dignity and human growth at work; and the aspiration to reduce technologies to be used for warfare. In other words, they have raised new questions about who should decide what will be produced, and how it should be produced.

These proposals seem abrasive, or even subversive because they challenge what management has considered to be its unquestioned right to make decisions about production. If, however, we are moving, in part, toward a human service-oriented post-industrial society where ethical questions become a central concern, then we can expect questions like these to be raised more frequently and with new

228

urgency. In fact, the kind of thinking initiated by the Lucas Shop Stewards has caught the imagination of people at work all over the world: in Australia; in European countries such as West Germany, France, Italy, Sweden, and in the U. S. A. in some auto workers unions, and in the Mid-Peninsula Conversion Project in California. A lot of important changes may go forward through collaborative arrangements; but bruising political battles will be an inevitable part of the transition when questions are raised which challenge prerogatives of the present holders of power.

The Combined Shop Stewards Committee's Corporate Plan proposals (1976) emerged as a response to the crises of industrial capitalism in England. Since it may be a forerunner of perspectives that will gain ground as we close out the century, we look briefly at the development of their vision of a new kind of "social productivity". [23]

Lucas Aerospace is part of Lucas Industries, a British-centered multi-national firm that produces electrical and mechanical systems, and components for the automobile, aerospace and engineering industries. (Lucas played a major role in production of the Concorde.) Approximately 13,000 workers are employed at seventeen sites throughout England, and include skilled engineers, designers, draftsmen, and technicians specializing in hydraulics, pneumatics, control engineering and aero-dynamics. They belong to thirteen different unions.

Key proposals for change came in 1972 from the Lucas Aerospace Combine Shop Stewards Committee formed from union representatives from the seventeen plants. The impetus for the Combine Committee was the threat of serious redundancies (lay-offs) due to proposed cuts in defense spending, and the rationalization of company production related to decisions for expanding production overseas. The rationalization policies led to a reduction in the work force from 18,000 in 1970 to about 13,000 in 1974. This came as a shock to Lucas's highly trained personnel.

In 1974, the Combine Committee created a "Science and Technology Advisory Service", to draw on the knowledge of workers to provide warnings about difficulties associated with the introduction of new technologies: technologies which could lead to skill fragmentation, stepped up work tempo, redundancies, and hazards in use of new processes. Developments at Lucas were part of the general trend of industries to become capital intensive through computerization and

robotization processes which resulted in structural
unemployment. The threat of lay-offs grew as Lucas,
in 1974, stated its intention to concentrate its major
capital investments in projects overseas.

The Combine Committee began to see that the
traditional trade union policy, of trying to protect
workers' interests by defensive responses to plans
initiated by corporate management, was not working.
As an alternative, they moved to the novel idea of
initiating their own corporate plan, independent of
the company, including detailed plans to create
alternative products which would preserve jobs. This
time, the plan would be presented directly to the
government by the union, to attract financial support.
After that, the plan would be negotiated with management through conventional collective bargaining.

Following the principle of self reliance, the
formidable task was launched by Shop Stewards Committees on each site. Workers, at all levels, were asked
to develop ideas for alternative products based on
their knowledge of the existing factory equipment,
services, sitings and layouts, and the total range of
skills of the work force. Detailed technical feasi-
bility and "state of the art" reviews were produced in
the energy, transport, economics and medical technology areas. In each case, an attempt was made to link
existing skills to the needs of the community and to
assess proposals on environmental grounds. Community
groups and trades councils were consulted with the aim
of identifying specific needs.

In 1976 a Corporate Plan was completed, con-
sisting of five 200 page documents, which outlined 150
new products and a number of tradition-breaking ideas
for how production should be organized.

An amazing array of proposals emerged. For
example, some were oriented towards high technology,
such as remote handling gear for undersea oil-rigging
maintenance aimed to reduce dangers of deep sea
diving; similar "telecheric" devices were proposed for
use in fire-fighting and mining. Alternative transport proposals included a hybrid electric-petrol
vehicle, and a light-weight rubber-wheeled road/rail
car capable of running on highways or rails. (A
prototype of this road/rail car has been produced and
widely exhibited.)

Ideas for "low and intermediate technologies"
also were brought forth: proposals for solar collec-
tor systems, wind generators and energy conservation
and technology projects, such as heat pumps for low
energy housing to be built in consultation with

230

community groups.

A variety of ideas came from the medical technology groups, such as kidney machines, portable life support systems for heart patients, and "hob carts" to enable children suffering from spina bifida to become self-transporting.

Many of these products were the joint product of cooperation between technicians and productions workers. In the case of the hob-cart, the multi disciplinary team included the collaboration of orthopedic specialists from the local hospital and a three year old boy, David, who was suffering from the disease.

Such collaborative efforts were related to the aim of restructuring all jobs, whether on the shop floor, in offices or in the design research departments, to overcome Taylorist type separation of brain and hand work. Thus the Corporate Plan includes new ideas for production organization and control, "in which the skill and ability of our manual and staff workers is continuously used in closely integrated production teams; where the experience and common sense of the shop floor workers would be directly linked to the scientific knowledge of the technical staff." Related to this was a call by the Stewards Committee for re-education programs, to help "our people to meet the technological and sociological challenges which will come during the next few years." Instead of laying off workers during transition periods of re-tooling, the Stewards argued that such times "could be transformed into a positive breathing space during which re-education programs could act as a form of work sharing." [24]

Behind all of these ideas was the general aim of enabling all members of the work force to exert influence, not only over the production process, but over the aims, goals and priorities of production. Such notions were in direct conflict with a managerial tradition where the only criterion in introducing new technologies is the reduction of costs and expansion of profits. Resistance was expected. It happened, and the ultimate response of top management was to reject the Stewards' Corporate Plan and to declare that the planning of new products rested with management. The interchanges were complex and prolonged, but the underlying basic issue centered on the challenge to the traditional prerogatives of management. An interesting development was that while top financial managers remained adamantly opposed, shop managers at local sites reacted favorably to many of the

231

proposals.[25]

The company has continued to resist mass production of the proposed products but prolonged struggle has had a number of concrete results. The creation of the Plan and efforts to implement it has had the educational effect of demonstrating the inventiveness that could come from the work force. The people at work responded with enthusiasm to the idea that they had "the right to work on products which actually help to solve human problems rather than create them".[26]

D.   The Philosophy of Work of the Lucas
Combine Stewards Committee

The direct effort of the Combine Stewards Committee was to propose alternative products as a response to threats of unemployment. It is clear, however, that the stewards were engaged not only in ideas for technical inventions but in ways of thinking and acting that represented bold and controversial social inventions.

One of the leading articulators of the philosophical framework behind the Stewards' Plan was Mike Cooley, a member of the Combine Committee. Cooley has been President of the Amalgamated Union of Engineering Workers/Technical and Supervisory Section (TASS) and Co-Director of the Centre for Alternative Industrial and Technological Systems (CAITS) in East London.

As I talked with Mike Cooley in London and read his writings, I saw parallels between his angers about the effects of "rationalization" on aerospace industry employees and the response of many American teachers to a related rationalization process in education. I also thought I could see parallels in Mike Cooley's efforts to conceptualize a human-centered concept of "social productivity" and Paulo Freire's way of thinking about education for critical consciousness.

Both resist tendencies which cut people off from their capacities to be whole persons in work or learning and to be creative actors in the world.

Freire said that the primary vocation of human beings was "to be more fully human". To fulfill that obligation persons have the duty, through critical dialogue, to develop awareness of aspects of social and personal life that thwart or enhance their vocation; and to act to replace what is oppressive with alternatives that are humanly freeing.

The Lucas shop stewards were developing that kind of awareness. When "rationalization" threatened lay-offs, they refused to become passive victims who "queued for the dole." They chose to gain insight about what confronted them, and to propose counter actions to preserve their dignity and social utility as people at work. As Cooley put it, "It seemed absurd to us that we had all this skill and knowledge and facilities and that society urgently needed equipment and services which we could provide, and yet the market economy seemed incapable of linking these two." [27] Their reflections on this situation, said Cooley, made them aware of a number of contradictions which "highlight the problems of our so called technologically advanced societies." [28]

The paramount contradiction is the growing gap that exists between what technology could provide for society and what it actually does provide. Technology produces systems as complex as the Concorde or space vehicles for scientific study of the planets, while at the same time in England 3,000 people per year die for lack of kidney machines; and pensioners suffer from hypothermia for lack of simple effective heating systems. We harness the energy of the atom and turn it into grotesquely expensive systems for self-destruction. Design engineers plan cars for aerodynamic stability at 120 mph in order to move through New York City at 6.2 mph (Horsedrawn vehicles in 1900 moved at 11 mph).

A second contradiction is, that while technologies are developed which could liberate people for more fulfilling tasks, there is an ugly wastage of the skill, ingenuity, creativity and sheer enthusiasm of ordinary people. This waste moves progressively higher into the ranks of technically skilled laboratory workers and white collar administrative personnel.

Cooley's commentary notes the relevance of a warning made decades ago by Norbert Wiener, father of cybernetics:

> It is easier to set in motion a galley or factory in which human beings are used to a minor part of their capacity only, rather than to create a world in which human beings fully develop. Those striving for power believe that a mechanized concept of human beings constitutes a simple way of realizing their aspirations to power. I maintain that this easy way to power not only destroys all ethical values in human beings, but also the very slight aspiration for the continued existence of mankind. [29]

This sense that technology is developing to the harm of nature and human beings, is leading to a third contradiction: a wide-spread skepticism about science/technology by the world's young. This, at the moment when the expansion of human knowledge and technique should be welcomed as a glowing achievement.

Looking at the gaps between the promise of science and its often de-humanizing results, Cooley and colleagues concluded that the so called neutrality of science/technology itself had to be called into question.

> Technological change has certainly been used, not merely to increase productivity, but to extend control over those who work within those processes....Science as practiced in the technologically 'advanced' countries, and I would include here the so called socialist countries, shares with Taylorism the methodological assumptions of predictability, repeatability and quantifiability.
>
> If one accepts these to be tenets of scientific method, it then follows that to be scientific implies eliminating human judgment, the subjective and uncertainty; yet skill, in the intellectual and also in the manual sense can be closely related to the ability to handle uncertainty. Skilled work we may say, is work of risk and uncertainty, whereas unskilled work is work of certainty. [30]

In Cooley's view it is linkage of a version of science with Taylorism, which produces a set of related conceptual and social dualisms that have disruptive and demeaning effects.

Conceptually, there is a separation of abstract theoretical thinking from tacit intuitive knowledge. This results socially in the subordination of ordinary workers to the expert. Personal subjective ideas for handling work by people in the work place are to be suppressed as possibly contaminating of "The Plan" of the experts. (The concept of "teacher-proof" instructional packages, insulated from the pedagogical hunches of experienced teachers, is an apt example.) "In my system", Taylor said, "the workman is told precisely what to do and how he has to do it and any improvement he makes upon the instruction given to him is fatal to success." ("It reminds me", Cooley wryly observed, "of some political leaders who claim that the mass has been subverted when it does not follow the direct party line.")[31] In that tradition of scientific management, all that counts is what can be

234

quantifiably measured within the prescriptions of the design-controller. People's value at work is determined by the time/motion measurements of the production engineers.

This bias in favor of the abstract, as Cooley sees it, is rooted in a feature of Western science based on the model of the natural sciences: a model with an assumption that scientific relationships must be seen as mathematically quantifiable. We are the beneficiaries of great advances made possible by the tools of abstractification. The problem, Cooley says, is when the methodology of this mathematically based version of science is accepted as the ruling principle for understanding and directing the complexities of human life.

Those working in the scientific field are themselves beginning to raise questions about the unreflective application of mathematically based science to the complex phenomena of the social sciences and public policy. Thus, Professor R. S. Silver in an article, "The Misuse of Science", identifies important discriminations that need to be made. There are certain risks, he says, in the scientific method which may abstract common features away from concrete reality in order to achieve clarity and systematization of thought. He points out that in science itself, "this tendency toward quantifiable abstraction has no adverse effects, because the concepts, ideas and principles are interrelated in a carefully related structure of ˉmutually supporting definitions and interpretations of experimental observation. The trouble starts when the same method is applied to situations where the number and complexity of factors is so great that you cannot abstract without doing some damage, and without getting erroneous results".[32]

Thus, the appropriate expression for the treatment of the dynamics of falling bodies is made in terms of mass, gravitational attraction, etc. It is dispassionately the same, whether for revolving planets, falling apples, or falling bombs. In contrast, concrete human experience is of incredibly complex, individual particular expressions, impossible to describe adequately in general terms. Dangerous distortions occur as abstract concepts, initiated by science and engineering for physical and mechanical phenomena, are transferred to human life. An obvious example is the difference in the treatment of "efficiency" by the physicist and the social engineer. For physicists, "efficiency" is a clear, well-defined abstract idea within a framework of related ideas such as conservation and transformation of energy. This is radically different from the talk about efficiency in industrial plants or education.

Serious damage occurs when planners assume that the human complexities of a social system can be treated analogously to the components of physical systems. Thus, Taylor's rationale, which aimed to increase industrial efficiency by assuming that human "production units" could be neatly divided into "idea generating parts" and "doing generating parts", is tragically out of touch with the realities of people at work. This was brought home to Mike Cooley as a member of the Combine Shop Stewards Committee when he witnessed the creative outpouring of workers at all levels in proposing imaginative ideas for socially useful products. He came to realize the serious damage done by the rationalizers of production who ignore such a rich source of creative thinking.

Cooley came to hold that the "abstractification" bias of the rationalizers blinds them to the subjective, personal, "tacit" experience of the "ordinary people", who bring large amounts of intelligence and knowledge to the performance of their daily tasks. Their kind of essential "savvy" tends to be denigrated, because of our tendency to confuse linguistic ability with intelligence. In Cooley's words,

Workers express their intelligence by the things they make and do, and the manner in which they organize themselves in producing these things. They have developed and utilized very high level and complex communications systems amongst themselves. When, for example, they are erecting a power station and are communicating with each other on the stages and processes they must go through in doing that, they convey in a few direct, simple words, whole bands of knowledge and experience. [33]

We may recall that Gyllenhammar of Volvo reached a similar conclusion in saying, "It is almost alarming to realize how much know-how and capability had been locked up in the work force, unavailable to managers who simply didn't realize what an important resource it was." [34]

When the "abstractification" bias of the planners leads them to ignore such powerful sources of ideas and energy, it would only be appropriate to "hold them accountable". Their blind-spot can probably be explained by Norbert Wiener's hunch, that their compelling need is to cling to control rather than to face the unsettling truths of a more complex reality.

Returning to his skepticism regarding the neutrality of science/technology, Mike Cooley points out that the unquestioned priority given to the abstract kind of knowledge is not without its political significance: "for if the mass of ordinary people are incapable of providing scientific reasons for their judgments (which are based on actual experience of the real world), ruling elites can then bludgeon their common sense into silence."[35]

What we need are epistemological and systems models which honor and integrate all aspects of our capacities for creative learning and doing. The power of abstract thought and tacit personal experience need not be pitted against each other. It is closer to the mark to see them as complementary dimensions of the capacity for creative thinking. Overemphasis of the abstract can cut people off from physical, concrete, personal experience; sole reliance on empirical experience limits theoretical understanding.

This symbiotic view of knowledge, as contrasted with the dualist tradition, has profound implications for our image of what makes for integrative social life in technological societies. In Cooley's words:

it implies a society which has a social structure capable of nurturing the co-existence of the subjective and the objective, tacit knowledge based on contact with the physical world, and abstracted scientific knowledge. In a word, a society which would link hand and brain, and permit people to be full human beings. This will mean challenging the assumptions of our present society and indeed the assumptions of societies such as exist in the so called socialist countries.[36]

As Cooley and the Combine Stewards Committee see it, we are confronted with a historical turning point with the revolution of computerization and robotization. The choice is whether the new techniques will be used to enhance human beings, or to de-skill and manipulate the many to enhance the power of the controlling few.

Their repeated warning is that science/technology is not neutral. As we design technological systems, we are, in fact, designing sets of social relationships. Computerization is not an isolated event. It is a mode of production that is part of a technological continuum emerging during the past 400 years, and has to be viewed in the context of the political, ideological and cultural assumptions that gave rise to it. When existing technical-social relationships are questioned, and attempts are made to design alternatives, challenges are being made to the power structure of the society.

Cooley, a design engineer himself, is active in groups which are heightening awareness of choices in concrete situations and who pioneer in the invention of "enhancing alternatives". An illustration or two of the kinds of analyses Cooley is making will have to suffice. One of his vivid examples concerns trends in the field of architecture, "The Queen of the Arts", assumed by its practitioners to be safe from the creeping proletarianization of white collar workers.[37] He describes how the relentless drive to extract human skills for transfer to computer storage and use has emerged in a software package for architectural design known as HARNESS. The core system idea is that building design can be systematized so that each building may be regarded as "a communication route". A number of predetermined architectural elements are stored within the computer system. These can be disposed around the communication route on a Visual Display Unit in order to produce different building configurations. Professionally trained architects are limited to choosing from these pre-determined elements.

Cooley finds appropriate a passage from Marx on the distinction between the architect and the bee. He turned it into the title of his newest book, Architect or Bee?:

> A bee puts to shame many an architect in the construction of its cells; but what distinguishes the worst of architects from the best of bees is namely this -- the architect raises in his imagination that which he will ultimately erect in reality. At the end of every labour process, we get a result that already existed in the imagination of the labourer at its commencement.[38]

Cooley points to the control motivation of multi-national corporations and State Socialism, to use the power of science/technology to control the "mode of intellectual production" of more and more technological and scientific workers. The new computerization can be used to extend the old division of labor concept to turn architects into bees. But Cooley refuses to accept the proposition that technology is so far advanced along the wrong path that it is too late to divert it into a different one.

At the technical level, Cooley and colleagues

238

have conceptualized alternative designs of high technology pointing toward human/machine symbiosis which enhances human freedom and imagination. For example, his colleague, H. H. Rosenbrock, works from the assumption that the computer and the human mind have quite different but complementary abilities.[39] The computer excels in analysis and numerical computation, the human mind in "pattern recognition, the assessment of complicated situations and the intuitive leap to new solutions." The obligation of the designer with humanist values is to design systems which are responsive to human judgments, and "which respond to the persons using them rather than acting upon them." Rosenbrock has attempted to counter the powerful de-skilling tendencies by creating alternative technologies for both manual and intellectual work.

Thus, a technical process of Analogic Part Programming has been designed for tool turners in Engineering workshops, which accepts as valid the tacit knowledge and experience of skilled workers and combines these with refined information from the computer to take advantage of both ways of knowing and doing.

The point is that basic value choices are at issue about human/machine relations. Decisions about technical design cannot be divorced from political and ideological choices.

Mike Cooley was sacked by Lucas Industries in 1981. In both his intellectual analyses and in his confrontational role as a leader in the Lucas Shop Stewards Combine Committee, he has clarified the conflict in values between the campaign for socially useful work and the value priorities of major multinational corporations. In terms of political/economic choices, there is no single blue-print model that the Combine endorses. Cooley himself has deep misgivings about the value orientations of both the multinational corporations and State Socialist economic enterprises.

As of this writing he works at the London County Council, where he can support his preference for helping create new human-centered industries based on cooperative worker-ownership principles.[40] Through the London County Council and several other City Councils in England, Cooley and colleagues are working on new plans to confront widespread unemployment. Contact is made with ailing companies. "Product and Equipment Banks" have been started which contain a wealth of ideas and processes, as well as inventions

of unutilized equipment, which companies may draw on
for fresh beginnings. Included are ideas for democratic community planning techniques. The structure
developed for company rehabilitation differs from case
to case. Ideally Cooley favors helping economic
enterprises become completely worker owned producer
cooperatives. Tax incentives and various types of
local government support, including seminars and
educational programs on worker-owned management
techniques, are made available. Where firms stay
under private ownership, a condition for local government assistance is that Planning Agreements be drawn
up with workers (hopefully with community participation) for short term and long term planning. The
Centre for Alternative Industrial Technological
Systems (CAITS) in East London, continues to be a
source of ideas for planning alternative technologies,
e.g., the prototype Road/Rail bus is located there.
It also develops ideas for social and economic alternatives.

Mike Cooley and colleagues have been sustained
through years of arduous and often discouraging
struggle, by the concern that we are confronted with
stark and profoundly significant choices about how
human beings will experience their lives in the
swiftly unfolding era of advanced technology.

Either we will have a future in which human
beings are reduced to a sort of bee-like
behaviour, reacting to the systems and equipment specified for them; or we will have a
future in which masses of people, conscious of
their skills in both a political and technical
sense, decide that they are going to be the
architects of a new form of technological
development which will enhance human creativity and mean more freedom of choice and
expression rather than less. The truth is we
shall have to make the profound decision as to
whether we intend to act as architects or
bees.[41]

There are powerful motivations to continue our bee-
like tendencies: to de-skill people at work, and to
"train for efficiency" instead of to educate our
children. The potential for a happier choice, however, resides partly in breakdowns of the present
arrangements, and partly in the creation of alternatives which demonstrate a capacity to transform
ourselves. There are leaders who are beginning to
accept the wisdom of Hazel Henderson's insight that
"For the first time in history, morality has become

pragmatic."[42] The Lucas Stewards have provided one example of taking seriously the values of treating people as ends, of putting people in touch with their creative, collaborative capacities to build for "permanence, health and beauty."

To take root, such experiments and policies will require both broad-based political support and new kinds of school and societal learning. The details of an appropriate political movement are hardly discernible. It probably would include a coalition of groups from the democratic left and center who draw inspiration from the populist, pluralist, democratic-participation traditions of the culture. Equally important is the need to create processes of education that will teach us to respect the well-being of nature and the integrity and creativity of persons. The issue is whether we can move from vulgar to integral efficiency - whether a society with our history can reach back into its democratic traditions to effect liberating transformation, or whether it will demonstrate the correctness of Marxist theory that a capitalist economy will never permit deviations from its profit-accumulation obsessions.

NOTES

1.   Denis Goulet, The Uncertain Promise. (New York: IDOC/North America, 1977), pp. 30, 28.

2.   Ernest Becker, The Structure of Evil: An Essay on the Unification of the Science of Man. (New York: The Free Press, 1968), p. 39.

3.   Philip G. Herbst, Socio-Technical Design. (London: Tavistock Publications, 1974), p. 203.

4.   Ibid., pp. 203-204.

5.   Ibid., p. 205.

6.   Ibid., pp. 205-206.

7.   Ibid., p. 208.

8.   Ibid., p. 206.

9.   Robert Howard, "Second Class in Silicon Valley," Working Papers (Sept/Oct 1981, Vol. VIII, No. 5) pp. 20-32.

10.   Herbst, op. cit., p. 211.

11.   Ervin Laszlo, The Inner Limits of Mankind. (Oxford: Pergamon Press, 1978), p. 16.

12.   Stewart Ewen, Captains of Consciousness: Advertising and the Social Roots of the Consumer Culture. (New York: McGraw-Hill Book Co., 1976).

13.   Howard C. Carlson, "A model of Quality of Work Life as a Developmental Process", in W. Warner Burke and Leonard D. Goodstein, eds., Trends and Issues in O.D.: Current Theory and Practice. (San Diego: University Associates, 1980), p. 115 and 92-115 et passim.

14.   John Logue (Saab/Trollhatten), "Reforming Work Life on the Shop Floor," Working Life In Sweden, (No. 23, June 1981), p. 3.

15.   Personal visit, Stavanger, May 1980.

16.   Mark A. Lutz and Kenneth Lux, The Challenge of Humanistic Economics. (Menlo Park, California: The Benjamin Cummings Publishing Co., 1979), pp. 230-240 et passim.

17.   Joep F. Bolweg, Job Design and Industrial Democracy. (Leiden: Martinus Nijhoff Social Sciences Division, 1976), p. 103. See also Bertill Gardell and Bjorn Gustavsen, "Work Environment Research and Social Change: Current Developments in Scandinavia," Journal of Occupational Behaviour, (Vol. I, 1980), pp. 3-17.

18.   Daniel Zwerdling, Democracy At Work. (Washington, D.C.: Association for Self-Management, 1978), pp. 168-171 et passim.

19.   Ibid., p. 172.

20.   Martin Carnoy and Derek Shearer, Economic Democracy: The Challenge of the 1980's. (White Plains, NY: M.E. Sharpe Inc., 1980), p. 375. (See also James M. Ellenberger, "The Realities of Co-Determinism," AFL-CIO American Federationist, October 1977, p. 15.)

21.   See Chapter III, pp. 38-39 (Footnote 24).

22.   See Chapter III, pp. 44-45 (Footnote 35).

23.   The account to follow is based largely on David Elliott, The Lucas Aerospace Workers' Campaign. (London: Fabian

Society, 1978).

24. Ibid., p. 8.

25. Interview with Mike Cooley, London, May 18, 1982.

26. Elliott, op. cit., p. 14. (For a recent elaboration see Hilary Wainwright and Dave Elliott, The Lucas Plan: A New Trade Unionism in the Making? (London: Allison and Busby, 1982)).

27. Interview with Mike Cooley, London, May 18, 1982.

28. Descriptions of contradictions from Mike Cooley, "Computerization -- Taylor's Latest Disguise," Economic and Industrial Democracy, Vol 1, 1980, pp. 523-525.

29. Ibid., p. 524 from Norbert Wiener, The Human Use of Human Beings. (New York: Doubleday, 1954).

30. Mike Cooley, Architect or Bee? (Boston: South End Press, 1981), pp. 96-97.

31. Ibid., p. 89.

32. R. S. Silver, "The Misuse of Science," New Scientist, (Vol. 66, 952, June 5, 1975), p. 555.

33. Cooley, op. cit., p. 95.

34. See Chapter III, p. 35. (Footnote 20).

35. Cooley, op. cit., p. 46.

36. Ibid.

37. Cooley, "Computerization," op. cit., p. 531.

38. Ibid.

39. Ibid., pp. 534-536.

40. Interview with Mike Cooley, London, May 18, 1982.

41. Cooley, Architect or Bee?, op. cit., p. 100.

42. Hazel Henderson, "A New Economics," in Dyckman Vermilye, ed., Work and Education. (San Francisco: Jossey-Bass, 1977), p. 235.

CHAPTER X

EDUCATION FOR "INTEGRAL EFFICIENCY":
NO LIMITS TO LEARNING

A theory of instruction is a political theory
in the proper sense that it derives from
consensus concerning the distribution of power
within the society - who will be educated to
fulfill what roles? In the very same sense,
...pedagogical theory must surely derive from
a conception of economics, for where there is
division of labor within the society and
exchange of goods and services for wealth and
prestige then how people are educated and in
what number and with what constraints on the
use of resources are all relevant issues. The
psychologist or educator who formulates
pedagogical theory without regard to the
political, economic, and social setting of the
educational process courts triviality and
merits being ignored in the community and
classroom. [1]   Jerome Bruner

The general position we have been arguing is
that disarray symptoms point to a need to move away
from the values and life-style of "modernism", before
we close out this century. We have argued that new
learnings are required across institutions; that for
schools to play their most effective role, they need
support and modeling from the master institution -
economic life; that the values emerging in work
redesign in socio-technical and quality of work life
theory represent a constructive development. They are
congruent with the democratic-humanist values of our
tradition as well as the conceptual needs of a technological era; they are congruent with shifts toward an
"ecological-symbiotic" world view, and the values of a
liberalizing view of learning. Finally we have
suggested, that while there is enormous complexity in
the order of shifts required, a significant contribution of work redesign is that it helps people in their
daily lives to escape the grip of ego-centered consumerism. It helps them to raise questions about the
quality of life: first by engaging in reflective
analysis about what is problematic in work life, then,
hopefully by raising ethical questions about policies
for people and the environment beyond the place of
work.

This general perspective coincides in major

245

respects with the 1979 Club of Rome Report, No Limits To Learning. The report took the position that the critical task for the eighties is to initiate new forms of human learning. They called for allies in mobilizing a large segment of public opinion to reflect on social and educational alternatives. Since this present book may be seen as one such ally, it is worthwhile to look at the juxtapositions between the two. No Limits To Learning may help to point to the larger arena of social change to which the redesign of schooling and work may be related.

No Limits To Learning was deliberately designed to see if thinkers from the East, West, and the Third World could agree on global priorities for the remaining years of this century. Its three authors, representing the "three worlds", identified both a substantive problem and a normative position on which they could agree. They saw the substantive problem rooted in the fact that humans act on the world to effect mutations, in the natural environment and their own condition, resulting in dangerous consequences which they do not adequately comprehend. The result is a widening human gap between an increasingly serious set of global problems (the world problematique), and the human insights, capacities and will to resolve them.

The Club of Rome identified the world problematique as an increasingly precarious "tangle of mutually reinforcing old and new problems, too complex to be apprehended by the current analytical methods and too tough to be attacked by traditional policies and strategies...plaguing all nations whether developed or developing, whatever their political regime and societal structure." The result is a growing realization that:

increasing world disorder and real or feared scarcities of natural resources exacerbate social tensions and trigger military build-ups of demential proportions, stifling peaceful developments; that in a polity where might is right the myth of national sovereignty but aggravates the inequalities among states, while social injustice coupled with inefficient, often corrupt institutions, breeds civil violence, which readily expands internationally; that polluted and impoverished environments, besides vitiating our life, also drag the economy downwards at a time when recession and inflation already conflow into stagflation, spawning unemployment, frustration and still more tension and disorder.[2]

Having called attention in earlier reports, such as The Limits to Growth (1972) and Mankind at the Turning Point (1974) to the complex of material problems in areas such as energy, population, and food, the Club, by the opening of the eighties, was ready to argue that an adequate attack on this web of interrelated problems depended on giving priority to support of the "latent capability of understanding and learning" of peoples across the world's societies. If there are "material limits to growth" there are potentially "no limits to learning". There is hope in the human potential for learning, but age-old habits inhibit the maximizing of the potential.

As the Report puts it:
Traditionally, societies and individuals have adopted a pattern of continuous maintenance learning interrupted by short periods of innovation stimulated largely by the shock of external events. Maintenance learning is the acquisition of fixed outlooks, methods, and rules for dealing with known and recurring situations. [3]

It is learning designed to maintain an existing or established way of life. Maintenance learning is indispensable to the functioning and stability of every society. But, in a time of unprecedented, disruptive global change, the conventional pattern of maintenance/shock learning is inadequate to cope with the complexity and gravity of the problems. The dangers of reliance on shock learning are too great. For example, to wait to do serious study of renewable sources of energy until we are struck by petroleum scarcities, higher prices, or nuclear accidents is intolerably risky. Furthermore, the onset of the complex challenges of the global problematiques marks the end of a period where learning can be denied to large portions of humanity without adverse effects.

Another type of learning, as a complement to desirable aspects of maintenance learning, increasingly becomes a top priority. The authors call it innovative learning.

It is no longer practical to rely on conventional learning at a time when people are increasingly conscious of their rights and of their capacity to support -- or impede -- measures handed down from above. Irrespective of any consideration of the immorality of restricting learning by race, sex, culture, or nation, no way has yet been devised to generate widescale understanding, cooperation, and

247

participation of some critical mass of the world's inhabitants in the short time period often required. Shock learning can be seen as a product of elitism, technocracy, and authoritarianism. Learning by shock often follows a period of over-confidence in solutions created solely with expert technical knowledge and perpetuated beyond the conditions for which they are appropriate. Should global shock occur, many of the positive accomplishments of science and technology are likely to be discarded in a reaction against elitism and technocracy.[4]

We, of course, have presented the hypothesis that we are beginning to experience the shock of dysfunctionality of the technocratic life style in both industry and education. We have pointed to leaders in both institutions who now hold that efforts to check declining productivity by stepping up technocratic controls is an effort to "cure" by "maintenance learning" remedies, which themselves may be the source of difficulties.

There are parallels between (1) the sociotechnical theory, which argues that "technical fix" type solutions are inadequate for handling the complexity and rapidity of technological and social change, and (2) the Club of Rome's arguments that maintenance learning is inadequate for meeting the impact of turbulent change.

The Report asks "What type of learning is required to bridge the human gap?" We present several key features of the type of innovative learning they argue for. These include:

1) Skills of <u>anticipatory learning</u> to reduce the trauma of learning by shock. By this they mean developing habits of spotting significant trends of change, evaluating the range of consequences, identifying key value choices, and projecting plans for action.

2) A second key feature of innovative learning is <u>participation</u>. It is required partly because major problems cannot be resolved by expert action alone, and partly because there is a global emergence of hitherto submerged groups who demand a role in the action.

If participation is to be effective, it will be essential that those who hold power do not block innovative learning. Participation is more than the formal sharing of decisions; it is an attitude characterized by cooperation,

248

dialogue, and empathy. It means not only keeping communications open but also constantly testing one's operating rules and values, retaining those that are relevant and rejecting those that have become obsolescent. [5]

A key requirement is that the skills of "anticipatory" learning and "participatory" learning be tied together.

3) It is not enough that only elites or decision makers are anticipatory when the resolution of a global issue depends on the broad-based support from some critical mass of people. Participation, however, without anticipation can be counter productive or misguided.

4) The seriousness of "the world problematique" which led to the argument for innovative learning means that it cannot be "value free". Learning aimed at identifying constructive change must be willing to question fundamental values, purposes and objectives of any system.

In view of the Report's view of the gravity of what is at issue, it announces that its concept of innovative learning is committed to support two normative values: human survival and human dignity. (1) Innovative learning is essential for human survival. The dictum of "learn or perish" is imperative for handling the survival needs of developing countries who have in their power the capacity to annihilate the human race. (2) The goal of survival, however, is not enough. Behind the rising calls for participation is the demand for human dignity. This is rooted in the need for individual self-respect, and beyond that, the according of respect to those in other roles and cultures.

The thesis then is that forms of innovative learning need to be developed in schools, and other institutions of the culture which involve both conceptual and normative dimensions. At the moment, a serious gap exists between what and how individuals learn and the changes societies must make.

The authors say that the key issue of how to get better linkage between individual and societal learning is not well established but they offer several recommendations about learning style which seem appropriate.

(1) Conceptually, the search for meaning - the desire to grasp a problem, to understand its significance, and to envisage solutions - is central in the present world. The reality in both developed and developing countries, in primitive or sophisticated

249

forms, is that enormous amounts of energies in schools are devoted to the ingestion of fragments of information; and, as Adam Curle put it, teaching students "to learn to compete for right answers so they can advance within the system."[6]   This motivates some, but it is neglect of meaning that creates the risk of alienating individuals from society. And the relative neglect of meaning in favor of information accumulation is the source of ineffective learning. The expansion of knowledge and access to media confront all of us with the problem of how to deal with information over-load.

The authors point to research which suggests that cognitive processes consist fundamentally in the matching of new information inputs with appropriate mental schemata created by past experience.

Our brain does not store memorized items in isolation, but keeps them in multiple copies according to the contexts associated with their arrival.... As the number of these contexts grow, understanding and learning are profoundly affected.[7]

Thus, significant obstacles to innovative learning derive from the neglect of context.   It cannot be reduced to the mere digesting of inputs resulting in outputs, or a simple additive process of connecting value judgments to things.   In order to enhance the capacity to act in new situations and to deal with unfamiliar events, innovative learning requires the absorption of vast collections of contexts. When contexts are restricted, the probability of shock learning increases.   Thus a key obligation is to enhance the ability of people to find, absorb, create new contexts - and to compare different contexts to reconcile their conflicts.

This exploring and extending of meanings is facilitated through reflective communication.   In dialogue, individual contexts are confronted, shared, expanded or changed.

(2) The conceptual meaning-seeking dimension of innovative learning in a time of change, tension, and cultural interaction requires a complementary normative dimension: practice in the examination and selection of value choices. As the authors put it:

The role of values distinguishes maintenance from innovative learning. Maintenance learning tends to ignore those values not inherent in the social or political structures it is designed to maintain, and even to keep its intrinsic values implicit and unexposed. Yet it is the tension created by the pressure

250

to select from among multiple values that
catalyzes innovative learning. This can be a
dramatic and stimulating process. It is one
that nearly every individual has experienced:
when one's values are being challenged, one's
learning comes to life. From this point of
view, values can be said to be the enzymes of
any innovative process. [8]

Space prohibits a more detailed analysis of
innovative learning but one final dimension is relevant. Value choices are related to the quality of
human relations which contribute to the participative,
context forming features of innovative learning. The
main obstacle to individual and societal innovative
learning, which robs us of enriched contexts, is the
asymmetry of interactions imposed by unequal power
relationships. Centralization, vertical relationships, and the perpetuation of unnecessary hierarchy
characterize societies still dominated by feudal
traditions or by organizational features of advanced
industrial societies. Top down relationships and
centralized control tend to suppress experimentation
and variety by imposing official or expert-made
solutions and contexts. The compelling need, therefore, is for multiple efforts at decentralizing,
including the need to create "smallness within
bigness".

Enough of the Report's orientation has been
presented to establish connections between its recommendations and the learning features for work and
schooling which we earlier had argued would be supportive of "integral efficiency". We are ready now for
some summary observations of our own about implications for education if "new work" philosophy and
practice become a serious development.

A. Summary Reflections on Education

We have entertained the idea that there are
significant connections between the quality of work
experienced by adults and the quality of education
experienced by their children. We have joined those
like The Club of Rome who assume that we stand at a
critical point of choice as we close the awesome
twentieth century. Science/technology carries us into
a post-industrial era with revolutionary changes in
areas like communications/cybernetics, robotics,
computers, nuclear power, genetic engineering, and
space exploration. These will change human experience
in ways we can but dimly surmise.

251

Whether we respond in terms of past tendencies to approach the world as a mechanism to be manipulated by a few, or whether we choose emerging alternatives which open more salutary possibilities, will be manifest in the designs we bring to the master institution of work. What happens there will have permeating effects on the rest.

The choices bring us up against the most profound philosophical questions - questions about how we conceive the nature of our world, the nature of human life and learning, the nature of science/ technology, and the quality of social and spiritual life we choose to embrace. We have referred only glancingly to these questions. The clarification and elaboration of the underlying philosophical problems will be the exciting intellectual work in the years ahead.

We have revealed our own bias and belief, that our best bet depends on a renewal of the values of our democratic tradition combined with an ecological perspective. ("Science", Renée Dubos reminds us, is "evolving from the description of concrete objects and events to the study of relationships as observed in complex systems.")[9]

Our thesis has been that a prototype of values for "good work" is emerging in democratic sociotechnical work theory. We end with some reasons why educators should find this concept of "good work" relevant for their own purposes. The case centers around two related features of the concept: first, its resistance to being reduced to a fixed formula and second, its nature as a hyphenated term.

There is an understandable hunger among educators for clear and precise answers to the question of "What do we do on Monday morning?" There has never been a lack of prophets rushing to fill the gap with answers; we have rarely failed to be disappointed with the results. It is refreshing, therefore, to find the articulators of democratic socio-technical theory refusing to offer formula type promises. Its essence is primarily a set of values and processes aimed at freeing capacities for learning and acting. Beyond that, its hyphenated nature is not without significance. At the most obvious level, it points to the need to take both technical learning and socio (human) involvement seriously. There is trouble when either side of the hyphen is neglected. The history of American education is filled with the litter of burnt out models which emphasized one extreme at the expense of the other.

252

In writing about education, however, it is very easy to point to the shortcomings of one dimension while ignoring its constructive features. If, for example, in the preceding chapters, I seemed to deplore the technical dimension of testing, it was only to point to the reductionist danger of narrowing teaching to "teaching for tests", i.e., of limiting teaching too exclusively to its technical aspects.

We need, of course, to have full access to the whole range of educational technologies to help improve the skill training of our youngsters. Under caring teachers, youngsters can rise to the challenge of learning how to perform well on appropriate tests. They can learn to take pride in growth in their individual and group performances. They can learn to be stimulated by the nature of the problems confronted and can be helpful to each other in mastering conceptual skills. Our schools need to invite children to test the limits of their personal abilities or areté (excellence). But they need opportunities to test their limits in a whole array of personal and group challenges: in the arts, in group problem-solving, in athletics, in service to the community and to each other. Competition, in the sense of seeking to excel over one's best effort as well as over others, is a zestful aspect of human experience. We all know, however, that it can degenerate into a corrupting desire to win at any cost. In schools, it is debased when learning is reduced to ugly impersonal pressures on teachers and schools "to get those scores up, no matter what." When pressures for technical quantitative results contaminate morale and caring, schools are turned into bad work places.

Beyond this obvious point, the hyphenated dimension points to a deeper issue - one identified by E. F. Schumacher as the difference between two fundamentally different types of problems: those which lend themselves to solutions by abstract logical reasoning (convergent problems) and those which do not (divergent problems). [10]

Convergent problems (such as those in geometry), when solved, can be written down and passed on to others. The techniques for solving these are enormously useful for certain technical/scientific problems. There is, however, a very different realm of problems in the area of human relations - in family life, education, politics, economics, and so forth, which do not lend themselves to neat solutions of logical thought. They involve the imprecise requirement of reconciling opposites, which in logical

253

thought cannot be reconciled. There is, for example, the need to reconcile the claims of freedom and discipline faced endlessly by parents and teachers. There is no one solution that one can write down, but countless parents and teachers work out salutary answers that accommodate their own needs and those of the children. Answers to such divergent problems have to be lived answers. They require more than recipe responses or logical reasoning. They require struggle and involvement by whole persons. Clever formula answers are always being proposed which promise easy short-cuts, but they don't work for long because invariably they neglect one of the two opposites and "thus lose the very quality of human life."[11]

From the hyphenated socio-technical perspective, those planners in industry or education who try to make divergent problems yield to convergent answers are guilty of the technological fix error. Educators who see that most of their problems are divergent may find it fruitful to consider the socio-technical concept. They will lose the pseudo-certainty promised by the rational control model; they will gain a refreshing sense that they are in honest contact with the whole range of exciting promises and disturbing frustrations of human reality.

We review now a few examples to illustrate how the socio-technical perspective is congruent with the need to "balance the opposites" required by divergent problems. The theme was, in fact, a recurrent one throughout the preceding chapters.

Thus, in one of the early efforts to introduce the socio-technical model in the U. S. A., Maccoby added the humanistic values of "democracy" and "individualism" to balance older trade union principles of "security" and "equity". To operationalize the principles, Core Planning Groups were created which combined the perspectives of union workers and management - to work on the task of reconciling improved quality of work life with production needs.

In education, we noted the early efforts of John Dewey to challenge the bureaucratic prescriptive style in big city educational systems. In spite of the fact that Dewey is often associated with "permissiveness", we noted Dewey's insistence on divergent type thinking for resolution of educational problems. In one of his influential tracts on education, The Child and the Curriculum (1902), Dewey held that efforts to force a choice between "the child" or "the curriculum" were misplaced. A meaning-seeking concept of education that will help learners "reconstruct

254

experience" so they will see the world or themselves differently requires, he said, that teachers take seriously the insight and meanings of the subject and the life experience and curiosities of the learners. There is no one right method or expert-designed program to accomplish this. Effective education requires imaginative utilization of the subjective experience of the teachers who have personally thought their way through to the meaning of their subjects, as well as intelligent use of educational programs, texts and technologies.

Dewey had a sense of the importance of recognizing the need to work out lived answers to balance the claims of the child and the subject matter; and to combine freedom and initiative of teachers, with concerns for academic quality.12 Dewey's affinity for divergent rather than linear control solutions was grounded in his broader philosophy. He had explored the values of the community of science to discern what made it such an effective model of human learning. The core values, he held, were individuality and community. The resolution of them required a never-ending creative "balancing of the opposites". In Dewey's mind that mode provided not only a model for creative learning, but for creative institutional and societal living. Individuality and community are core values of democracy rooted in primary human needs for sane living; thus, Dewey's conclusion that effective schools should be democratic learning communities for teachers, administrators and students.

We found concurrence with the Deweyan tradition in the educational ideas of the contemporary socio-technical theorist, Philip Herbst. In order to deal with the challenge of change in a technological era, Herbst argued for a shift away from the "production process" models of learning of earlier industrialism to "research process" models, although he accepted the necessity for a balance of both. Herbst also argued that institutions viable enough to cope with post-industrial turbulence must themselves be institutions capable of learning. He was, therefore, critical of school systems whose programs are rigidly prescribed by centralized authority. He called for more autonomy for individual schools, with Boards of Education whose consultative and facilitative roles would grow, while their prescriptive, control functions would diminish.

We found similar ideas in the thinking of a leading scholar of contemporary American education, John Goodlad, who charged that educational planning, based on the production models of industry, is out of touch with realities of work in schools. As he identified historic examples of "schools of excellence" he found they were schools with a great deal of autonomy, and a sense of mission, unity, identity and wholeness that came from a dynamic tension between strong principal leadership and vigorous teacher participation.

As we enter the eighties, we find a new group of "revisionists" in educational administration who are bringing under criticism the orthodox injunctions to follow industrial rationalization models. Thus, Karl Weick argues that schools have been managed with an incorrect "tightly coupled" model in mind. Schools are in reality, he says, marked by "loose coupling" that demands a judicious balance of teacher or teacher group autonomy and initiative, with imaginative administrative leadership to provide the "glue" to hold things together.[13]

The "loose coupling" concept recognizes that effectiveness requires a framework that can capitalize on a wide range of human uniqueness and creativity. To tap that range requires taking the risk to move from monologue-type control to a kind of communication that opens the whole range of human complexity - confrontation of cantankerousness, anger and irritation as well as imaginative innovation and problem-solving. It takes a commitment to a never-ending search for a fine balance between administrative direction and decision making, and support of freedom of initiatives by the staff. "Tight coupling" brings "order" at a price that undermines educational effectiveness.

That reach for a balance between "freedom and order" for adults in schools has its counterpart, of course, in the work of students. John Bremer, founder of the Philadelphia Parkway School Without Walls program, one of the productive innovators of the late sixties, observed that a basic axiom of teaching is:
There is no learning without structure...and ...there is no learning without 'unstructure'. The function of the educator...is to provide that combination of order and disorder, of structure and unstructure which will, on the one hand, support the student as he learns, and on the other hand, provide him with something to learn.[14]
We know something when we order it, bring it into relationship with other things.

In my own experience some of the most effective teaching I have seen occurred when teams of four

teachers representing English, Mathematics, Social
Studies and Science in a junior high school functioned
as "autonomous work groups". Each team was responsible for about a hundred students. Teachers operated
within the general curriculum guidelines of the
district which included a testing program. Beyond
that, the teachers had a good deal of autonomy in how
they would relate to create structure/unstructure type
learning experiences for students. One team had
relatively little interaction and stayed within
boundaries teacher members were comfortable with.
Families who favored this style could choose it.
Another team emphasized parental activity both in
class instruction and in joint educational/social
events such as week-end canoe trips. Students were
encouraged to move toward the "research project-type"
learning activities but only after they demonstrated a
capacity to handle responsibilities in more structured
learning situations. "Structure and unstructure" were
involved in both teams but in ways that accommodated
the differing styles and needs of teachers and
students.

Reflection on the subtle complexities of
significant learning gives the lie to the simplistic
notion that we can get effective education by "making
school hard and flunking a lot of them." What we need
is an education that challenges all of them. That can
happen only if we have teachers who find fulfillment
and challenge in their own work. The creative ones
won't remain if they are offered only technocratic
straight-jackets that stifle their personal
enthusiasms.

Behind the question of styles of teaching are
questions about the nature of learning itself. Here,
too, we encountered ideas which embraced the divergent
perspective. Thus, Erich Fromm distinguished
intelligence involved in the capacity to acquire and
apply information, from reason, which he associated
with a person's capacity to win understanding through
a personal appropriation of meanings. Since both
dimensions are vital for human growth, "either/or"
solutions are self-defeating.

Mike Cooley, in his awareness of the waste
involved in neglecting the personal, experiential
learning of work place personnel, found clarification
in Michael Polanyi's concept of the importance of the
tacit dimension of knowing, in both its inarticulate
and articulate manifestations. To try to separate the
inarticulate tacit dimension of our knowing from
articulate abstract thinking is to cripple our

257

capacity to learn and understand in both our personal and social lives. Polanyi reminds us, too, that the ideal of detached impersonal knowledge is out of touch with the reality of human understanding or comprehension. The alternative to the empiricist idea of knowing is an ideal of knowledge which recognizes that "the participation of the knower in shaping his knowledge ...is now recognized as the true guide and master of our cognitive powers."[15] In Polanyi's words, the human need for comprehension is rooted in a personal craving for understanding. It entails an active grasping of disjointed parts into a comprehensive whole. This coincides with Dewey's image of learning as an active reconstruction of experience, a reaching forward into the world for meaning. The image is of the person as homo poeta, the meaning maker.[16]

The dignity of our person is dependent on our having access to the opportunity to develop this distinctive capacity of our being. It is true for children and for adults.

Paulo Freire's rejection of the monologic conveying of information to passive peasants by agricultural extension experts was rooted in his sense of how that diminished the dignity of both the peasant and the expert. The alternative was an active process of dialogue in which the tacit knowledge of the peasants could interact fruitfully with the abstract knowledge of the experts. The process of dialogue which brings together the personal and technical dimensions of learning could enhance the dignity of both.

We could note additional ways in which the divergent concept of "good work" bears on the problems of education. It is fit, however, to stop on an unfinished note. The essence of the concept is that it is a process for securing more sane, productive development. It is not a finished product.

It is appropriate to end with a reminder by Philip Herbst. Current efforts to solve problems of productivity in work and education by nervous accelerations of mechanistic control methods are foundering. They fail because they ignore the necessity of an ethical concern - an ethical concern for the entheos, the personal enthusiasms that are the sources of creativity and commitment. Such efforts make the category error of treating human subjects as objects. They fail to see the relation of that to the observation of Renée Dubos that alienation and chaos in human affairs and relations have the same origin as chaos between man and his natural environment.

258

When man truly enters the age of science he
will abandon his crude and destructive efforts
to conquer nature. He will instead learn to
insert himself into the environment in such a
manner that his ways of life and technologies
make him once more in harmony with nature.[17]

NOTES

1. Jerome Bruner, "Culture, Politics and Pedagogy,"
Saturday Review, (May 18, 1968), p. 69.

2. James W. Botkin, Mahdi Elmandjra, and Mircea Malitza,
No Limits To Learning. (Oxford: Pergamon Press, 1979), p. xiv.

3. Ibid., p. 10.

4. Ibid., p. 11.

5. Ibid., p. 13.

6. Adam Curle, Education for Liberation. (New York: John
Wiley and Sons, 1973), see Chapter I.

7. Botkin, op. cit., pp. 22-23.

8. Ibid., p. 40.

9. Renée Dubos, The God Within. (New York: Charles
Scribner's Sons, 1972), pp. 41-42.

10. E. F. Schumacher, Small Is Beautiful: Economics As If
People Mattered. (New York: Harper Torchbooks, 1973), pp.
89-90.

11. Ibid., p. 91.

12. See Arthur G. Wirth, John Dewey as Educator. (New York:
John Wiley and Sons, 1966), Chapter 5.

13. Karl E. Weick, "Administering Education in Loosely
Coupled Schools," Phi Delta Kappan, (June 1982, Vol 63, No. 10),
pp. 673-676.

14. John Bremer, A Matrix For Modern Education. (Toronto:
McClellan and Stewart Ltd., 1975), pp. 11, 15.

15. Michael Polanyi, The Study of Man. (Chicago: The
University of Chicago Press, 1959), p. 26.

16.   Becker, op. cit., p. 172.

17.   Dubos, op. cit., pp. 149–150.

BIBLIOGRAPHY

Apple, Michael, "Curriculum Form and the Logic of Technical Control," Economic and Industrial Democracy, 2, 3 (August 1981).

Becker, Ernest, The Structure of Evil. New York: The Free Press, 1978.

Bell, Daniel, "Schools in American Society." In Louis Rubin, ed., The Future of America: Perspectives on Tomorrow's Schooling. Boston: Allyn and Bacon, 1975.

Berger, Peter, et.al., The Homeless Mind. New York: Vintage Books, 1974.

Berlak, Ann and Harold Berlak, Dilemmas of Schooling: Teaching and Social Change. New York: Methuen, 1981.

Bernstein, Harry, "Democracy Moves into the Work Place." Los Angeles Times, October 23, 1980.

Bernstein, Richard J., The Restructuring of Social and Political Theory. Philadelphia: University of Pennsylvania Press, 1976.

Bettelheim, Bruno, "Why Children Don't Like To Read", Atlantic Monthly, 248, 1 (November 1981).

Blichfeldt, Jon F., "Relations Between School and the Place of Work," School and Community, OECD (CERI), Paris, 1975.

Bluestone, Irving, "A Changing View of Union-Management Relationships." Vital Speeches, 43, 4 (December 11, 1976).

_____, "Quality of Work Life: Its Status and Its Future." Proceedings, 1980, Executive Conference on Quality of Work Life (General Motors).

_____, "UAW-Loosening the Chains." The Harvard Crimson, February 21, 1979.

Bolweg, Joep F., Job Design and Industrial Democracy. Leiden: Martinus Nijhoff Social Sciences Division, 1976.

Bookchin, Murray, The Ecology of Freedom. Palo Alto: Cheshire Books, 1982.

Botkin, James W., Mahdi Elmandjra, and Mircea Malitza, No Limits To Learning (A Report to the Club of Rome). Oxford:

Pergamon Press, 1979.

Bowers, C.A., "Cultural Literacy in Developed Countries."
Prospects, VII, 3, 1977.

_____, "Emergent Ideological Characteristics of Educational
Policy," Teachers College Record, 79, 1 (September 1977).

Bowra, C.M., The Greek Experience. Cleveland: The World
Publishing Co., 1957.

Braverman, Harry, Labor and Monopoly Capital: The Degradation of
Work in the Twentieth Century. New York: Monthly Review
Press, 1974.

Burnett, Joe, "John Dewey and the Ploys of Revisionism."
Educational Considerations, 7, 2 (1980).

Bremer, John, A Matrix for Modern Education. Toronto: McClellan
and Stewart, Ltd., 1975.

Business Week, "A Solution: A New Social Contract." No 2643 (June
30, 1980).

Callahan, Raymond E. Education and the Cult of Efficiency.
Chicago: University of Chicago Press, 1962.

Carlson, Howard C., "A Model of Quality of Work Life as a
Developmental Process." In W. W. Burke and L.D. Goodstein,
ed., Trends and Issues in OD: Current Theory and Practice.
San Diego: University Associates, 1980.

Carnoy, Martin and Derek Shearer, Economic Democracy: The
Challenge of the 1980's. New York: M.E. Sharpe, Inc., 1980.

Cohn, Marilyn, "Back to Basics: A Case Study of Student
Learning." Unpublished, Washington University, St. Louis,
1980.

Cooley, Mike, Architect or Bee? Boston: South End Press, 1981.

_____, "Computerization -- Taylor's Latest Disguise,"
Economic and Industrial Democracy, 1, 4 (November 1980).

Cork, Jim. "John Dewey, Karl Marx and Democratic Socialism."
Antioch Review, IX, 4 (December 1949).

Cronbach, Lee J. and Suppes, Patrick, eds., Research for
Tomorrow's Schools. Toronto: MacMillan, 1969.

Curle, Adam, <u>Education for Liberation</u>. New York: John Wiley and Sons, 1973.

Davis, L.E. and Cherns, A.B., eds., <u>The Quality of Work Life, Vol. I</u>. New York: Free Press, 1975.

Davis, Louis E. "Optimizing Organization-Plant Design: A Complementary Structure for Technical and Social Systems", <u>Organizational Dynamics</u>, 8, 2 (Autumn, 1979).

Dewey, John, <u>The Child and the Curriculum and School and Society</u>. Chicago: University of Chicago Press, 1943 ed.

_____, <u>Democracy and Education</u>. New York: MacMillan, 1916.

_____, <u>Education Today</u>. New York: Putnam, 1949.

_____, <u>Ethics</u>. New York: Henry Holt, 1908.

_____, <u>How We Think</u>. Boston: D.C. Heath and Co., 1933 rev. ed.

_____, <u>Individualism Old and New</u>. New York: Capricorn Books, 1962.

_____, <u>Intelligence in the Modern World</u>. Ed. Joseph Ratner. New York: Modern Library, 1939.

_____, <u>Liberalism and Social Action</u>. New York: Capricorn Books, 1963.

_____, "Plan of Organization of the University Primary School." Published in Appendix of Arthur G. Wirth, <u>John Dewey As Educator</u>. New York: John Wiley and Sons, 1968.

_____, <u>Problems of Men</u>. New York: Philosophical Library, 1946.

_____, "Progressive Education and the Science of Education." <u>Progressive Education</u>, Vol. 5 (July 1928).

_____, <u>The Public and Its Problems</u>. Chicago: Swallow Press, 1954.

_____, <u>Reconstruction in Philosophy</u>. New York: The American Library, 1950.

_____, <u>School and Society</u>. Chicago: University of Chicago Press, rev. ed., 1923.

263

_____, The Sources of a Science of Education. New York: Horace Riverwright, 1929.

Dickson, Paul, The Future of the Workplace. New York: Weybright and Talley, 1975.

Dubos, Renée, The God Within. New York: Charles Scribner's Sons, 1972.

Duckles, M. M., et.al., "The Process of Change at Bolivar." (Available from the Harvard Project on Technology, Work, and Character, 1710 Connecticut Avenue N.W., Washington, DC, 20009).

Elden, Max, Sharing the Research Work. Trondheim: Institute for Industrial Social Research, Norwegian Technical University, 1977.

Ellenberger, James M., "The Realities of Co-Determination," AFL-CIO American Federationist (October 1977).

Elliott, David, The Lucas Aerospace Campaign. London: The Fabian Society, 1978.

Eliot, Charles W., "Industrial Education as the Essential Factor in Our National Prosperity." National Society for the Promotion of Industrial Education, Bulletin, No. 5, 1908.

Emery, Fred and Einar Thorsrud, Democracy At Work, Leiden: Martinus Nijhoff Social Sciences Division, 1976.

_____, Form and Content in Industrial Democracy. London: Tavistock, 1969.

Emery, Fred E., and Eric L. Trist, Towards a Social Ecology. New York: Plenum/Rosetta, 1973.

Ewen, Stuart, Captains of Consciousness: Advertising and the Social Roots of Consumer Culture. New York: McGraw-Hill Book Co., 1976.

Fay, Brian, Social Theory and Political Practice. London: George Allen and Unwin, 1975.

Feuer, Lewis, "John Dewey and the Back to the People Movement." Journal of the History of Ideas, XX, (October-December 1959).

Fish, Frederick, "The Vocational and Industrial School." N.E.A. Proceedings, 1910.

264

Freire, Paulo, Education for Critical Consciousness. New York: The Seabury Press (A Continuum Book), 1974.

Fromm, Erich, The Revolution of Hope: Toward a Humanized Technology. New York: Harper and Row, 1968.

_____, The Sane Society. New York: Rinehart and Co., 1955.

Fuller, Stephen H., "Corporate Approaches to the Quality of Work Life." Personnel Journal, 59, 8 (August 1980).

Gardell, Bertil and Bjørn Gustavson, "Work Environment Research and Social Change: Current Developments in Scandinavia," Journal of Occupational Behaviour, I, 3-17, 1980.

Giddings, Franklin, Principles of Sociology. New York: MacMillan, 1896.

Gilder, George, Wealth and Poverty. New York: Basic Books, 1980.

Goodlad, John, "Can Our Schools Get Better?" Phi Delta Kappan, 60, 5 (January 1979).

Goulet, Denis, The Uncertain Promise. New York: IDOC/North America, 1977.

Green, Thomas F., Work, Leisure, and the American Schools. New York: Random House, 1968.

Guest, Robert H., "Quality of Work Life -- Learning from Tarrytown." Harvard Business Review, 57, 4 (July-August 1979).

Gyllenhammar, Pehr G., People at Work. Reading, Ma.: Addison-Wesley Publishing, Co., 1977.

Hackman, J.R. and G. R. Oldham, Work Redesign. Reading, Ma.: Addison-Wesley Publishing Co., 1980.

The Harmon Mirror, Bolivar, Tennessee: Harman International Industries, June, 1977.

Harrison, Ordia, "Education as Practice for Freedom and Socio-Technical Theory", Unpublished paper, Washington University, St. Louis, MO, 1981.

Hays, Samuel P., The Response to Industrialism: 1885-1914. Chicago: University of Chicago Press, 1957.

Henderson, Hazel, "A New Economics", In Vermilye, Dyckman, ed.,

Work and Education. San Francisco: Jossey-Bass, 1977.

Herbst, Phillip B., _Alternatives to Hierarchies_. Leiden: Martinus Nijhoff Social Science Division, 1976.

_____, _Socio-Technical Design_. London: Tavistock Publications, 1974.

Hirschhorn, Larry, "The Soul of a New Worker," _Working Papers Magazine_, 9, 1, January/February, 1982.

Horner, Bill, "UAW Involvement." _Proceedings_ 1980 Executive Conference on Quality of Work Life (General Motors).

House, Ernest R., "Evaluation as Scientific Management in U.S. School Reform." _Comparative Education Review_, 22, 3 (October 1978).

Howard, Robert, "Second Class in Silicon Valley", _Working Papers_, 8, 5 (September/October 1981).

Jackson, Philip W., _Life in the Classroom_. New York: Holt, Rinehart and Winston, 1968.

Johansen, Ragnar, "Democratizing Work and Social Life on Ships: A Report from the Experiment on Board M. S. _Balao_." Ship Research Group, Work Research Institutes, Oslo, Norway, 1979.

Kolakowski, Leszek, _Main Currents of Marxism: Its Rise, Growth and Dissolution_. Oxford: Clarendon Press, 1978.

Landen, Delmar L., "Labor-Management Cooperation in Productivity. April 21, 1980. Available from Organization Research and Development Division, G.M.

_____, "The Real Issue: Human Dignity." _Survey of Business_, 12, 5 (May-August 1977).

_____, Article in _Los Angeles Times_ (October 23, 1980).

Laszlo, Ervin, _The Inner Limits of Mankind_. New York: The Pergamon Press, 1978.

Leavitt, Frank M., "How Shall We Study the Industries for the Purpose of Vocational Guidance." U.S. Bureau of Education _Bulletin_, #14 (U.S. Government Printing Office, 1914).

Lerner, Max, _America as a Civilization_. New York: Simon and Schuster, 1957.

Levin, Henry, _Education and Work_. Stanford: Institute for Research on Educational Finance and Governance, December, 1982.

Logue, John, "Reforming Work Life on the Shop Floor", _Working Life in Sweden_, No. 23, June 1981.

Lortie, Dan, _School Teacher_. Chicago: University of Chicago Press, 1975.

Lovejoy, Owen R., "Vocational Guidance and Child Labor." U.S. Bureau of Education _Bulletin_, #14 (U.S. Government Printing Office, 1914).

Luttwak, Edward N., "A Critical View of the U.S. Military Establishment." _Forbes_, 125, 11 (May 26, 1980).

Lutz, Mark A. and Kenneth Lux, _The Challenge of Humanistic Economics_. Menlo Park, California: The Benjamin Cummings Publishing Co., 1979.

Maccoby, Michael, "The Quality of Working Life -- Lessons from Bolivar." Available from Harvard Project on Technology, Work and Character, 1710 Connecticut Ave. N.W., Washington, DC 20009.

_____, "What is Productivity?" Cambridge: Harvard Project on Technology, Work and Character, 1979.

Marx, Karl, _Economic and Philosophical Manuscripts_. London: Lawrence and Wishart, 1971.

Mayhew, Katherine C. and Anna C. Edwards, _The Dewey School_. New York: Appleton-Century-Crofts, 1936.

McLaughlin, Milbrey W., _Evaluation and Modern Reform_. Cambridge, Ma.: Ballinger, 1975.

Mecklenberger, James, _Performance Contracting_. Worthington, Ohio: Charles A. Jones Publishing Co., 1972.

Merkle, Judith A., _Management and Ideology_. Berkeley: University of California Press, 1980.

Miller, Ernest C., "GM's Quality of Work Life Efforts ... An Interview with Howard C. Carlson, Reprint from _Personnel_, July-August, 1980 (Available from Organizational Research and Development, General Motors, General Motors Building, Detroit, MI 48202.

Morros, Boyd, "The Concept of Community in John Dewey's
Educational Philosophy." Unpublished Ph.D. Dissertation,
Washington University, 1978.

Neuman, David, "Work and Technology in Telephone." _Dissent_,
(Winter, 1982).

Palermo, James, "The Stagnation of Positivist Education Theory."
Unpublished Manuscript (State University College of New York
at Buffalo), 1980.

Piaget, Jean, _To Understand Is to Invent_. New York: Grossman
Publishers, 1973.

Pirsig, Robert, _Zen and the Art of Motorcycle Maintenance_. New
York: Bantam Books, 1974.

Polanyi, Michael, _Personal Knowledge_. Chicago: University of
Chicago Press, 1958.

_____, _The Study of Man_. Chicago: The University of Chicago
Press, 1959.

Popper, Karl R. "Of Clouds and Clocks: An Approach to the
Problem of Rationality and the Freedom of Man." In Popper,
Karl, _Objective Knowledge: An Evolutionary Approach_.
Oxford: Clarendon Press, 1972.

Radice, Giles, _The Industrial Democrats: Trade Unions In An
Uncertain World_. London: George Allen and Unwin, 1978.

Reese, Elmer, "A QWL Direction to Delco-Remy's Future."
Proceedings, 1980 Executive General Motors Quality of Work
Life Executive Conference, April 11, 1980.

Ricoeur, Paul, "Ethics and Culture," and "The Hermeneutical
Function of Distantiation." _Philosophy Today_, 17, 2 (Summer,
1973).

Rivlin, Alice M. _Systematic Thinking for Social Action_.
Washington DC: Brookings Institute, 1971.

Roth, Rita, _Literacy Acquisition, Schooling and Knowledge
Control_. Unpublished Ph.D. Dissertation, Washington
University, St. Louis, MO 1982.

Savall, Henri, _Work and People: An Economic Evaluation of Job
Enrichment_. Oxford: Clarendon Press, 1981.

Schaefer, Robert, _The School As a Center of Inquiry_. New York:

Harper and Row, 1967.

Schroyer, Trent, "Marx and Habermas." Continuum 8, 1 & 2 (Spring-Summer 1970).

Schumacher, E.F., Good Work. New York: Harper and Row, 1979.

_____, Small is Beautiful: Economics As If People Mattered. New York: Harper Torch Books, 1973.

Silver, R.S., "The Misuses of Science," New Scientist. 66, 952 (June 5, 1975).

Silvert, Kalman H., The Reason For Democracy. New York: The Viking Press, 1977.

Simons, Diane, George Kerschensteiner. London: Methuen, 1966.

Skinner, B.F., The Technology of Teaching. New York: Appleton-Century-Crofts, 1968.

Smith, Joan K., Ella Flagg Young: Portrait of a Leader. Ames, Iowa: Educational Studies Press and the Iowa State University Research Foundation, 1979.

Snedden, David, "Education for a World of Teamplayers." School and Society, 20 (November 1, 1924).

_____, "Fundamental Distinctions Between Liberal and Vocational Education." N.E.A. Proceedings, 1914.

_____, "Teaching History in Secondary Schools." History Teachers Magazine, 5, 9 (November 1914).

_____, The New Republic. Vol. 3, May 15, 1915.

_____, Toward Better Educations. New York: Bureau of Publications, Teachers College, Columbia University, 1931.

Stanley, Manfred, The Technological Conscience: Survival and Dignity in An Age of Expertise. New York: The Free Press, 1978.

Tanner, David and L.N. Tanner, Curriculum Development: Theory into Practice (Second ed.). New York: MacMillan, 1980.

Taylor, Frederick, The Principles of Scientific Management. New York: Harper, 1911.

Thorsrud, Einar, "Breaking Down Bureaucracy." In Dyckman W.

269

Vermilye, ed., <u>Relating Work and Education</u>. San Francisco: Jossey-Bass Publishers, 1977.

_____, "Listening to the Workers Produce Results." <u>International Management</u>, 35, 2 (February 1980).

Wainwright, Hilary and Dave Elliott, <u>The Lucas Plan: A New Trade Unionism in the Making?</u> London: Allison and Busby, 1982.

Weick, Karl, "Administering Education in Loosely Coupled Schools." <u>Phi Delta Kappan</u>, 64, 10 (June 1982).

Weisenborn, Howard, "The Next Step." <u>Proceedings</u>, 1980 Executive Conference (General Motors).

Wiebe, Robert, <u>The Search for Order</u>. New York: Hill and Wang, 1967.

White, Lynn Jr., <u>Dynamo and Virgin Reconsidered</u>. Boston: M.I.T. Press, 1968.

Wirth, Arthur G., <u>John Dewey as Educator</u>. New York: John Wiley and Sons, 1966.

_____, <u>Education in the Technological Society</u>. Washington: University Press of America, 1980.

Wirtz, Willard, "Education for What?" In Dyckman W. Vermilye, ed., <u>Relating Work and Education</u>. San Francisco: Jossey-Bass, Publishers, 1977.

Wise, Arthur E., <u>Legislated Learning: The Bureaucratization of the American Classroom</u>. Berkeley: University of California Press, 1979.

Wolin, Sheldon S., "The People's Two Bodies." <u>Democracy</u>, I, 1 (January 1981).

_____, "Why Democracy?" <u>Democracy</u>, I, 1 (January 1981).

Zager, Robert and Michael P. Rosow, <u>The Innovative Organization</u>. New York: Pergamon Press, 1982.

Zwerdling, Daniel, <u>Democracy at Work</u>. Washington, DC: Association for Management, 1978.

learning, 128, 133, 153

Bowra, C.M.: 136; 154

Braverman, Harry: degradation of work, 12

Bremer, John: 256

Bruner, Jerome: 245

Buber, Martin: 140; 195

bureaucratic rationality: 16-17; versus "wholeness of persons", 19, 120, 214-216

Callahan, Raymond: Taylorism, 11-13

Captains of Consciousness: 219

Carlson, Howard C.: Quality of Work Life theorist, 56-58; 220

Carnoy, Martin: re Economic Democracy, 226

Centre for Alternative Industrial and Technological Systems (CAITS): 232; 240

The Child and the Curriculum: 101; 254

Club of Rome: 246-251

Co-determinism: 223-224

Cohn, Marilyn: research on "back to basics", 144-152; reflections on her research, 152-155

Community: in Dewey's concept of democracy, 87-90; school as community, 100

competency based education: 118-119; 124

competition: 253

consumerism: 219; 245

computerization: 171-172; 237-239

continuous learning: as aspect of socio-technical work, 32-35

Cooley, Mike: philosophy of Lucas Combine Stewards Committee, 232-241; 257

cost/benefit principles: 1, 15; applied to education, 134, 140-142

Crazy: from root word krasa, 15

cultural tension: between rationality and wholeness, 19-20

Curle, Adam: 250

cybernation: 167-169; 171

Davis, Louis: 38; high technology, 171

democratic socio-technical theory: See socio-technical theory

democracy: as social living, 85-87, 219; related to ecological perspective, 252

Democracy and Education: 78; industrial life and schools, 99; education as reconstruction of experience, 102-103

Dewey, John: opposes narrow vocational training, 77-80; opposing dualisms, 83-85; on social democracy, 95-97; science and social reform, 85-87; relation of science and democratic humanism, 87-88; two

272

views of science, 97-98; on dialogue,90; science, liberalism and capitalism, 91-92; genetic method, 90; on economic liberalism, 90-92; vision of industrial democracy, 92-103; science and democracy, 95; democracy and Marxist-Leninism, 94; experimentalist education in Laboratory School, 95-100; as "freeing of intelligence", 97-99; teaching 3R's, 101; curriculum and children, 101-102; teachers, 101-103; testing, 156; schools for "freeing intelligence", 182, 254-255; learning as reconstruction of experience, 258

desegregation: and accountability, 109-110

de-skilling: of teachers, 126-128

dialogue: in Dewey, 90; in Buber, 140, 195; in work redesign, 190; in Freire, 194; with minority children, 195-196

Dickson, Paul: Future of the Work Place, 14

Douglas Commission Report on Industrial and Technical Education: 73

Dubos, Renée: 252; 258

Duffy, William: 15

ecological world view: 245

economic democracy: 223-228

education/work relations: 13-14; Marxist theory of school/work "correspondence", 165

efficiency: "vulgar" vs. "integral", 16-18; integral efficiency defined, 19; social efficiency philosophers, 73-77; social efficiency criticized by Dewey, 78-79; and systems analysis, 115; efficient child learning, 119-120; effects of "passion for efficiency" in schools, 155-157; in physics and social sciences, 235-236; education for integral, 245

Elden, Max: research on work redesign in Norwegian bank, 180-181

Elementary and Secondary Education Act (1965): 109-111

Eliot, Charles: education for "probable destinies", 74

Emery, Fred: 214

employee participation groups: in General Motors plants, 187-188; 221

energy transition: to post-petroleum society, 9

entheos: as root of enthusiasm, 14, 258

ethical concern: in socio technical work, 35; to maintain public good in economic activity, 37; of Quality of Work Life, 64, 69; of Greeks, 136; Habermas, 140; right to learn in work, 184; and technological choice, 227; for entheos, 258

"Evaluation as scientific management in U.S. School Reform": 107-110

Ewen, Stewart: 219

Feuer, Lewis: on Dewey's

273

social philosophy, 83, 87

Fish, Frederick, advocate of practical education, 76

Ford, Franklin: "socializing of intelligence" with John Dewey, 84

Fraser, Douglas: 59

Freire, Paulo: ideas about teaching, 192-196; 258

Fromm, Erich: principles of The Sane Society as influence on Michael Maccoby, 39-42; sane society defined, 42-43; 257

future of work: two scenarios, 60-61

Galileo: mathematization of nature, 137

Gardner, John: HEW Secretary, 110

General Motors: Quality of Work Life at Tarrytown, 49-54

German vocational education: 70

Gilder, George: subordinating work to cognitive style of industrialists, 24

Gompers, Samuel: 2; 12

Goodlad, John: skeptical of accountability, 121, 122; criticizes accountability, 202-205; compared to Philip Herbst, 207, 255

"good work": Schumacher's definition, 10; criteria of according to Einar Thorsrud, 36-37; in schools, 202, 252

Goulet, Denis: efficiency – "vulgar" vs. "integral", 17-18, 213, 218

Green, Thomas: distinguishes work from job, 69-70

Gyllenhammar, Pehr: President of Volvo and work reform leader, 25-28; quality of participation in good work, 37, 236

Habermas, Jürgen: on positivist science, 140

Harman International Industries: union/management structure at Bolivar plant, 48-49; learning at work, 185; The Harmon Mirror, 185-186

Harman, Sidney: President Harman International Industries, 39, 46

Harrison, Ordia: applies Freire to teaching, 192-196

Henderson, Hazel: 240

Herbst, Philip: alternatives to hierarchy theory, 33; socio-technical work and education, 174-176; compared to Goodlad, 207; socio-technical as fore-runner of social change, 213-218, 255, 258

high technology: and education, 167-173; at Three Mile Island, 168-169, 216

Hirschhorn, Larry: analysis of Three Mile Island accident, 167-169

The Homeless Mind: 108; technological consciousness, 126

homo poeta: the meaning maker,

274

275

Luttwak, Edwin M.: efficiency in the military, 157-158

Maccoby, Michael: philosophical principles of work, 38-39; as definer of "social productivity" vs. "economic productivity", 43, 44; "The Quality of Working Life", 44-45; his principles at General Motors, 53, 219, 227, 254

maintenance learning: 247

management ideology: and competency based education, 116-117; features of rationalistic model, 121-122, 124, 128; and teachers, 218; prerogatives, 223-225; loose coupling vs. tight coupling, 256

mandated learning: 118

Marxism: and industrial democracy, 2; Marxist-Leninism and Dewey, 94; social relations of capitalism, 136; skepticism of socio-technical theory, 165-166; schools reproducing capitalism, 166, 241

mathematics: teaching of, 146-147

matrix organization: in Norwegian shipping, 31-37

McLaughlin, Milbrey: author of Evaluation and Reform, 110-112

McNamara, Robert: influences on HEW, 111

Mead, George: concept of self and democratic values, 80

meaning: search for, 249

Methods Time Management: work model, 25

Miles, H.E.: advocate of German model of vocational training, 70-73

"modernism": defined, 10-11, 214, 219

Murray, Philip: 50

National Assessment of Educational Progress: 204

National Association of Manufacturers (N.A.M.): advocates of vocational training, 70-72

National Society for the Promotion of Industrial Education (NSPIE): 73; clash of vocational educators and "progressives", 77-79

Net National Strength (NNS): as opposed to Gross National Product (GNP), 38

No Limits to Learning: as congruent with socio-technical perspective, 246-251

Norway: Work Research Institutes, 29; Norwegian ship life as example of integral efficiency, 31-35; socio-technical influences on learning, 173-181, 219

Palermo, James: criticism of positivism, 135

People at Work: 25-26

performance contracting: 118

phenomenologists: critique of

positivist ideology, 135-138

Piaget, Jean: principles used at Bolivar, 47; learning as discovery, 165, 176

Pirsig, Robert: on technological ugliness, 158-161

Planning, Programming, and Budgeting System (PPBS): 110; 116; 133

Polanyi, Michael: tacit learning, 114, 251

Popper, Karl: freedom and control, 16

positivism: and education, 136; positivist science, 138; value free, 141

post-industrialism: 215; 252

problems: convergent and divergent, 253

problematizing: in Freire's educational theory, 195, 200

productivity: free market vs. social productivity, 43

public good: and economic activity, 37

The Public and Its Problems: Dewey on requirements for democracy, 88-91

Prosser, Charles: founder of vocational education, 73-74; creator of rationale for vocational education, 76

Quality of Work Life (QWL): at General Motors, 49-54; training sessions, 53; contrasted with job

enlargement, 54; and collective bargaining, 55; as on-going process, 56-58; compared to European industrial democracy, 58-59; employee participation groups, 187-189, 220

reading: teaching of, 142-144, 153; Freire's method, 191-195; a black teacher applying Freire's methods, 196-202; Bettleheim's ideas, 201

The Reason for Democracy: See Kalmar Silvert

Reconstruction in Philosophy: 79

reductionism: of rationalistic model, 161

re-industrialization: as perversion of industrial democracy, 24

research-type learning: Herbst's theory, 179-181, 216-217

Ricoeur, Paul: criticism of positivism, 138

"right answer" schools: 107, 154

Rivlin, Alice: systems efficiency evaluator at HEW, 111-113, 133, 139

Rosenbrock, H.H.: 239

Roth, Rita: 133; 142-143

SAAB: 222

The Sane Society: See Erich Fromm

scenarios: two scenarios for the future of work, 60-62

school as work place: 191; 202; 207

Schumacher, E.F.: creating "good work", 10; on convergent and divergent problems, 253

science: as model of creative learning (Dewey), 85-88; science instruction (prepackaged), 126-127; positivist, 138; as mechanistic, 214-215; science - Taylorism linkage, 234, 258

scientific management: Taylor, Frederick W. as creator of, 11-14; compared with sociotechnical theory, 15, 19; as related to technocratic ideology, 107-108; and federal reform efforts, 108-113; rational efficiency model of education, 134; as a technical production function, 158

secondary education: affected by socio-technical theory in Norway, 179-180

Silicon valley: 217

Silver, R.S.: on "misuse of science", 235

Silvert, Kalmar: a democratic political economy defined, 23, 38

Skinner, B.F.: ideas for teaching, 140-142

Snedden, David: founder of vocational education 73-75; relation of vocational and liberal education, 76; in debate with Dewey, 79-80

Social Darwinist philosophy: 71; 74

social ecology: 216-217

socialism: 5; 226; state socialism, 238

socio-technical theory: democratic principles, 4; as challenger to scientific management, 13-14; as hyphenated concept, 20; as paradigm of "good work", 23; Scandinavian versions, 25-29; compared to cost efficiency model, 25; and turbulent environments, 28; distinguished from job enrichment, 37; at Harman International Industries, 38-48; and Quality of Work Life, 49-60; as model for learning in Norway, 173-183; in the United States, 185-191; as "leading edge" for social change, 213-218; hyphenated nature, 253-256

social learning: in sociotechnical work, 33-34

Socio-Technical Design: 195-196

state legislation for accountability in education: 116-119

Sweden: 25-28; 222; Labor Organization, 224

Systems analysis: features and influence on schools, 107-108; perspective, 110, 114-115, 116, 120, 140

tacit knowledge: 114; 234

Tavistock Institute of Human Relations: pioneer in socio-technical theory, 25

Taylor, Frederick W. (Taylorism): creator of scientific management, 11-13; 54; influence of scientific management at Department of HEW, 113; resistance to